W9-DAL-116

JUN 1 1 2012

Welcome Katie, to *RIM 101: Fundamentals of Professional Practice!*

To Begin Your Course:

1. Go to **My ARMA**
2. Log in with your e-mail address and password
3. Click on "My Education"
4. Click the "View" link in the "*Online Course*" section associated with *RIM 101: Fundamentals of Professional Practice*

Your progress is bookmarked, so you can return to your course at any point and begin where you left off.

Need Assistance?

Contact ARMA International from 8:30 a.m. to 5:00 p.m. (CT) at +1 800.422.2762 (U.S. & Canada), +1 913.341.3808, or e-mail education@armaintl.org.

For information about your member or customer account, go to My ARMA. To ensure that we can serve you efficiently and effectively, please verify the information on your account.

Records and Information Management: Fundamentals of Professional Practice

William Saffady

ARMA International
Lenexa, Kansas

Consulting Editor: Mary L. Ginn, Ph.D.
Composition: Rebecca Gray Design
Cover Art: Jason Vannatta

ARMA International
13725 West 109th Street, Suite 101
Lenexa, KS 66215
913.341.3808

ISBN: 1-931786-17-8

Contents

Chapter 4   Managing Inactive Records I: Records Centers   77

Chapter 5   Managing Inactive Records II: Micrographics   97

Chapter 6   Vital Records   123

Chapter 7   Managing Active Records I: Document Filing Systems   143

Preface

Records and Information Management: Fundamentals of Professional Practice deals with principles and practices for systematic management of recorded information. It is intended for newly appointed records managers, experienced professionals who want a review of specific topics, supervisors whose oversight responsibilities include records management functions, planners and decision-makers who develop strategies and tactics for managing their organizations' information assets, and undergraduate and graduate students of records management or allied disciplines—such as library science, archival administration, information systems, and office administration—concerned with the storage, organization, retrieval, retention, or protection of recorded information.

This book is organized into eight chapters that reflect the scope and responsibilities of records management programs in corporations, government agencies, academic institutions, professional services firms, and other organizations:

- Chapter 1 examines the role of records management as a business discipline. It begins with a summary of the conceptual foundations of systematic records management, followed by an overview of the most important components of a records management program and an evaluation of records management's contribution to organizational effectiveness.

- Chapter 2, the first of two chapters about records retention, discusses the records inventory, a fact-finding survey that identifies and describes an organization's records. It explains inventory work steps, emphasizing important considerations for records managers who must plan and conduct inventories for retention scheduling.

- Chapter 3 deals with the purpose, content, and format of records retention schedules, the core component in a systematic records management program. It emphasizes legal and administrative factors that determine how long an organization's records must be kept and provides examples of legal retention requirements for commonly encountered types of records. The chapter also discusses the implementation of retention schedules, including secure destruction methods for confidential records and the importance of auditing retention practices for compliance with schedules.

- Chapter 4 surveys the characteristics and components of records centers, which provide economical off-site storage for inactive records. It emphasizes factors that records managers must consider when planning, implementing, and operating in-house records centers or when evaluating the facilities and capabilities of commercial storage providers. Topics covered include records storage containers, shelving, fire-protection requirements, environmental controls, material handling equipment, and retrieval operations.

- Chapter 5 examines the role of micrographics technology, products, and services in records management. It explains the distinctive characteristics and advantages of micrographics technology for managing recorded information, particularly inactive records. It also describes microfilm production methods as well as equipment for viewing, printing, and scanning microfilm images. The chapter concludes with a discussion of microfilm service bureaus as an alternative to in-house production of microforms.

- Chapter 6 deals with vital records, which contain information that is indispensable to an organization's mission-critical operations. Placing vital records protection into the context of an organization's business continuity and disaster preparedness initiatives, it discusses the components of a systematic program for identification and protection of vital information assets, including methods for assessing risk and reconstructing records in the event of a disaster.

- Chapter 7, the first of two chapters about the organization and retrieval of active records, examines filing principles and methods for paper records and, where applicable, other media. It begins with a discussion of centralized filing, followed by surveys of file arrangements, filing equipment, and filing supplies. Rather than explaining how to file, it presents essential concepts from an analytical and managerial perspective.

- Chapter 8 deals with computer-based document storage and retrieval systems that employ indexing rather than filing concepts. It begins with an overview of document indexing concepts, including the identification of indexing parameters and selection of index values. The chapter describes electronic document imaging, computer-assisted microfilm retrieval, and text retrieval technologies, emphasizing their advantages and limitations for records management applications.

In every chapter, the treatment is practical rather than theoretical. Where applicable, this discussion of specific topics emphasizes best practices, which are defined as the most advisable courses of action for particular recordkeeping problems or processes. Published standards, the embodiment of best practices, are cited where applicable.

Although terms and concepts are defined when first introduced in the text, Appendix A provides a glossary of important definitions for convenient reference. Appendix B contains suggestions for finding additional information about records management concepts and practices.

William Saffady

Chapter 1

Introduction

Records management is a specialized business discipline concerned with the systematic analysis and control of **recorded information**, which includes any and all information created, received, maintained, or used by an organization in accordance with its mission, operations, and activities. Records are physical objects that contain such information. ISO 15489-1, *Information and Documentation—Records Management, Part 1: General,* emphasizes the role of records as "evidence of and information about business activities and transactions."

By definition, records contain information that is "written down" as opposed to merely memorized or exchanged verbally. In this context, "written down" encompasses a variety of recording methods, including, but not limited to, handwriting, typewriting, drawing, computer data entry, photography, audio recording, and video recording. Thus, handwritten notes or voice recordings made during a meeting are examples of recorded information as are any subsequent transcriptions made from them. In some cases, however, confidential information—discussed "off the record"—is intentionally excluded from such records. Excluded information may be very important and have a decisive impact on an organization's operations and activities, but it is not within the scope of records management authority or initiatives unless and until it is written down.

The definition of a **record** presented here is intentionally broad; records may contain information recorded in any format on any medium by any method, manual or automated. The Federal Records Act (44 U.S. Code 3301) provides a useful model for other organizations to follow. It defines U.S. government records as:

> "all books, papers, maps, photographs, machine-readable materials, or other documentary materials, regardless of physical form or characteristics, made or received by an agency of the U.S. Government under Federal law or in connection with the transaction of public business and preserved or appropriate for preservation by that agency or its legitimate successor as evidence of the organization, functions, policies, decisions, procedures, operations, or other activities of the Government or because of the informational value of the data in them."

Similarly, the Canadian Access to Information Act (R.S. 1985, c. A-1, s-1) defines records as "any correspondence, memorandum, book, plan, map, drawing, diagram, pictorial or graphic work, photograph, film, microform, sound recording, videotape, machine readable record, and any other documentary material, regardless of physical form or characteristics, and any copy thereof." Other government agencies have adopted comparably broad definitions.

The concepts and methods discussed in *Records and Information Management: Fundamentals of Professional Practice* apply to recorded information created and maintained by organizations of all types and sizes, including the following:

- Federal, state, and local government agencies, including public authorities and other quasi-governmental organizations;

- Corporations, partnerships, sole proprietorships, and other businesses;

- Law firms, accounting firms, consulting firms, and other providers of professional services;

- Schools, colleges, universities, and other educational institutions;

- Museums, libraries, and other cultural institutions;

- Medical clinics, hospitals, and other healthcare facilities; and

- Not-for-profit organizations such as professional associations, philanthropic foundations, religious institutions, learned societies, social service agencies, and charitable organizations.

The ISO 15489-1 standard recognizes the global importance of systematic recordkeeping and the international applicability of records management principles. Although this book principally addresses records management practice in North America, the concepts and methods presented here have been successfully implemented by government agencies, corporations, and other organizations throughout the world. The global validity of records management concepts and methods is an important advantage for multinational companies and other organizations that operate in more than one country. Such organizations can adopt consistent records management principles and practices throughout their operations, subject to variations required by local laws and regulations that apply to certain records.

This chapter examines the purpose and scope of records management as a business discipline. It begins with a summary of the conceptual foundations of systematic records management, followed by an overview of the most important components of a records management program and an evaluation of the contribution made by records management to organizational effectiveness. The chapter concludes with a discussion of the role of records management as a staff function. Topics introduced in this chapter are examined in detail elsewhere in this book.

Conceptual Foundations

Corporations, government agencies, and other organizations have been creating and maintaining records for centuries. However, the volume and complexity of recorded information have risen dramatically, even exponentially, in recent decades. Contributing factors include:

- The expanded scope and increased complexity of business and governmental activities;

- A growing white-collar workforce that relies on recorded information for the completion of assigned tasks, management decision-making, and other purposes;

- The increased prominence and economic significance of information-intensive service industries such as banking, insurance, management consulting, litigation support, and healthcare;

- Increased governmental regulations and their associated recordkeeping requirements;

- The widespread availability and adoption of computers, high-speed printers, photocopiers, data communications, and other technologies that can quickly generate large quantities of recorded information in a variety of formats.

Records management principles and practices have developed in response to the increased pervasiveness of information-related activities that characterize modern work environments and the corresponding need for systematic approaches to recordkeeping requirements. As a professional discipline, however, records management dates from the early 1950s, although its concepts and methods have been expanded and refined considerably since that time. Today, records management is a multifaceted field with tens of thousands of practitioners. It incorporates ideas and practices from such related fields as computing, telecommunications, knowledge management, information science, library science, archival administration, and industrial engineering.

The following sections review the most important principles on which systematic records management is based. These principles provide a firm conceptual foundation for the development and implementation of effective records management initiatives. They must be clearly articulated in an organization's records management policies.

Ownership of Records

A corporation, government agency, academic institution, or other organization is the owner of all records created, received, and/or maintained by its employees—and, subject to predetermined exclusions, by contractors, temporary employees, and unpaid employees such as student interns and volunteers—in connection with the organization's mission, business operations, and other activities. Such records are sometimes described as *official records*, although that phrase may have other meanings in specific situations. Terminology aside, an organization's records are its property. As the owner of its records, an organization is solely empowered to make decisions about their storage, distribution, control, protection, retention, destruction, or use. From an ownership perspective, an organization's authority over its records is identical to its authority over real estate, equipment, inventory, or other property. An organization's decisions about recordkeeping are, of course, subject to legal and regulatory mandates that may affect the making, use, or retention of records as discussed later in this book.

When permitted by records management policies and procedures, so-called personal files may be established for the convenience of individual employees, but this practice is done without any connotation of personal ownership. Such personal files may be kept in employees' offices or desks. They may be unique records or copies of selected documents that reside in other files. Because these records pertain to an organization's mission, operations, and activities, personal files are the organization's property and are subject to the organization's records management policies and procedures, including retention guidelines discussed in Chapter 3. When employees retire, resign, or otherwise leave an organization, they cannot take personal files with them.

The concept of ownership of records applies to all information, but it may require elaboration or clarification in special situations. In the United States, for example, medical records are generally treated as the property of the healthcare agency or clinician that creates and maintains them, but most states have enacted laws that give patients access to their medical records. In some states, patients are said to own the information in their medical records as opposed to the actual records, but this concept of ownership confers limited authority. Patients can obtain copies of their medical records for their own use, to give to other healthcare providers, for review by attorneys, or for other purposes. Patients cannot make decisions about the storage, retention, or destruction of their medical records by healthcare agencies or providers.

Confusion sometimes arises about the status of personal papers as distinct from personal files, which were defined previously as copies created for the convenience of individual employees pursuant to the employees' duties as permitted by policies and procedures. As previously explained, personal files are the property of the employer not the employee. True personal papers, by contrast, are unrelated to the conduct of an organization's business or to an employees' duties. Such papers may pertain to an employee's professional affiliations, volunteer activities, personal interests, or other matters. They are the property of their creators and are consequently excluded from records management authority. As discussed next, personal papers are considered nonrecords. If personal papers are kept in employees' offices, they should be clearly designated as such and maintained separately from the organization's records.

Records as Assets

Broadly defined, an *asset* is something of value. Although recordkeeping is often treated as a tedious clerical chore or, at best, a necessary evil, systematic records management takes a different view. Records contain information that is needed by and, in some cases, is indispensable to the organization that creates and maintains them. Recorded information is an asset not a burden. Systematic records management is an aspect of asset management, which seeks the most effective deployment of an organization's assets to support its mission, operations, and activities. Records contain information essential for transaction processing, the development and delivery of products and services, planning, decision-making, legal and regulatory compliance, and other purposes. In government, recorded information protects the rights of citizens, property owners, taxpayers, and others. In the private sector, recorded information protects the rights of shareholders, partners, or other owners.

All Formats

Records management concepts and methods apply to recorded information in all formats, including the following:

- Paper documents such as office files, business forms, engineering drawings, charts, maps, patient records, student records, project files, legal case files, technical or managerial reports, and computer printouts;

- Photographic records, including photographic negatives and slides, motion picture films, and filmstrips, as well as microfilm, microfiche, aperture cards, and other microforms produced from paper documents or computer data;

- **Electronic records**, including computer files and databases, word processing files, e-mail, voice mail, instant messages, electronic document images, computer-generated graphics, audio recordings, and video recordings.

In some cases, ordinary or unusual objects may also be considered operating records. In many localities, for example, construction projects must be preceded by analysis of soil samples from the proposed building site for specific environmental characteristics. The analysis is embodied in a written report for which the soil samples serve as supporting material. Similarly, pharmaceutical research organizations take biopsy tissue samples from laboratory animals when evaluating the safety of drugs under development. The tissue samples serve as supporting materials for written toxicology reports and other test documentation. In these situations, the soil and tissue samples are treated as records and are within the scope of records management activities.

Information Life Cycle

Although records are assets, their value is subject to change over time. The concept of an **information life cycle** is well established in records management theory and practice. Recorded information is subject to changing requirements for timely retrieval, convenient distribution, and cost-effective storage from its creation or receipt through destruction or permanent retention. As depicted in the accompanying graph in Figure 1-1, the business significance of many, if not most, records varies inversely with the age of the records. Typically, records maintained by corporations, government agencies, and other organizations are referenced frequently for a relatively brief period of time following their creation or receipt while the transactions, projects, events, or other matters to which they pertain are under active consideration. As time passes, reference activity diminishes, either gradually or abruptly:

- Some records have short life cycles. Notes of telephone calls and junk mail are often discarded after an initial reading. Other records, such as routine office correspondence, are filed for a brief period then discarded, usually within several years of creation or receipt.

- Many transaction-oriented documents, such as purchase orders and insurance claims, are referenced frequently for several weeks or months following their creation or receipt, but only occasionally after the matters to which they pertain are

Information Life Cycle
The information life cycle, showing reduced reference activity for recorded information with passage of time.

Figure 1-1

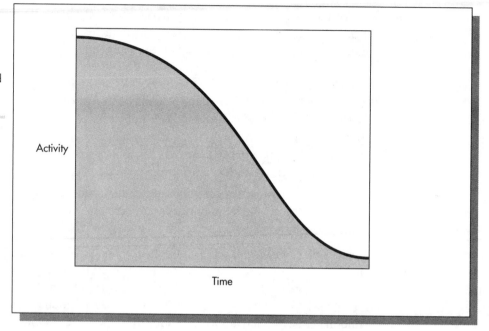

Activity

Time

resolved. As discussed in Chapter 3, such records are typically kept for six to ten years to satisfy legal or audit requirements.

- Certain records retain their business value for longer periods. Their retention parameters may be determined by the life cycles of objects or the duration of events or activities to which the records pertain. Engineering drawings of manufacturing facilities or equipment, for example, are retained as long as the facilities or equipment remain in service. Records that relate to pharmaceutical products are retained as long as the products are marketed and often longer as continuing proof of safety or efficacy. Project documentation is retained as long as a project is active and for some period of time thereafter. Medical records and academic transcripts are retained for a human lifetime. Certain pension and trust records are retained until all beneficiaries are deceased and payment issues resolved.

- Some records have continuing administrative or scholarly value that warrants long-term retention, either by business offices or by cultural agencies. Government agencies, for example, keep birth records, death records, marriage records, court records, and property records permanently, and such records may remain useful for decades. A title search, for example, may require access to deeds, mortgages, liens, judgments, and other documents that date back 30 years or longer. Government and corporate archives preserve records of scholarly value, even though such records may experience limited reference activity. In fact, records of high scholarly value are often of interest to a limited audience of subject specialists. For reasons of confidentiality, some records retained for their scholarly value may not be made available to researchers for many years. Even some cases of records, such as certain court records, are retained permanently, but they are sealed to prohibit access.

The information life cycle is divided, by frequency of reference, into active and inactive (less active) stages. Each stage has distinct requirements. The *active stage* is concerned with the timely availability of information to support an organization's business operations. By contrast, the *inactive stage* is principally concerned with cost-effective, reliable retention of information, often for long periods of time. These life cycle concepts apply to paper documents, microforms, and electronic records. They are the basis for records management initiatives described in subsequent chapters.

Records vs. Nonrecords

All records contain information, but not all information-bearing objects are considered records. Broad as they are, the definitions presented at the start of this chapter impose an important qualifier: **Records** contain information that is directly related to an organization's mission, operations, and activities. In records management practice, information-bearing objects that meet this requirement are described as having "record status." Those objects that do not have record status are categorized as **nonrecords** and are excluded from records management policies, procedures, and initiatives discussed in this book. Some widely cited examples of nonrecords include:

- Library materials and other publications, such as departmental copies of books or periodicals, that are acquired and maintained solely for general reference purposes rather than to support a specific business operation.
- Unsolicited brochures, catalogs, pamphlets, and other documents, usually received through the mail, that describe specific organizations, events, products, or services and that have no substantive business value.
- Unsolicited e-mail, instant messages, and voice mail that have no substantive business value.
- Information received from Internet list services and news groups.
- Personal papers that may be kept in an employee's work area, and even filed in the same cabinets as records, but that were not created or received in the course of business and do not relate in any way to the employee's duties.
- Excess inventory of annual reports, bulletins, circulars, employee newsletters, brochures, posters, handbooks, publications, and other materials intended for sale or distribution.
- Blank copies of purchase requisitions, travel reimbursement requests, and other forms that, when completed for a specific business purpose, would be considered records.

Some organizations broaden this list to include drafts of documents once the final versions are completed, shorthand notes once they are transcribed, worksheets from which data is extracted, and other records that lose their value once their contents are incorporated into other records.

Differentiating records from nonrecords can be difficult. Although lists of nonrecords are helpful, they are never conclusive. An information-bearing object may be considered a nonrecord in some circumstances and have record status in others. As an example, scientific books, journals, and other publications acquired by a pharmaceutical company's library for unspecified reference purposes are considered nonrecords. Photocopies of journal articles that individual scientists may keep in their work areas for general reference and professional development are also considered nonrecords. On the other hand, a pharmaceutical company's intellectual property department may keep patent application files that include copies of journal articles or other publications that contain information about the novelty of a claimed invention. Those publications are considered records because they are directly related to a specific business activity.

Although nonrecord designations exclude certain information-bearing objects from the scope of records management authority, policies, and procedures, they do not affect the status of those objects as an organization's property. With the notable exception of personal papers, most if not all nonrecords on the previous list relate to an organization's business, were paid for by the organization or acquired with the organization's resources, and are the property of the organization that creates, receives, or maintains them. Thus, undistributed copies of annual reports or other publications are properly considered the organization's property and are subject to the organization's authority, even though they are classed as nonrecords from a records management perspective. Thus, an organization may have policies and procedures for distributing or disposing of excess inventory of publications, but such policies and procedures would not be developed by the records management function.

Deteriorative Nature of Recordkeeping Problems

Records management is a problem-solving discipline. In the absence of systematic controls, the following problems with recorded information are all too familiar:

- Records occupy valuable office space that is needed for other purposes.
- Expensive equipment and supplies must be purchased to accommodate the rapid growth of recorded information.
- Recorded information is difficult to organize for effective retrieval.
- Records needed for a given purpose—be it decision-making, transaction processing, litigation support, regulatory compliance, product development, or some other activity—cannot be located in a timely manner, often with devastating consequences.
- Information handling is labor-intensive, time-consuming, and costly.
- Information indispensable to mission-critical activities is lost or destroyed and cannot be reconstructed.

Traditionally, these problems have been closely associated with paper documents, but they apply to recorded information in all formats, including electronic formats. Records accumulate on computer media as they do in file cabinets. In many organizations, the voluminous accumulation of daily e-mail, voice mail, and instant messages alone can push online storage to its limits. Preparation of information for computer storage and processing can be labor-intensive, time-consuming, and costly. Computer-processible records can be damaged or inappropriately deleted. Computerization is often viewed as a solution to the problems of paper filing systems, but the mere fact that information has been computerized is no guarantee that it can be retrieved when needed.

The records management problems previously cited are never self-limiting. Unless corrective action is taken or business operations are discontinued, increasing amounts of space, equipment, supplies, and other resources will be required to accommodate new records. Information will never organize itself for retrieval, essential records will be irrevocably lost, and the cost of recordkeeping will continue to escalate.

Program Components

Systematic records management is principally concerned with five aspects of information management:

1. Determining how long recorded information should be kept
2. Ensuring compliance with recordkeeping laws and regulations
3. Managing inactive records
4. Organizing active records for retrieval when needed
5. Protecting vital records

These aspects apply equally to paper and nonpaper records. All have a significant impact on an organization's mission, business processes, operations, and activities. The following sections survey these aspects briefly. They will be examined more fully in subsequent chapters.

Records Retention

Corporations, government agencies, and other organizations have long been concerned about the needless retention of obsolete records. In the United States, the Cockrell Committee (1887-1889) and the Keep Commission (1905-1909), two of the earliest bodies to examine the impact of recordkeeping practices on the cost of federal government operations, criticized the retention of unnecessary records. Early records management initiatives, such as the General Records Disposal Act of 1889, emphasized the destruction of federal government records when no longer needed. Equally important, however, is the identification of records that must be kept to satisfy legal or regulatory requirements, to address operational needs, or to preserve information of enduring value.

In every organization, the disposition of recorded information is a critical business activity that must be governed by formalized policies and procedures rather than the discretion of individual employees. Determining how long recorded information needs to be kept and developing effective procedures for implementing retention policies are defining responsibility of records management as a business discipline. Records retention policies and implementation procedures are core components in a systematic records management program. By ensuring the availability of record information for appropriate periods of time, these policies and procedures provide the foundation upon which other records management activities discussed in this book are based.

Compliance with Laws and Regulations

As discussed in Chapter 3, various laws and government regulations specify that certain types of records must be created and retained for minimum periods of time. Going beyond retention, recordkeeping laws and regulations may also specify storage conditions, acceptable media formats, retrieval requirements, and restrictions on disclosure for records associated with activities subject to government regulation. Some recordkeeping laws and regulations apply to commonly encountered business operations such as hiring employees and paying taxes. Others apply to specific industries or business activities, such as financial services or pharmaceuticals, that are regulated by one or more government agencies.

Recordkeeping laws and regulations apply to all private and public organizations that operate within a specific governmental jurisdiction. U.S. corporations, for example, are subject to recordkeeping requirements contained in federal laws and in the laws of every state or locality where they do business. Similar requirements apply in other countries. Multinational organizations must conform to recordkeeping requirements in all countries where they maintain business operations. The previously cited ISO 15489-1 standard identifies an organization's regulatory environment as a determining factor in records management initiatives. As one of its key responsibilities, a systematic records management program must identify legal and regulatory requirements that bear upon the creation, storage, retrieval, and retention of records and implement policies and procedures to ensure compliance with them.

Cost-Effective Management of Inactive Records

Records management programs include a combination of elements that address both active and inactive records. Used in this context, active and inactive status are determined by the frequency with which records are referenced or consulted to support specific business processes or operations. The determination is admittedly imprecise: **Active records** are consulted frequently; **inactive records** are not, but many inactive records must be retained for some period of time to meet legal or audit requirements or in anticipation of future retrieval, however occasional or unlikely that future need may be. Distinctions between active and inactive records need not be precisely drawn to be meaningful. According to the previously discussed concept of an information life cycle, all records become less active and ultimately inactive as time passes. At any given time, some records are clearly identifiable as active or inactive, while others are at some stage in the transition from active to inactive status.

For records in the inactive phase of the information life cycle, the principal goal is space conservation with resulting minimization of storage costs. These considerations are particularly important where large quantities of inactive records must be retained for long periods of time. In such situations, records management methodologies, such as off-site storage and microfilming, provide economical storage solutions while ensuring reasonably responsive and convenient retrieval when and if the records are needed for specific business purposes.

Organization and Retrieval of Active Records

For records to be useful, they must be accessible. Effective organization of recorded information for retrieval when needed is the principal concern for records in the active phase of the information life cycle. By definition, active records are consulted frequently to support specific business processes or operations. Space conservation and economical storage, although important, are usually secondary considerations. Records management initiatives for organization and retrieval of active records range from the development of filing systems and procedures for paper documents to the implementation of computer databases, document imaging systems, and text retrieval technologies that employ sophisticated indexing methodologies and provide rapid display of retrieved information at online workstations.

Protection of Vital Records

Protection of information assets has long been recognized as an important component of records management practice. Among the earliest records management initiatives of the U.S. government, the Archives Act of 1810 provided for the construction of fireproof rooms to store the records of executive departments. The law's underlying principle recognizes the obligations of records custodians: Citizens have a reasonable expectation that government agencies will safeguard essential records, but concerns about the safety of recorded information are not limited to government. Similar expectations apply to corporate shareholders, to clients of professional services firms, to medical patients, to students in academic institutions, and to any other persons or organizations that may be affected by the recordkeeping practices of others.

In every organization, certain records contain information that is indispensable to the continuity of **mission-critical operations**; that is, to business processes and activities essential to an organization's purpose and obligations. Such records are termed **vital records.** For many organizations, information contained in vital records is their most valuable asset. A corporation may place a high value on its computing equipment, for example. However, compare the impact of a calamitous event that irrevocably damages a network server but leaves a mission-critical database intact with the impact of a system malfunction that destroys the database but leaves the server operational. As discussed more fully in Chapter 6, a systematic records management program includes effective methods for identifying and safeguarding vital records against damage or loss as well as for recovering information contained in vital records if damage or loss occurs.

The Business Case for Records Management

In a section that lists the benefits of records management, the ISO 15489-1 standard emphasizes the importance of recorded information as a business asset and cites the role of systematic recordkeeping for the orderly and efficient conduct of an organization's business operations. Recorded information is a strategic asset that makes direct, significant, and indispensable contributions to an organization's objectives, efficiency, and effectiveness. When properly managed, records will ensure compliance with legal and regulatory requirements, promote continuity of business operations in the event of a disaster, support policy formulation and decision-making, and protect the rights and interests of an organization's stakeholders.

In U.S. government agencies, the benefits of systematic records management were accepted decades ago and are now beyond discussion. The First Hoover Commission on the Organization of the Executive Branch of Government (1947-1949) included a task force that examined recordkeeping practices in federal agencies and recommended legislation for the systematic management of all government records. The previously cited Federal Records Act specifies that heads of federal government agencies "shall establish and maintain an active, continuing program for the economical and efficient management of the records of the agency." At the state and local levels, government agencies are similarly obligated to implement records management policies and procedures, usually under the direction of a state archives or another designated unit. The South Carolina Public Records Act (Code of Laws of South Carolina 1976, Volume 10, 355-363, and 1988 Cumulative Supplement, 229-231, as amended) is typical. It specifies that:

> "A records management program directed to the application of efficient and economical management methods and relating to the creation, utilization, maintenance, retention, preservation, and disposal of public records must be established and administered by the Archives . . . The head of each agency, the governing body of each subdivision, and every public records custodian shall cooperate with the Archives in complying with the provisions of this chapter and to establish and maintain an active, continuing program for the economical and efficient management of the records of the agency or subdivision."

In nongovernmental organizations and the private sector, however, systematic records management is mandated by policies and executive directives rather than by law, if it is mandated at all. Ultimately, the business case for systematic records management depends on its contribution to an organization's effectiveness, for which recorded information is essential.

The need for recordkeeping is indisputable—it is an ordinary and necessary component of virtually all business operations. In some cases, laws and regulations specify that certain records must be created and maintained for designated periods of time. Legal requirements aside, records are a necessary aid to memory. They document an organization's decisions, actions, transactions, and other activities. Records management concepts and methods provide systematic, well-developed approaches to recordkeeping operations that individual departments would otherwise perform themselves, without direction and, presumably, with less knowledge, skill, and effectiveness. Thus, the business case for systematic records management is based on its instrumental value for effective recordkeeping.

Systematic records management must provide demonstrable, quantifiable benefits for essential business operations or activities. Further, the quantified value of the benefits must exceed the cost to develop and implement systematic records management initiatives. The difference between the quantified value of benefits and the cost of records management initiatives is the value added by systematic records management.

Systematic records management can deliver demonstrable, quantifiable benefits by reducing operating costs, by minimizing legal exposure, and by increasing revenues. These benefits are discussed briefly next and examined more fully in subsequent chapters.

Reducing Operating Costs

Recordkeeping is a necessary but expensive activity. Recordkeeping costs are an important, if often unrecognized, component of an organization's operating costs. Cost reduction has been an attainable objective of systematic records management for over half a century. The earliest records management initiatives emphasized cost-effective storage and retrieval of operating records in large corporations and government agencies. For many organizations, cost reduction remains the principal motive for systematic records management. In for-profit businesses, systematic records management can deliver savings that have a direct, beneficial impact on the bottom line. When justifying costs, money saved is the same as money earned. Efficient recordkeeping contributes to profitability by lowering the cost of doing business. In government agencies and not-for-profit organizations, cost-reduction initiatives have a direct, beneficial impact on mission. Money saved through more efficient recordkeeping can be directed to essential programs and services.

Systematic records management can reduce recordkeeping costs in several ways:

1. Many business processes generate voluminous records that require large amounts of storage space as well as expensive equipment and supplies. Corporations, government agencies, and other organizations frequently complain that they have too many records. Although recorded information is a valuable business resource, many organizations waste money by retaining older records—such as customer correspondence pertaining to long-closed accounts, database records associated with completed business transactions, and obsolete versions of revised reports—that are no longer needed. A systematic records management program can reduce storage requirements and costs by identifying and discarding such records. For records that must be kept, off-site storage or microfilming can be used to minimize office space requirements and reduce retention costs as explained in Chapters 4 and 5.

2. Recorded information is useless if it cannot be retrieved when needed. The organization of recorded information for effective retrieval is a difficult task, and many file maintenance operations are labor-intensive and consequently expensive. Systematic records management adds value to actively referenced information by making it easier and less costly to retrieve and use. Through a combination of manual and automated approaches, systematic records management initiatives can reduce labor costs and improve the retrievability of recorded information. Well-developed filing systems and procedures, for example, reduce operating costs by making efficient use of administrative labor, filing equipment, and supplies.

They also improve productivity by minimizing time-consuming file searches, expediting tasks that depend on the timely availability of recorded information, and preventing needless duplication of previously completed work. For business operations with complex document retrieval and control requirements, computer-based methods can reduce costs by minimizing labor requirements for file creation, maintenance, and control and by speeding document retrieval, thereby expediting business operations and improving employee productivity.

3. For mission-critical information, records management concepts and methods emphasize improved security precautions, combined with the off-site storage of backup copies, to minimize risk, simplify the reconstruction of recorded information, facilitate the resumption of business operations, and otherwise reduce the potentially costly consequences of adverse events.

Minimizing Legal Exposure

As previously noted, laws and government regulations specify retention requirements for records associated with certain business operations. Such requirements promote the enforcement of laws by ensuring that government auditors will have access to required information about specific business activities. Failure to comply with legally mandated recordkeeping requirements can be costly. At a minimum, an organization may be subject to fines or penalties for failure to produce records requested by government auditors. In tax audits, claimed deductions may not be accepted, and higher assessments, with penalties and interest, may be levied. In pharmaceuticals, telecommunications, utilities, and other industries, the approval of products or services that are subject to government regulation may be delayed or rescinded.

By consulting appropriate reference tools and working with legal counsel, systematic records management initiatives identify laws and regulations that apply to specific records. To minimize exposure, legally mandated recordkeeping requirements are incorporated into records management policies and procedures, thus ensuring that the requirements are observed by employees responsible for disposition of operating records.

Systematic records management can also reduce an organization's exposure in civil litigation and government investigation. Recorded information plays a critical role as evidence in product liability, personal injury, breach of contract, wrongful dismissal, and other lawsuits as the opposing parties seek to use documents, data, and other information to prove their contentions. Systematic records management initiatives can identify records that may be relevant and useful for future litigation, ensuring that those records will be available when needed. Effective retention practices can also reduce the logistic burdens and costs of legal discovery by discarding obsolete records in a timely manner before lawsuits or government investigations are initiated.

Increasing Revenues

Systematic records management can add value to business operations by increasing an organization's revenues. This increase in revenues can occur in several ways:

- *Systematic records management initiatives can create business opportunities.* When managed effectively, recorded information can have marketable, quantifiable value in certain business situations. Mailing lists and customer intelligence information, including demographic or other data about purchasing habits, preferences, and patterns, are obvious examples. These information resources are, in effect, products that can be sold to interested parties.

- *Recorded information is an important component of a marketable object or service.* As an example, effective recordkeeping systems support the profitable exploitation of an organization's intellectual property such as proprietary technologies, trade secrets, patents, product formulations, trademarks, and copyrights. Technology transfer agreements involving the sale or licensing of patented or unpatented inventions or manufacturing processes depend on accurate, complete records that describe the inventions or manufacturing processes in detail. The availability of thorough documentation for these highly valued knowledge assets can also be an important consideration in mergers and acquisitions.

- *Systematic recordkeeping practices confer competitive advantages that can lead to increased revenues.* Records management's contributions to competitive advantage are based on widely cited value chain concepts, which view the creation of a product or service as a series of interdependent activities, each of which adds value and costs to the final offering. The *value chain model* treats recorded information as a critical supporting element in business operations. From a value chain perspective, an organization with effective recordkeeping practices must enjoy a competitive advantage over an organization with less-effective or ineffective ones. By organizing and expediting the retrieval of valuable information and by eliminating irrelevant information through formally developed retention policies and procedures, systematic records management facilitates procurement, order processing, accounting, product scheduling, marketing, post-sale service, and other value chain activities. As its principal value contribution in such situations, recorded information reduces uncertainty, thereby enabling better management decisions.

The Records Management Function

In most organizations, records management is a staff function. Other examples of staff functions include accounting, human resources, purchasing, public relations, information systems, telecommunications management, reprographic services, the legal department, and the library. Staff functions provide enterprise-wide capabilities that would otherwise have to be replicated in many departments. Presumably, those capabilities can be provided more knowledgeably, consistently, efficiently, and economically on a centralized basis. In most organizations, individual departments do not have their own attorneys, telecommunications specialists, or librarians. They rely on staff functions for those capabilities when needed.

Organizational Placement

In government, the records management function is often based in an archival agency. The rationale for such arrangements is straightforward: Through its involvement in records management policies and procedures, an archival agency can ensure the preservation of records of enduring value. The National Archives and Records Administration (NARA) is the model for archives-based records management programs. According to 44 U.S. Code 2904, NARA is to "provide guidance and assistance to federal agencies to ensure economical and effective records management." NARA is further authorized to "promulgate standards, procedures, and guidelines with respect to records management" and to conduct "inspections or surveys of the records and the records management programs and practices within and between federal agencies." Similarly, the National Archives of Canada Act (R.S., 1985, c. 1, s-3) directs the Archivist "to advise government institutions concerning standards and procedures pertaining to the management of records."

Comparable laws define the records management authority of state and provincial archives. In New York, for example, the Arts and Cultural Affairs Law (Chapter 11-C of the Consolidated Laws) authorizes the State Archives to "review plans submitted by state agencies for management of their records" and "to provide technical assistance in records management for state agencies." Similarly, the Archives of Ontario develops records management policies, standards, and procedures for ministries and provincial agencies. Its authority is based on the province's Archives Act (Revised Statutes of Ontario, 1990, Chapter A.27) and on a subsequent policy directive on recorded information management issued by the province's Management Board.

In a few states and provinces, the records management function resides outside of an archival agency, even where such an agency exists. In California, for example, the State Records Management Act (Government Code, Chapter 5, Sections 14740-14774) requires the Director of the Department of General Services to "establish and administer, in the executive branch of government, a records management program which will apply efficient and economical management methods to the creation, utilization, maintenance, retention, preservation, and disposal of state records." The California State Archives is responsible for the state's local government records program, however. The State of Tennessee's Records Management Division, which is based in the Department of General Services, operates under the direction of the State's Public Records Commission, which has ultimate authority over records management policies and procedures for state government records. In Vermont, the Division of Public Records is based in the Central Services unit of the Department of Buildings and General Services. In Montana, the Records Management Bureau, which reports to the Secretary of State, administers the Public Records Management Act (Montana Code Annotated, Section 2-6-201 through 2-6-213). In many cases, state and provincial records management programs have authority over records created and maintained by local governments and quasi-governmental agencies, including counties, cities, towns, villages, school districts, and public authorities.

In colleges, universities, cultural institutions, philanthropic foundations, social service agencies, and other not-for-profit organizations, the records management function is typically based in an archives department, where such a department exists. The Harvard University Archives, for example, has responsibility for recordkeeping and retention procedures "to ensure the prudent maintenance and efficient disposition of University records." The University of Delaware's archives and records management policy clearly states the dual purpose of such archives-based records management programs: "to establish general procedures for the permanent preservation of University records of enduring value and for achieving economy and efficiency in the creation, maintenance, use, and disposition of University records."

Organizational placements are more varied in corporations, professional service firms, and other for-profit entities. The records management function may report to business services, to the legal department, to information technology, or to some other organizational unit. Each of these organizational placements has advantages and limitations. For example:

- Early in its history, records management was categorized as an administrative support function. An organizational placement in business services recognizes the role of records management as a service-oriented support activity that contributes to corporate efficiency and effectiveness. Often, however, a corporate business service unit includes activities that have little or no relationship to recorded information. Records management may be part of the same organizational unit as photocopying, printing, graphic arts, corporate travel, conference coordination, building maintenance, parking, and the mail room. In these situations, little opportunity is available for synergy between records management and other operations in the business services unit.

- An organizational placement in a corporate legal department recognizes the importance of litigation support, regulatory compliance, environmental issues, and other legal and quasi-legal concerns as powerful motivators for systematic records management. The close association of records management and corporate legal departments makes sense, given the latter's necessary involvement in records retention decisions. An organizational placement in a legal department gives records management high visibility. The legal department is just one step below the top in many large corporations and is likely to have considerable authority, influence, and resources. On the negative side, records management programs that report to legal departments may have a narrow scope, focusing on records retention to the exclusion of other records management activities.

- The growing importance of electronic records and technology-based document management systems underscores the roles and shared interests of records management and information technology as information management disciplines. A reporting relationship to an information technology unit is increasingly viewed as a modern organizational placement that clearly distances records management from its historical association with filing and other administrative activities. As a more substantive advantage, a reporting relationship with corporate information technology, which is typically influential and well-funded, can extend a records management program's scope and impact, while promoting records management's involvement in technology-based projects to which it can provide valuable input about retention issues and other matters. As a potential limitation, however, information technology personnel may have limited interest in the management of paper records, which continue to account for a large percentage of an organization's recorded information.

- Other organizational placements, such as having the records management function report to a finance, internal audit, tax, or security department, for example, are less commonly encountered. Some conceptual basis exists for these reporting arrangements. Some records management programs grew out of narrowly focused initiatives to define retention requirements for accounting and tax records. In some companies, the security department is responsible for information protection, disaster recovery, business continuity, and other activities related to protection of corporate assets, including information assets. Nevertheless, these organizational placements are difficult to evaluate. Often, their success or failure depends on the personal interactions of supervisors and subordinates.

Staffing and Duties

Generalizations about the records management function's employees and their duties are complicated by the considerable variety in staffing levels among records management programs. In most organizations, the records management function is administered by a department head that has the job title of *records manager* or some close approximation thereof. Where the head of an archival agency is nominally the records manager, as is sometimes the case in government, the actual responsibilities are typically delegated to a subordinate who functions as the records management department head. In that capacity, the records manager is responsible for representing the records management function in dealings with other organizational units, setting program priorities, developing records management policies and procedures, determining employees' work assignments and schedules, supervising staff, working with advisory committees where they exist, and performing a variety of general administrative functions, including preparation of budgets and reports.

In a one-person program, the records manager is necessarily responsible for all managerial and operational tasks. Most records management programs, however, employ one or more records analysts who work with departments or other organizational units to inventory records, determine retention requirements, and advise about the destruction of records, off-site storage, microfilming, protecting vital records, filing and retrieval methods, and other matters discussed in subsequent chapters. If a records management program has more than one records analyst, each may be assigned to work with specific departments. Alternatively, analysts may specialize in particular tasks or aspects of professional practice such as managing electronic records, electronic document imaging applications, training, or compliance determination.

Most records management programs have one or more employees who provide general administrative support and may perform other tasks such as data entry. Some records management programs have a part-time or full-time technology specialist for software, database, or Web site development.

If a records management program operates an off-site storage facility, as described in Chapter 4, a coordinator, one or more laborers, and administrative support are usually assigned to that activity. Although outsourcing off-site storage to a commercial provider can reduce in-house staffing requirements, it does not eliminate them. In most cases, a designated records management employee handles all business dealings with the commercial storage provider. That employee also works with departments to coordinate the transfer and retrieval of records, authorizes destruction of records in off-site storage, reviews monthly charges, and performs related tasks.

Some records management programs provide document imaging services or operate central file rooms or other document repositories. Those programs employ microfilm camera operators, imaging technicians, and records clerks, as well as one or more supervisors. Often, these operational personnel outnumber records analysts.

In addition to the staff described previously, records management programs may employ consultants, contractors, or temporary personnel to work on short-term projects or, when funds are available, to supplement regular staff. Further, some records management programs have informal working relationship with employees who perform filing, document scanning, or other records management tasks in other departments. Although those employees do not report directly to the records management program, they may take some direction from it.

Advisory Committee

In some corporations, government agencies, and other organizations, an advisory committee has oversight responsibilities for the records management function. The advisory defines program objectives, reviews records management policies and initiatives, and is involved with records retention issues, particularly the review and approval of retention policies. In some cases, the advisory committee also reviews records eligible for destruction. Committee members typically represent organizational units that have a strong interest in systematic recordkeeping. Examples include the legal department, finance or tax department, internal audit group, regulatory affairs, information technology, and, less commonly, human resources, quality assurance, and corporate security. Departments with large or important records collections, such as regulatory affairs in a pharmaceutical company or the registrar in an academic institution, may also be represented.

Departmental Coordinators

As discussed previously, records management is a staff function in most organizations. As such, it develops recordkeeping policies and procedures and provides guidance that others must implement. To succeed, the records management function requires the cooperation and assistance of knowledgeable persons in departments where records are kept. Many organizations have established a formal network of departmental coordinators—variously known as *records management coordinators, records facilitators, departmental records representatives,* or *departmental liaisons*—that are designated to work with the records management function for all matters relating to their departments. These employees report to supervisors in their own departments, but they take direction from the records management function for records-related matters. Their principal responsibilities include deployment of retention schedules, preparation of inactive records for transfer to off-site storage, and implementation of protection guidelines for vital records. As discussed in subsequent chapters, departmental coordinators may also perform records inventories or assist the records management program in conducting such inventories.

Departmental coordinators are typically designated by department managers. In most cases, they are administrative support personnel who are familiar with departmental operations and recordkeeping practices. Often, they supervise filing operations or have other involvement with departmental records.

Records Management and Related Fields

Records management is closely related to other information management disciplines and activities, including computing, telecommunications, knowledge management, library science, and archival administration. Collectively, these disciplines are involved in the systematic management of information resources.

In some organizations, records management is part of an administrative structure that encompasses multiple information-related specializations. Since the 1980s, some corporations, government agencies, and other organizations have consolidated their computing, telecommunications, records management, the library, and other information-related activities in a single business unit headed by a chief information officer (CIO) or other top management official. Such consolidated business units are sometimes described as *information management directorates* or *information resource management departments*. Properly organized and administered, they promote coordination of responsibilities, encourage the exchange of ideas, and foster cooperative rather than competing relationships among information-oriented operations, while preserving the distinctive characteristics, methods, and business objectives of each.

Regardless of organizational structure, information management initiatives that support complex business operations require the collaboration of multiple disciplines. Records management has a long history of successful interaction and cooperation with other information-related fields.

Information Technology

Records management's relationship to computing and telecommunications is clearly complementary and collaborative. Technology plays a key role in systematic management of recorded information, but the various information management disciplines are involved with technology in different ways. Computing and telecommunications are responsible for the selection, implementation, operation, and administration of an organization's information technology resources, including computer hardware, computer software, and networking facilities. Records management makes use of computing and telecommunication concepts and technologies, but its focus is on recorded information rather than the machines that process it.

Some records management concepts and methods, particularly those relating to active records, incorporate technological solutions, and records management responsibilities extend to the growing accumulation of electronic information produced by computers and related technologies. As discussed in Chapter 8, records managers are principally interested in the application of computing and telecommunications concepts and technologies to specific information management problems such as the timely retrieval of documents or database records to support particular business operations. Records management seldom has operational responsibility for computer systems or telecommunication networks. Instead, it typically draws on the expertise and technology resources provided by an organization's information systems department.

Knowledge Management

Knowledge management is concerned with the systematic management, utilization, and exploitation of an organization's knowledge resources. A multifaceted field with wide boundaries, **knowledge management** encompasses the creation, storage, arrangement, retrieval, and distribution of knowledge. Drawing on information technology, education, and other disciplines, knowledge management initiatives emphasize the value of an organization's intellectual capital—its inventions, patents, trade secrets, product formulations, customer intelligence, and well-established business processes. Knowledge management deals with *explicit knowledge*, which is codified in documents and databases, and *implicit knowledge*, which is embodied in employee's education and skills.

A close relationship exists between knowledge management and records management as business disciplines. Records and recordkeeping systems are valuable knowledge resources. From the perspective of knowledge management, recorded information is an important embodiment of an organization's intellectual capital. It is the principal manifestation of explicit knowledge, which is externalized in documents and data repositories. Records management concepts and activities complement and promote knowledge management. By providing systematic control of recorded information throughout its life cycle, records management paves the way for knowledge management, while successful knowledge management initiatives presuppose and affirm the strategic and operational importance of effective records management policies and procedures.

Library Science

Records management has a similarly close relationship to library science, on which some records management concepts are based. This relationship is most evident in document filing and indexing methodologies, which are discussed in Chapters 7 and 8. Records management and library science are equally concerned with the systematic analysis and control of recorded information, but each discipline has distinctive responsibilities that are complementary rather than competitive.

Records management is principally responsible for an organization's unpublished or proprietary information as contained in office documents, business forms, project files, databases, engineering drawings, and other resources. This information may be created by an organization itself or received, by physical delivery or electronic transfer, from other organizations. Often, the information is unique or exists in a limited number of copies. Libraries, by contrast, are repositories for books, periodicals, and other published information, much of which is purchased from external sources and exists in many copies.

Archival Administration

The close relationship between records management and archival administration is readily observed in government where records management authority is often based in archival agencies. A similar relationship between records management and archival administration is also the case in academic institutions and not-for-profit organizations; many university archives, for example, have records management responsibilities. In corporations and professional service firms where formal archival programs are less commonly encountered than in the not-for-profit sector, records managers are sometimes responsible for preserving records that reflect a company's history, products, and accomplishments.

Although they are allied disciplines, records management and archival administration have different missions. Records management is principally concerned with the usefulness of recorded information for an organization's ongoing business operations. Records management's clients are the employees who need information to do their jobs. Archivists, by contrast, seek to preserve information of enduring value for cultural, scholarly, or other research purposes. Their clientele includes historians, sociologists, public policy analysts, and genealogists, among others.

Records may have considerable business significance but no archival value. Conversely, records may have archival value even though their business significance has elapsed. Records management and archival administration are complementary activities. When addressing life cycle issues and making retention decisions, records management concentrates on the business significance of recorded information while relying on archivists for determination of research value.

Chapter 2

Preparing Retention Schedules I: Inventorying Records

A **records inventory** is a fact-finding survey that identifies and describes records maintained by all or part of an organization. The purpose of conducting an inventory is to gather information about the quantity, physical characteristics, storage conditions, use, and perceived value of records the organization maintains. As explained in Chapter 1, records management is a problem-solving activity. Recordkeeping problems cannot be successfully addressed until those problems are clearly delineated and fully understood. A thorough inventory is the initial step in a scientific approach to systematic control of recorded information. It is an essential component of an effective records management program.

Properly conducted, a records inventory provides detailed information about the nature and number of records maintained by a corporation, government agency, educational institution, professional services firm, or other organization. A records inventory is a means to an end rather than an end in itself. Information collected during the inventory is used to prepare records retention schedules, which, as discussed in the next chapter, indicate the lengths of time that specific types of records are to be kept. **Records retention scheduling** is an aspect of records management work that determines how long records need to be kept.

As an alternative to the inventory methods discussed in this chapter, retention schedules can be based on preformulated lists of generic records types that are presumably associated with commonly encountered business activities such as accounting, purchasing, human resources, engineering, or sales. This approach, which reduces the time and effort to prepare retention schedules, can be effective in some circumstances. It is best suited to straightforward business processes that are performed in more or less the same way from one organization to another and that have well-established recordkeeping requirements. A reasonable assumption, for example, is that an accounting office will have vouchers, an accounts payable department will have invoices, a purchasing department will have purchase orders, a human resources department will have master personnel files, an engineering department will have drawings and specifications, or a sales department will have customer order records. Further, retention requirements for these commonly encountered record types have been extensively analyzed; they are routinely included in retention schedules published by government agencies, for example. For purposes of preparing retention schedules, time-consuming empirical examination of such records contributes little, if any, new understanding about them.

As a potential shortcoming, however, retention schedules based on generic record types can be vague and incomplete. They sometimes contain highly generalized descriptions of record types that may be difficult to match against the records that a given department actually possesses, and they necessarily omit records associated with business processes or activities that are unique to a given organization. Only an inventory based on the empirical methods discussed in this chapter can reliably identify and describe such records. Nonetheless, lists of generic record types and predetermined retention periods are a useful starting point for inventorying records associated with commonly encountered business operations. When inventorying records in an accounting department, for example, having a preformulated list of the kinds of records likely to be encountered in that department is undeniably helpful. In particular, preformulated lists of generic record types can help focus the inventory process on unique records or those records with special retention requirements.

This chapter emphasizes the role of a records inventory in preparation of retention schedules, but inventory information may also be useful for other records management initiatives. In addition to confirming the existence of specific types of records held by an organization and describing their most important attributes, a records inventory can identify inactive records that might be discarded, transferred from office locations to off-site storage, or microfilmed. A comprehensive records inventory can also identify vital records and provide potentially valuable information about the quantity, arrangement, and use of an organization's active records.

Inventorying concepts and methods have been well-established components of records management practice for over half a century. A comprehensive records inventory consists of the following work steps:

1. Develop an inventory strategy—that is, a plan for conducting the records inventory.
2. Prepare a survey instrument for collecting inventory information.
3. Conduct the inventory according to plan.
4. Tabulate or otherwise write up the inventory results, collecting additional information and performing other follow-up tasks as necessary.

These work steps are described and discussed in this chapter. Practical considerations for records managers who must plan and conduct inventories for retention scheduling are emphasized.

Inventory Strategy

An inventory identifies and describes records maintained by all or part of an organization. At a minimum, an inventory strategy must address the scope of the inventory, and the procedures to be used to identify records. To accomplish its intended purpose in a reasonable amount of time with usable results, an inventory must have a manageable scope, where *scope* denotes the specific types of records and/or parts of an organization to be included in the inventory. Records are inventoried at the series level in the program units where they are maintained. Each program unit creates, receives, uses, and maintains groups (or series) of logically related records. The records management function works with departmental coordinators to identify records and gather data about them. The inventory process can be time-consuming. A reasonable amount of time must be allowed to complete the work.

Limiting an Inventory's Scope

To be considered comprehensive, an inventory must encompass recorded information in all formats—paper, photographic, and electronic—in every division, department, or other unit of an organization where records are kept. However, enterprise-wide inventories involving all types of records in a single initiative may not be advisable or practical. Enterprise-wide inventories may be workable for small-to-medium-size organizations— a company or government agency with fewer than 100 departments, for example—but ambitious inventory strategies pose significant logistic and analytical complications in large organizations with many business units and complex administrative structures. Inventorying records, as described next, is a labor-intensive activity that requires painstaking attention to detail. In large organizations, enterprise-wide inventories that attempt to cover all records and business units in a single initiative can take a long time to complete; multiyear inventorying projects are not unheard of. The principal problem with such lengthy inventories is that preparation of retention schedules and other tasks that depend on inventory data, and are the rationale for conducting an inventory, will be correspondingly delayed.

Management and participants alike can easily lose enthusiasm for initiatives that fail to show results in a reasonable time frame. Although information gathering can be accelerated by hiring temporary workers, forming special project teams, or otherwise augmenting a records management program's personnel resources, information gathering is just one part of an inventory project. The inventory's findings must be synthesized and analyzed. That intellectual activity can rarely be expedited. If useful results are to be obtained, an inventory cannot be rushed. Further, some information collected during early stages of a lengthy enterprise-wide inventory may become obsolete before the project is completed. Business operations may be added or discontinued, business processes may change, or departments or other organizational units may merge, expand, or be dissolved. In such cases, recordkeeping practices will be affected, and inventory work must be redone.

As a more effective approach, the records of large organizations should be inventoried in stages, beginning with a single division or business function, then adding others as the work progresses and specific inventory tasks are completed. In a pharmaceutical company, for example, a records inventory might begin in corporate headquarters. When that work is completed, the inventorying initiative can proceed to research and development, marketing, manufacturing, and other organizational units in succession. In a hospital, a records inventory might be initially limited to accounting, human resources, and other administrative departments, with patient records held centrally or in clinical departments to follow in a second stage. In multinational companies, an inventory project might be limited initially to domestic operations. Alternatively, an inventory might be limited to a specific type of recorded information, such as financial records in a corporation or government agency, case files in a law firm, engineering project records in a manufacturing company, property-related records in local government, or student records in an academic institution. Limitations on record types can be combined with organizational limitations. As an example, an inventory might be limited to the domestic research and development division of a pharmaceutical company and, initially, to regulatory records within that division.

An inventory's scope can be limited by record format, but conducting the inventory of paper, photographic, and electronic records simultaneously is often advisable, particularly in organizations where systematic records management is a new activity and formal records retention schedules are incomplete or nonexistent. Multiformat inventories are also recommended for organizations that need to update retention schedules. Among its advantages, the multiformat approach can simplify the logistics of inventorying by reducing the number of required site visits and meetings when compared to separate inventories of paper, photographic, and electronic records. Multiformat inventories can also provide useful insights into the interrelationship and redundancy of information in various formats. As an example, word processing software may be used to transcribe audio recordings created by voice dictation equipment. The resulting documents are then printed for filing or distribution and saved as word processing files on hard drives, with backup copies on magnetic tape, floppy disks, or other media. The printed versions may be photocopied multiple times, and the originals or any of the copies may subsequently be microfilmed or even digitized for storage and retrieval.

Under the best circumstances, inventorying records is a difficult and time-consuming task. Meetings must be scheduled. Information must be collected and analyzed for completeness and usability. Follow-up discussions may be necessary to verify information or clarify specific points. Limiting an inventory's scope will make it more manageable and permit faster completion. Results and benefits will be obtained more quickly, although they will admittedly impact only a segment of the organization.

Identifying Program Units

Regardless of scope, records inventories are typically conducted on a program-unit basis. For purposes of this discussion, a **program unit**, perhaps better described as a *recordkeeping unit*, is broadly defined as a division, department, section, or other administrative unit that maintains recorded information. As a generic designation, *program unit* avoids confusion associated with varying names that identify organizational units and their differing hierarchical relationships. In some organizations, for example, departments are subordinate to divisions; in other cases, the reverse is true. A department or division may be divided into offices, branches, or sections. Alternatively, a section, branch, or office may be the highest level in an organization's administrative hierarchy, and departments and divisions may be subordinate to them.

Within a corporation, government agency, educational institution, or other organization, program units vary in size, complexity, and hierarchical interrelationships, as well as in the number and types of records they create, maintain, and use. Some program units may be large departments with hundreds of employees and huge quantities of records in multiple formats. Other program units may be small offices staffed by one or two persons who maintain a few paper files or electronic records. When planning a records inventory, the program units to be included must be identified. This identification is typically done by consulting organization charts, directories, or administrative handbooks. In many cases, however, such documents are out-of-date, and additional program units may be discovered while the inventory is in progress or after it has been completed.

The Records Series Concept

A program unit's mission and responsibilities are presumably related to and supported by its records. For each program unit, inventorying, retention scheduling, and related operations are applied to records at the series level, as opposed to the document, folder, or item level. Broadly defined, a **records series** is a group of logically related records that support a specific business or administrative operation performed by a given program unit. A records series typically consists of multiple documents, folders, or items, which are used, indexed, and/or filed together. In some cases, a records series may exist in several different media—active records from a given series may be kept in paper form, for example, and inactive records stored on microfilm.

Properly conducted, a records inventory identifies and describes each records series maintained by a given program unit. Examples of records series include:

- Open purchase orders in a corporate purchasing department
- Construction contracts in an engineering project management office
- Employee benefits records in a human resources department
- Closed claims in an insurance company
- Invoices in an accounts payable department
- Property records in a municipal building department
- Patient records in a hospital
- Patent files in a pharmaceutical company's intellectual property office
- Applications pending file in a college admissions department.

Role of Departmental Coordinators

A records inventory cannot succeed without top management support and the cooperation of individual program units. To encourage support, the inventory's objectives and its relationship to the systematic control of recorded information must be explained to, and appreciated by, appropriate levels of management. To demonstrate its support, an organization's top management should send a directive to all program units that will be affected by a records inventory. The directive should announce that an inventorying initiative has been authorized, and it should solicit the cooperation of program unit personnel.

Presented as a management memorandum, the directive is typically drafted by the records management staff for top management's signature. At a minimum, the memorandum should:

- Acknowledge the value of recorded information as an organizational resource;
- Emphasize the importance of managing recorded information in a systematic manner;
- Explain briefly the role of the records inventory as an essential data-gathering activity and the critical first step in the systematic control of recorded information;
- Indicate when the inventory will begin, who will conduct it, and approximately how long it will take; and
- Instruct each program unit to designate a departmental coordinator who will assist the records manager in inventorying recorded information.

Departmental coordinators are crucial to the success of records inventories and other records management initiatives. As discussed briefly in Chapter 1, these coordinators are knowledgeable about the records maintained by their program units. Departmental coordinators are the principal contact persons for all records management activities within their program units. They will assist the records manager in conducting inventories and in formulating retention and disposition recommendations for their program units. Once retention schedules are finalized, the departmental coordinators will be responsible for implementing them.

Consultation vs. Questionnaires

Information collected during a records inventory will be used to prepare retention schedules, as explained in the next chapter. An inventory's success is determined by its suitability for that purpose. Inventories must be conducted systematically and efficiently. Inventory procedures must be well planned. A formalized survey instrument will ensure the usefulness, uniformity, and completeness of information collected during the inventory process. The survey instrument, described in detail next, delineates the descriptive data and other items of information that must be collected for each records series.

The survey instrument may be distributed as a questionnaire to departmental coordinators, with completed questionnaires to be returned to the records management unit by a specified date. Alternatively, records management staff can consult with individual program units to conduct physical inventories of records series. Assisted by departmental coordinators, records managers will personally collect the information required by the survey instrument. The questionnaire and consultative methods are applicable to records in all formats. Five decades of records management theory and practice have identified the advantages and limitations of each approach.

The obvious advantage of the questionnaire method is shorter elapsed time for the information-gathering phase of a records inventory. This reduction in time is achieved through distribution of the inventory workload among departmental coordinators. Multiple program units can consequently be inventoried simultaneously. The consultative method, by contrast, relies on the records management staff or, in many cases, a records analyst as solo practitioner who must inventory program units sequentially. As its principal shortcoming, the questionnaire method provides limited opportunities for direct interaction between program-unit personnel who conduct the inventory and the records management staff who must prepare retention recommendations based on inventory data. Even under the best circumstances, obtaining sufficiently clear and detailed information to be analyzed by others is difficult. Misinterpretations, discrepancies in calculations, and some marginally useful responses are to be expected. If the questionnaire method is selected, records management staff must provide orientation sessions for departmental coordinators, supplemented by detailed written instructions, to explain the questionnaire's purpose and content. The orientation sessions should review the data elements to be collected and provide examples of appropriate responses to specific questions. Records management staff must also be available to answer questions or clarify issues that may arise during the inventorying process.

Although the consultation method takes longer than the questionnaire method and involves a greater commitment of time and resources by the records management function, it usually yields more accurate, reliable, and immediately usable information. It produces more detailed responses, and it minimizes the potential for misinterpretation; confusing points can be clarified during the inventory itself. The consultation method relies on two techniques that are well established in information systems analysis: (1) direct observation of a program unit's recordkeeping practices by the records management staff and (2) interviews with program-unit personnel who create, maintain, and use recorded information.

As noted previously, the records management staff work directly with departmental coordinators in each program unit to identify and describe records series. Presumably, departmental coordinators are knowledgeable about the way in which specific records series are created, stored, and used in their program units. During the inventory, the records manager meets with the departmental coordinator to discuss the characteristics of records series maintained by a given program unit. A formalized survey instrument serves as an interview script. If more detailed information about specific records series is required, departmental coordinators will arrange interviews with other program-unit employees. The records manager also has the opportunity to inspect files, examine paper documents, view microfilm, or retrieve samples of electronic records for display or printing.

Although the questionnaire and consultation methods are presented here as opposites, they are not mutually exclusive. As a potentially effective combination of the two approaches, records management staff may distribute survey instruments to individual program units for completion, then conduct site visits and interviews with departmental coordinators to review, clarify, or expand the program units' responses.

In some cases, the questionnaire method is the only practical approach to inventorying records. Because of time or economic constraints, for example, records management staff may be unable to conduct site visits and interviews at field offices, branch locations, international subsidiaries, or other geographically remote program units. If an organization has multiple field offices or branch locations with similar recordkeeping practices, a site visit and interviews may be conducted at several of the locations, and the remainder surveyed by the questionnaire method.

Two examples of inventory questionnaires are shown in Figures 2-1a and 2-1b.

Records Inventory Worksheet

Examples of forms used to inventory records.

Figure 2-1a

Records Inventory Worksheet		
Records Title / Series		
Company	Department	
Record Copy ☐ Yes ☐ No	If no, where is it?	If yes, where is it?
Description		
Dates	Retention, If Known	
Format and Size ☐ Paper _____ ☐ Electronic _____ ☐ Bound _____ ☐ Video _____ ☐ Photo _____ ☐ Microfilm _____ ☐ Other _____	Volume Cubic Feet _____ Filing Inches _____	
Reference Citation	Legal Requirement ☐ Yes ☐ No	Tax Requirement ☐ Yes ☐ No
Person Taking Inventory	Telephone / E-mail Address	Date Inventory Taken
Contact Name	Telephone No. / Ext.	E-mail Address
Remarks		

Inventory Timetable

Regardless of the method employed, sufficient time must be allotted to complete a records inventory. Although a sense of urgency may stimulate productivity, unrealistic deadlines are not compatible with quality work. If the consultation method is used, site visits and interviews will likely require at least one-half day per program unit, exclusive of preparation, travel time to the program-unit location, and follow-up work. These

**Records
Inventory and
Analysis**

Figure 2-1b

Records Inventory and Analysis

Department	Division/Office		
Location	Person	Telephone / E-Mail	Date

Record Title

Record Description

Purpose of Record

Type of Record
☐ Original – Location of Duplicate _____
☐ Duplicate – Location of Original _____

Record Format
☐ Letter   ☐ Plans/Drawings   ☐ Card File   ☐ Printout   ☐ EDP Tape
☐ Legal   ☐ Video Tape   ☐ Photograph   ☐ Microfilm   ☐ EDP Disk/Diskette
☐ Ledger   ☐ Audio Tape   ☐ Other _____

Filing Method
☐ Alphabetic   ☐ Numeric   ☐ Chronologic   ☐ Subject   ☐ Alphanumeric
☐ Geographic   ☐ Other _____

Type of Filing Equipment
☐ Vertical   ☐ Lateral   ☐ Shelf   ☐ Other _____

Is Record Microfilmed? ☐ Yes   ☐ No | If not, could microfilm be used? ☐ Yes   ☐ No   ☐ Unknown

Inclusive Dates of Records _____ Thru _____	Retention Period _____ Years in Office _____ Years at Records Center	Does Record Have Historical/ Archival Value? ☐ Yes ☐ No ☐ Unknown
Rate of Accumulation _____ Cubic Inches / Year _____ Cubic Feet / Year	Total Accumulation _____ Cubic Inches _____ Cubic Feet	Special Characteristics ☐ Vital Record ☐ Confidential Record Statutory Retention Period P.A. _____ Year _____
Reference Activity Rate First Year _____ Per Week in Office _____ Per Month _____ Per Year	Reference Activity Rate Subsequent _____ Per Week Years _____ Per Month in Office _____ Per Year	Reference Activity Rate Years at _____ Per Week Records _____ Per Month Center _____ Per Year

Cubic Foot Measurements   (1 cu. ft. = 1728 cu. in)
Letter-Size Drawer (Lateral) 2.0 cu. ft.......(Vertical) 1.5 cu. ft.   Microfilm, 100, 16mm Reels...........1.2 cu. ft.
Legal-Size Drawer (Lateral) 2.5 cu. ft.......(Vertical) 2.0 cu. ft.   4x6″ Card File, Single Row 12″......0.2 cu. ft.
Records Center Carton..1.2 cu. ft.   5x8″ Card File, Single Row 12″......0.3 cu. ft.
Shelving, 4 ft. Letter Size.......................................2.3 cu. ft.   Shelving, 4 ft. Legal Size................3.0 cu. ft.
Tab Card Drawer, Single Row 25″.........................0.3 cu. ft.   Computer Tape (7 Reels).................1.2 cu. ft.

Comments

(Source: Sample Forms for Archival & Records Management Programs, published by ARMA International and the Society of American Archivists)

tasks can double or triple the time required to inventory records in a given program unit. Several days and multiple site visits may be required to complete an inventory in large program units. Some interviews and site visits can take much longer. Given the wide variety of situations in which records are kept, reasonable estimates of completion time can only be made in the context of specific work environments. As discussed at the end of this chapter, additional time will be required to tabulate or otherwise write up the inventory's findings from notes taken during interviews and site visits. Follow-up interviews or telephone calls will often be necessary to clarify specific points raised during interviews.

Thus, an inventorying initiative in an organization with 100 program units will require at least 200 to 250 working days (about one calendar year), exclusive of the time required to analyze inventory results and draft retention schedules as discussed in the next chapter. That estimate may be optimistic. Site visits may prove difficult to schedule. Cancellations and rescheduling are inevitable and will delay the work. Follow-up requirements are unpredictable and can prove time-consuming. Inventories that involve records in multiple formats will take longer to complete.

Even when the questionnaire method is used, inventorying records is a time-consuming process. Some responses will be late. Repeated telephone calls may be necessary to obtain the completed questionnaires. Information provided by departmental coordinators must be reviewed and, where necessary, clarified by records management staff. Systematic, thorough inventories cannot be rushed. Top management must understand that time spent obtaining reliable, detailed inventory findings will facilitate the preparation of appropriate retention recommendations for recorded information as well as the identification of vital records and other records management activities that depend on accurate, complete inventory data.

Special Issues for Electronic Records

Inventories of electronic records are complicated by the fact that such records are invisible and consequently difficult to identify. Electronic record characteristics cannot be easily determined by observation, as they can with paper files. Empirical methods may be useful for magnetic tapes, diskettes, optical disks, and other removable media, but many electronic records are stored, out of view, on nonremovable hard drives.

When inventorying records in individual program units, the existence of electronic records can often be determined by inquiring about electronic counterparts when paper or photographic records are identified. That approach, however, will not identify electronic records that have no paper or photographic counterparts. Some records managers consequently recommend that electronic records be inventoried by identifying and analyzing the automated information systems with which they are associated.

Broadly defined, an **automated information system** consists of hardware and/or software components designed to perform one or more information processing operations. To identify electronic records associated with computer-based information systems, a records manager must first identify the application software utilized by a given program unit. Both custom-developed computer programs and prewritten software packages must be considered. Data files, text files, or other electronic records series associated with such software can then be identified. This method is easiest to implement for electronic records created and maintained by computers installed in and operated by a given program unit. It can also be used for electronic records associated with information processing applications that run on mainframes, minicomputers, and network servers installed outside the program unit. Such computers, which create and maintain electronic records on a program unit's behalf, may be operated by a centralized information technology department or by a commercial computer service bureau.

The same method can be used to inventory electronic records created and/or used by audio and video recording and playback equipment, as well as by data recorders and other specialized instrumentation encountered in certain scientific, engineering, and medical applications. As with computer-based information systems, the records manager must first determine the type of devices employed by a given program unit, then identify the electronic records associated with such devices. If a program unit has camcorders or other video recording equipment, for example, the records manager should inquire about videotapes or other media produced by such equipment. Similarly, records managers should inquire about video recordings produced for the program unit by centralized video departments or video service companies.

As a potentially significant limitation, inventories conducted on a program-unit basis may fail to identify electronic records associated with enterprise-wide information systems that serve multiple departments. Such records may support interdepartmental communications, budget preparation, multidepartmental transaction processing, and such analytical activities as knowledge management, data mining, and decision support. Examples include electronic mail, Web pages posted on the public Internet or organizational intranets, computerized document repositories created by electronic document imaging and document management software, and centralized databases and data warehouses of financial, personnel, customer, product, and other information. Although these centralized information resources serve multiple program units, they are not the property of any single program unit. The records they create and maintain usually reside on computers operated and administered by centralized information technology departments. Individual program units access these enterprise-wide electronic records, but they are not responsible for storing, protecting, or otherwise managing them. The records are not stored locally. Consequently, they may not be mentioned when inventorying a program unit's records.

The Survey Instrument

Recorded information is inventoried at the series level, where a records series is a group of logically related records that support one or more business processes or operations performed by a given program unit. Presumably, departmental coordinators can identify and describe the major records series maintained by their program units. Major records series are notable for both their quantity and importance to program-unit operations. Records analysts must usually work harder during interviews and site visits to identify minor records series, which are less important and less voluminous. No matter how diligent the inventory procedures, some minor series may be overlooked.

As discussed in the preceding section, a *survey instrument* specifies the descriptive data and other items of information to be collected for each records series maintained by a given program unit. Depending on the inventory method employed, the survey instrument may be formatted as a questionnaire to be distributed to departmental coordinators in individual program units. If the consultative method is used, the survey instrument is treated as a script and checklist to be followed when conducting site visits and interviewing program-unit personnel.

Regardless of approach, the following discussion lists and explains the types of information to be collected about each series maintained by a given program unit during a records inventory. Typically, an inventory begins with general information about the scope, purpose, and quantity of a records series. Other information describes the physical and technical characteristics of records, their storage locations, reference patterns, business value, and retention requirements.

Series Title

The series title is the name by which a records series is known to the program unit where the records are kept. The title will identify the records series in retention schedules, reports, tabulations, analyses, and other documents prepared from inventory data. Consequently, it should be as descriptive as possible. At a minimum, the title must accurately represent the content of the records series and clearly distinguish it from other series maintained by the program unit. Examples of acceptably descriptive series titles include:

- Employee Benefit Files – for records maintained by a human resources department about insurance and other benefits elected by individual employees;
- Accounts Payable Files – for invoices and related records maintained by an accounting department;
- Litigation Files – for case files maintained by a corporate legal department;
- Property Records Cards – for a card file of property descriptions maintained by a municipal assessor's office;
- Plant Drawing Files – for engineering drawings relating to power generation facilities in a utility company;
- Active Student Files – for records maintained by a registrar's office for currently enrolled college students;
- Patient Files – for patients' medical records maintained by a hospital;
- Collection Object Files – for records about art works maintained by the curatorial department of a museum.

Some records series may also be identified by alternative titles, which should be noted. Thus, property records cards may also be known as *assessment cards* or they may be identified by their color as *yellow cards* or *green cards*. Where a records series consists of standardized forms, the form number often serves as an alternate title.

Summary Description

A brief description, perhaps a paragraph in length, should summarize the business purpose, scope, and content of the records series. With some records series, such as the Active Student Files example cited previously, the title describes the content of the series, but additional details can clarify its business purpose and scope. The additional details might indicate the specific types of students—graduate or undergraduate, for example—covered by the series, the types of documents included in student files, and the series' relationship to other records series maintained in the registrar's office or elsewhere in the organization. Similarly, a brief descriptive paragraph for the Property Records Cards series might indicate the specific properties covered and give examples of the type of information included on each card. In every case, a statement of purpose should indicate the records series' relationship to the program unit's mission, administrative activities, and business operations.

Dates Covered

During inventories, records analysts must determine the inclusive (beginning and ending) dates for information contained in each records series. Records series that support ongoing business operations will have open-ending dates, which are noted in inventories as "to the present." This notation is the norm for most operating records. Closed records series, to which no new documents are being added, may be associated with discontinued or divested business operations, defunct program units, organizational realignments, or acquired companies that cease to operate independently. With electronic records, closed series may consist of legacy data associated with computer systems that have been replaced.

Format

Three principal physical formats are used for recorded information: (1) paper documents; (2) photographic records, including still-image negatives and plates, slides, motion picture films, X-rays, and microforms; and (3) electronic records, including computer records, audio recordings, and video recordings. As discussed in Chapter 1, certain other objects that are not normally considered records may come within the scope of a records management program and inventorying initiative if they are closely associated with research and development reports, contracts, product specifications, architectural renderings, engineering drawings, medical tests, environmental tests, or other records. Examples include biological specimens, architectural models, soil samples that relate to construction projects, and product samples.

For descriptive purposes, paper records are often categorized by page size. Table 2-1 lists commonly encountered paper sizes for office records in the United States. Table 2-2 lists commonly encountered international paper sizes. U.S. paper sizes are measured in inches. International paper sizes, which have metric measurements. are identified by alphanumeric designations defined by the International Organization for Standardization (ISO). Most U.S. paper sizes have an international counterpart

Commonly
Encountered
North American
Paper Sizes

Table 2-1

Commonly Encountered North American Paper Sizes		
	Dimensions	
Page Type	Inches	Millimeters
Letter	8.5 × 11	216 × 279
Legal	8.5 × 14	216 × 356
Printout	11 × 14	279 × 356
Ledger	11 × 17	279 × 432
Index Card	3 × 5	76 × 127
Index Card	4 × 6	102 × 152
Index Card / Invoice	5 × 8	127 × 203
Engineering Drawing A	11 × 8.5	279 × 216
Engineering Drawing B	11 × 17	279 × 432
Engineering Drawing C	17 × 22	432 × 559
Engineering Drawing D	22 × 34	559 × 864
Engineering Drawing E (new)	34 × 44	864 × 1118
Engineering Drawing E (old)	36 × 48	914 × 1219

Commonly
Encountered
International
Paper Sizes

Table 2-2

Commonly Encountered International Paper Sizes			
	Dimensions		
ISO Designation	Millimeters	Inches	Typical Uses
A4	210 × 297	8.25 × 11.7	Office documents
B4	250 × 353	9.8 × 13.9	Computer printouts
A3	297 × 420	11.7 × 16.5	Ledgers
A5	148 × 210	5.8 × 8.3	Index cards
A6	105 × 148	4.1 × 5.8	Index cards, microfiche
A2	420 × 594	16.5 × 23.4	Engineering drawings
A1	594 × 841	23.4 × 33.1	Engineering drawings
A0	841 × 1189	33.1 × 46.8	Engineering drawings

that is slightly larger or smaller but is intended for the same business purpose. Multinational companies, universities, cultural institutions, government agencies, and other organizations with international activities or operations will likely have records in both U.S. and international paper sizes. Although comingled U.S. and international papers cannot be neatly stacked, the size variations pose no significant problems for filing, microfilming, scanning, or other records management activities.

In the United States, 8.5 by 11 inches (U.S. letter size) is the most commonly encountered page size for correspondence, reports, and other office records. Its international counterpart is the A4 size, which is slightly narrower and longer (approximately 8.27 by 11.7 inches). In the 1930s, the U.S. government, the world's largest purchaser of office papers, adopted an 8-by-10.5-inch page size for correspondence and other office documents generated by federal agencies, but that practice was discontinued in the 1990s.

Since the 1980s, the records management profession, led by ARMA International, has strongly opposed the use of U.S. legal-size (8.5-by-14-inch) papers, which were once commonplace for contracts, legal briefs, depositions, and other documents. When compared to letter-size papers, legal-size pages require larger, more expensive filing cabinets that occupy more floor space. Legal-size documents also require larger, more expensive file folders, and they must be microfilmed at higher reduction ratios than their letter-size counterparts. Legal-size pages are typically reduced to letter-size when scanned for display or printing.

U.S. computer printout pages, which measure 11 by 14 inches, are the largest office records that can be packed into cubic foot containers without folding. The closest international paper size is B4, which measures approximately 9.8 by 14 inches. Increasingly, computer reports are printed in a reduced format on 11-by-8.5-inch paper.

The U.S. ledger-size page is the largest office document that can be digitized by a desktop scanner or recorded onto 16mm microfilm at a reasonable reduction in a single exposure. Its international counterpart is the A3 page size, which measures approximately 11.7 by 16.5 inches.

Apart from size, a records inventory should collect information about the physical attributes of paper documents, including thickness, color of pages and ink, legibility, fragility, and two-sided pages. These attributes are particularly important if retention recommendations will include microfilming or document scanning.

Although original engineering drawings may be created on polyester, vellum, or other nonpaper materials, they are treated as paper records for inventorying purposes. U.S. and international page sizes for engineering drawings, architectural plans, and other large-format documents are specified in ASME Y-14.1, *Decimal Inch Drawing Sheet Size and Format*, and ASME Y-14.1M, *Metric Drawing Sheet Size and Format*. Both standards are published by the American Society of Mechanical Engineers (ASME International).

U.S. drawing sizes are identified by alphabetic designations, while international drawing sizes use alphanumeric identifiers in the ISO A Series. The most commonly used drawing sizes are U.S. D and E and their international counterparts, A1 and A0. The E and A0 sizes are the largest drawings that can be readily digitized or recorded onto 35mm microfilm in a single exposure. E and A0 drawings are also the largest sizes that can be filed flat in a drawer or hanging cabinet. Although U.S. letter designations are available for them, drawings larger than E size are sometimes collectively categorized as O (oversize). Such large drawings are typically rolled for storage, and they must be digitized or microfilmed in segments.

Photographic records include, but are not necessarily limited to, still-image negatives, photographic plates, slides, X-rays, microforms, and motion picture films. These records are usually described by type, size, format, color status, and special attributes. Examples include 4-by-5-inch black-and-white negatives, 2-by-2-inch color slides in paper mounts, and 35mm color motion picture film on reels. Note that photographic prints are considered paper records for inventorying purposes. They may be filed separately or comingled with other paper documents in folders. As previously noted, microforms are considered photographic records. They include 16mm and 35mm reels, 16mm cartridges, microfiche, microfilm jackets, and aperture cards. When inventorying microforms, the reduction ratio, image placement, and film type are typically noted. These attributes are discussed more in Chapter 5.

Electronic records media include computer, video, and audio disks and tapes. As with photographic records, these media are described by type, size, format, and special attributes. Examples of computer disks include 3.5-inch, double-sided, double-density floppy disks; proprietary floppy disk products, such as Zip cartridges and LS-120 SuperDisks; older 5.25-inch and 8-inch floppy disk formats; 3.5-inch or 5.25-inch magneto-optical disk cartridges; and compact disks and DVDs in read-only and recordable formats. Examples of computer tapes include 9-track magnetic tape on reels, half-inch data cartridges in 34xx and 3590 formats, digital linear tape (DLT), 8mm data cartridges, linear tape open (LTO) media, and digital audio tape (DAT). Examples of video media include VHS and Beta tapes, 8mm videotapes, digital video cartridges, and DVDs. Examples of audio media include compact discs and audio tapes on reels and in cassettes.

Arrangement

The **arrangement** is the physical sequence of records or groups of records within a series. In paper filing systems, documents pertaining to a given person, case, subject, or other matter are typically grouped in folders, which are arranged by their principal retrieval parameter. In a hospital, for example, folders containing patient records may be arranged alphabetically by the patient's name. In a law office, case folders may be arranged sequentially by case number. In a municipal building department, folders containing building permit applications and related documents may be arranged by a geographic designator such as property address or tax map identifier. In a sales department, folders containing order documents may be arranged by customer name or order number. Many program units maintain general subject files with folders arranged alphabetically by topical headings. These and other filing arrangements for active records are discussed more fully in Chapter 7.

Microforms are often arranged in the same sequence as the paper records from which they were made. Thus, microfiche copies of student records may be arranged by student name, while aperture cards produced from engineering drawings may be arranged by drawing number. Arrangement concepts are also applicable to magnetic tapes, optical disks, or other removable media that contain electronic records. In computer installations, for example, backup tapes may be shelved chronologically or by a serially assigned number. Similarly, videotape recordings of building inspections may be arranged by building number or project number, while dictated correspondence and other office documents may be arranged chronologically within a series of audio tapes, which may themselves be arranged chronologically in cabinets or on shelves.

Arrangements are rarely meaningful for computer records stored on hard drives. The computer's operating system determines where such records will be stored, often on a space-available basis. Access is provided by directories and indexes; users are unaware of the physical sequence in which information is recorded within a given medium. In many cases, unrelated documents and files are intermingled within a disk, and a given file may be fragmented among several disk locations.

Quantity

For each records series, the inventory must collect information about the quantity of records as well as the locations and conditions in which the records are stored. Quantity estimates provide useful information about the amount of physical storage space required by a given records series. In particular, such measurements alert the records manager to potential storage space problems posed by voluminous records series.

For office documents and other paper records, quantity is customarily measured in cubic feet, a practice that facilitates the tabulation and comparison of records regardless of paper size or the cabinets in which they are stored. In records management, a **cubic foot** is defined as the contents of a container with interior dimensions of 10 inches high by 12 inches wide by 15 inches deep, which is slightly greater than one cubic foot. That container can conveniently store the three most commonly encountered sizes of office records: letter-size pages, legal-size pages, and computer printouts. It can also store index cards and other small records packed or stacked in multiple rows and layers.

Active records are rarely packed in cubic foot containers; they are typically stored in drawer or shelf-type filing cabinets. To determine the number of cubic feet in such cases, measure the number of linear inches of drawer or shelf space occupied by the records and apply the following simple conversion rules:

1. For letter-size pages, 15 linear inches of records equals 1 cubic foot.

2. For legal-size pages, 12 linear inches of records equals 1 cubic foot.

3. For 11-by-14 inch computer printouts, 10 linear inches of records equals 1 cubic foot.

Thus, a file cabinet drawer with 26 linear inches of filing space contains slightly less than 2 cubic feet of letter-size pages or 2.5 cubic feet of legal-size pages when completely full. Because many file drawers are partially filled to facilitate inserting and removing folders, a reasonable volume estimate is 1.5 cubic feet of letter-size pages or 2 cubic feet of legal-size pages per drawer, which results in 6 cubic feet of letter-size files or 8 cubic feet of legal-size files per four-drawer cabinet.

For small records, which may be packed in cubic foot containers in the most practical manner, reasonable volume estimates are as follows:

- 3-by-5-inch cards – 12,000 per cubic foot
- 4-by-6-inch cards – 6,000 per cubic foot

- 5-by-8-inch cards – 4,500 per cubic foot
- tabulating-size cards – 10,000 per cubic foot

Quantity estimates for engineering drawings and other large-format documents are usually based on the number of individual items. The same method applies to photographic and electronic storage media. Estimates of the number of film negatives, slides, motion picture reels, microforms, disks, tapes, or other media are typically included on an inventory. With high-capacity computer disks and tapes, several records series may be comingled within a given medium, in which case the percentage occupied by each series should be indicated.

When inventorying records, emphasizing the most voluminous series and surveying them first is often advisable. When retention recommendations are developed and implemented, large records series usually offer the greatest potential for floor space reduction, elimination of new filing equipment purchases, and other savings.

Estimated Growth

Information about the annual growth of records is essential for planning future storage requirements. In presentations to management, growth estimates can also encourage a sense of urgency about records management initiatives, particularly for records series growing at a rapid rate. As discussed in Chapter 1, recordkeeping is an ordinary and necessary aspect of all business activities. Unless the operations they support are discontinued or severely curtailed, the quantity of records created and maintained by a corporation, government agency, university, or other organization will increase over time.

Anticipated annual growth rates for a given records series are most easily and conveniently determined when the series is subdivided by year or other chronologic periods, a practice known as *breaking files*. Subdividing a series is often the case with financial records and other transaction-oriented documents. The sizes of annual segments can be measured and compared to calculate growth. Thus, if a series of vouchers in an accounting department occupied 15 file drawers in the 2002 fiscal year and 18 file drawers in the 2003 fiscal year, the growth rate from one year to the next is 20 percent.

Where a given records series is not subdivided by year, the annual growth rate must be estimated in other ways such as relating the growth of records to some measurable factor. The creation of records never occurs in a vacuum. Records are typically linked to events or transactions such as the receipt of orders in a sales department, the issuance of policies or receipt of claims in an insurance company, the acceptance of new clients in a social services agency, the admission of students in an academic institution, the hiring of new employees in a human resources department, or the initiation of projects in an engineering firm. If such events or transactions are increasing at a specific annual rate, records associated with such transactions will consequently grow at a corresponding rate. Thus, if a file is created each time a college enrolls a new student and if enrollment is increasing by 10 percent per year, the number of files for newly admitted students should also increase by 10 percent, all other things being equal. If 5,000 new student files were created this year, 5,500 files will be created next year.

Where the foregoing methods are inapplicable, paper files, database records, or other records can be examined, their creation dates determined, and a tabulation of annual quantities prepared, but that procedure is labor-intensive, time-consuming, and difficult to apply. Methods aside, unusual circumstances often defy estimation. None of the methods discussed here could have predicted the explosive growth of e-mail, for example.

Storage Location(s) and Equipment

Records may be stored in departmental offices, in file rooms or other centralized repositories, in off-site warehouses, or in other facilities. Records from a given series may be stored in multiple locations; active records may be kept in departmental offices, while older records are transferred to off-site storage. An inventory should indicate all storage locations for each records series and for all copies of a given series. If storage facilities have special security or environmental characteristics, whether suitable or unsuitable, they should be noted.

An inventory should also indicate the types, quantities, and physical conditions of file cabinets or other containers that house a given records series. This information is important because records retention initiatives typically result in the destruction of inactive records or their transfer from office areas to off-site storage. As part of that process, file cabinets may be emptied. Using information collected during an inventory, a records manager can estimate the number of file cabinets that will be made available and are suitable for reuse, thereby eliminating the need to purchase an equivalent quantity of new cabinets. Certain types of file folders may also be reusable.

Reference Activity

Reference activity means the frequency with which a given records series is consulted for business or other purposes. An analysis of reference activity should consider the business processes or operations that a given records series supports, the departments or other organizational units that use the records, and access privileges or restrictions associated with specific users and/or business operations.

This information is best obtained by interviewing knowledgeable users of a records series. Ideally, a knowledgeable user will be able to make a reasonable estimate of the number of times that all or part of a given records series is consulted per month, year, or other time period. With most recorded information, frequency of reference diminishes over time. Within a series, the newest records—the current year's accumulation, for example—are consulted most frequently. Records typically become less valuable and are consulted less often as they age. The oldest records in a series may be consulted very occasionally, if at all.

During interviews with program-unit personnel, the records analyst should identify events—such as the end of a fiscal year, expiration of a contract, or completion of a project—that may cause records within a given series to become less active and, ultimately, inactive. The records analyst should also determine the users' speed expectations when retrieving information from a given records series, because such requirements will dictate locations and/or media for records storage. Information that must be immediately and continuously available for unpredictable but urgent consultation will be handled differently than information for which retrieval delays, measured in hours or days, are tolerable.

Retention Requirements

A records inventory is a means to an end, rather than an end in itself. Its principal purpose is to provide the information necessary to prepare retention schedules for records covered by the inventory. As explained in the next chapter, many retention recommendations rely on the perceived requirements of employees who create, maintain, and use records. Such requirements are typically based on operational experience with records and their relationship to specific business processes or operations. Knowledgeable persons in a program unit contend that they must retain a given records series for seven years, for example, because they have consulted records from the series that were seven years old. During the inventory, records analysts must ask about the program unit's operational retention requirements.

The analyst must also ask about the program unit's existing retention practices. In the absence of systematically developed retention schedules, some program units formulate their own retention guidelines. In such a situation, the time period and appropriateness of existing retention practice must be determined. In particular, the records analyst must ask about the program unit's reason for adopting the existing practice.

Sensitivity

Records containing personally identifiable information, trade secrets, business plans, competitive intelligence, or other confidential or sensitive information, must be identified and access restrictions, including any restrictions imposed by privacy legislation, fully understood.

Duplication

An inventory must determine whether copies of all or portions of a given records series are kept by other program units, and the business purpose and relationship of such copies must be identified. During inventories, some records managers differentiate originals from copies for purposes of determining the **official copy**—that is, the copy that will satisfy an organization's retention requirements for information that exists in multiple copies—also known as the **record copy**. Official copy concepts are explained more fully in the next chapter.

As part of an organization's computer security and disaster recovery precautions, backup copies are routinely produced for electronic records that are stored on centralized computers or network servers. As discussed in subsequent chapters, such backup copies are typically stored off-site, but their existence should be noted during inventories. Backup copies are much less common for electronic records stored on desktop or mobile computers.

The same records may exist in multiple formats. Many electronic records are related to, and often duplicate, human-readable information recorded on paper or microfilm. In most word processing applications, for example, paper file copies are printed from computer-processible files. Electronic mail may be printed for reference purposes. Databases are used to print paper reports that provide a snapshot of database records at a particular point in time or for a particular set of variables. Whenever paper or microfilm records are encountered during an inventory, a records analyst should inquire about electronic records with identical or similar contents. Whenever electronic records are encountered, the records analyst should inquire about corresponding paper or microfilm records.

Hardware and Software Requirements

Electronic records and microforms require specific hardware and/or software components for reference or other uses. An inventory must include descriptions of all equipment and software required to retrieve or process a given records series. In some cases, a generic description will suffice. Examples include: "a 16mm microfilm cartridge reader/ printer with 24× magnification," "a Windows-compatible computer system with a CD-RW drive," "a videocassette recorder with Super-VHS playback capabilities," or "an audiocassette deck with Type IV tape compatibility." Some electronic records, however, require specific brands and/or models of computers, storage peripherals, and software. Further, inventories may encounter older electronic records that can be read only by discontinued hardware or software components.

Supporting Files

An inventory should identify and briefly describe any related records that support the creation, maintenance, or use of a given records series. As an example, a litigation file arranged by case number may be supported by an alphabetic index that permits retrieval by the litigant's name if the number is not known. Such indexes are essential, and their retention periods should be coordinated with retention recommendations for the records series they support.

Vital Record Status

As discussed more fully in Chapter 6, **vital records** contain information that is essential to an organization's mission-critical operations. To eliminate the need for a separate survey of vital records, potentially vital records should be identified during a records inventory conducted for retention purposes.

Execution and Follow-Up

Inventory information will be used to prepare retention recommendations for specific records series. Consequently, responses to questions contained in the survey instrument

---

Suggestions for Conducting Records Inventory Interviews

- *Ask brief questions and, when necessary, clarify them with succinct explanations.* The purpose of an inventory is to obtain information necessary to draft retention recommendations for records created and maintained by a given program unit. Therefore, the interviewee must be talking, and the records analyst must be listening.
- *Begin the interview by briefly describing its purpose, methods, and intended outcome.* Emphasize the need to obtain information from knowledgeable persons in order to prepare retention recommendations that meet the program unit's requirements.
- *Emphasize that the inventory is limited to recorded information.* Interviewees may be concerned that their duties and job performance are being evaluated. Specifically disavow any interest in evaluating the job descriptions or work performance of departmental employees. When describing the interview's purpose, avoid words such as *investigate* and *inspect* that have evaluative connotations.
- *Work with a preformulated interview script based on the survey instrument.* After a few interviews have been completed, reevaluate the interview script for effectiveness and make any necessary modifications.
- *Ask the interviewee for a brief description of the program unit's mission and an overview of the types of records the program unit creates and maintains before asking detailed questions about specific records series.* The

continued on page 44

overview will reveal the records series that the interview must cover.

- *Explain that you have a list of questions about each records series but that you are interested in whatever the interviewees have to say about the creation and use of recorded information in their program units.* Let the interviewee talk, but you are responsible for keeping the interview on track and the responses on point.

- *Take notes during the interview.* Tape recording inhibits open discussion. Note-taking forces the records analyst to be involved and attentive. It also confirms for interviewees that the analyst is listening to and interested in their responses.

- *Be honest about your lack of knowledge.* The lack of knowledge is the reason that a records inventory is necessary. Ask the interviewee to define specialized terms and describe unfamiliar business processes or operations.

- *Remember that the purpose of the interview is to obtain information not give it.* Until the inventory is completed and its findings are evaluated, a records analyst cannot knowledgeably advise program units about their recordkeeping practices. Such advice should be deferred until draft retention recommendations are prepared.

- *Avoid criticizing a program unit's recordkeeping practices during an interview.* Unacceptable practices should be noted, and corrective actions incorporated into retention recommendations.

- *Visit the file rooms, storage areas, or other locations where records are kept and used.* These visits may be done at the beginning of the interview to provide an overview of the program unit's records or at the end of the interview after the records have been described in detail. In particular, ask to see any unfamiliar records series or unusual storage conditions.

- *Ask for copies of written policies and procedures for recordkeeping if the program unit has such policies and procedures.*

- *Plan to complete the inventory in 90 minutes or less and inform the interviewee at the time the meeting is scheduled.* Work tends to fill the time allotted for its completion. Longer sessions are often difficult to arrange and will likely disrupt the interviewee's work schedule. If additional time is required for large or complicated collections of records, schedule a follow-up meeting.

must be both accurate in content and correctly interpreted by the records analyst. If the questionnaire method is used, the records analyst should review the responses with departmental coordinators or others responsible for completing the questionnaire in each program unit. To avoid misunderstandings that can lead to inappropriate retention recommendations, the records analyst's interpretation of major points should be confirmed by knowledgeable persons in the program units where records are kept and used. Clarification should always be requested for vague or incomplete responses.

If the consultation method is used, interview technique will have a significant impact on the success of an inventory. Above all, the records analyst must elicit useful responses to questions about recorded information. Although a comprehensive discussion of interviewing techniques is beyond the scope of this book, the points in the sidebar summarize widely cited interviewing suggestions for records inventories. Most of the suggestions are also applicable to interviews associated with other records management activities, such as the development of filing systems or computer-based document storage and retrieval systems, that depend upon interviews to obtain information about business processes, operations, and requirements associated with recorded information.

When the interview is completed, the records analyst should prepare a written summary of information obtained during each interview with departmental coordinators or other program-unit representatives. The summary can be written as if it were the minutes of a meeting. The written summary should be submitted to the interviewee for examination and, where necessary, correction or clarification. Such follow-up work steps will increase the time required to inventory records, but they are highly advisable. The time and effort required to conduct thorough inventories and accurate interview summaries will be repaid in appropriate retention recommendations that are less likely to require time-consuming negotiation and revision.

Chapter 3

Preparing Retention Schedules II: Making Retention Decisions

As discussed in Chapter 2, *records retention* refers to the length of time that records need to be kept or retained. The principal purpose of a records inventory is to collect the information needed to prepare retention schedules for records covered by the inventory. Broadly defined, a **retention schedule**—variously described as a *retention and disposal schedule* or, simply, a *disposal schedule*—is a list of records series maintained by all or part of an organization together with the period of time that each records series is to be kept. Some retention schedules also include information about the reasons records are kept for specified time periods, as well as instructions regarding the locations and conditions under which records are to be retained. Retention schedules may be maintained as paper copies or as computer files. In the latter case, they may be printed for reference purposes, although corporations, government agencies, and other organizations are increasingly posting Web-based versions of retention schedules on intranets as alternatives to printed copies.

Retention schedules may be general or program-specific in scope. A **general retention schedule** specifies retention periods for designated records series, regardless of the particular program units where the records are maintained. General retention schedules are sometimes characterized as **functional retention schedules** because they categorize records series by the business functions to which they pertain rather than by the program units where they are maintained as shown in Figure 3-1. Examples of functional categories include administrative records, accounting records, procurement records, human resources records, legal records, product development records, manufacturing records, and sales and marketing records. An organization may issue separate general schedules for specific functional categories or prepare a single general schedule that groups records for the entire organization by functional categories. Such enterprise-wide functional schedules are sometimes described as *master retention schedules.*

By definition, a general schedule provides one set of retention guidelines for all program units in an organization. A given program unit will have some, but not all, of the

Sample General
Retention
Schedule

Excerpt from general
retention schedule

Figure 3-1

Sample General Retention Schedule
1. Budget Correspondence Files
Correspondence files in formally organized budget offices pertaining to routine administration, internal procedures, and other matters not covered elsewhere in this schedule, EXCLUDING files relating to agency policy and procedure maintained in formally organized budget offices.
Destroy when 2 years old.
2. Budget Background Records
Cost statements, rough data, and similar materials accumulated in the preparation of annual budget estimates, including duplicates of budget estimates and justifications and related appropriation language sheets, narrative statements, and related schedules; and originating offices' copies of reports submitted to budget offices.
Destroy 1 year after the close of the fiscal year covered by the budget.
3. Budget Reports Files
Periodic reports on the status of appropriation accounts and apportionment.
a. Annual report (end of fiscal year).
Destroy when 5 years old.
b. All other reports.
Destroy 3 years after the end of the fiscal year.
4. Budget Apportionment Files
Apportionment and reapportionment schedules, proposing quarterly obligations under each authorized appropriation.
Destroy 2 years after the close of the fiscal year.

(Source: National Archives and Records Administration)

records series enumerated in a general schedule. A **program-specific retention schedule**, by contrast, is limited to those records series that are actually held by a specific department, office, or other program unit. Sometimes described as *activity-oriented* or *departmental retention schedules* (See Figure 3-2), program-specific retention schedules are custom-prepared for each program unit within an organization. Many organizations require departmental retention schedules to be approved by their tax and legal departments before implementation. An approval request form (See Figure 3-3), along with a copy of the schedule, is transmitted to these departments.

As their principal advantage, program-specific retention schedules are highly prescriptive. They list only those records series that a given program unit maintains, with unequivocal retention designations for each. Each program unit has direct input into the determination of retention periods. Being tailored to the requirements of individual program units, program-specific retention schedules are easy to understand and may include detailed implementation instructions. General schedules, which are often lengthy, may be difficult for individual program units to interpret.

Sample Departmental Retention Schedule

Typical format for a departmental retention schedule.

Figure 3-2

Records Retention Schedule

Division	Department	Records Coordinator	Issue/Revision Date	Page 1 of ____	Schedule No.

Records Title	Records Description	Retention Period			Office of Record	Remarks
		Office	Storage	Total		

Key for Retention Codes:

01 – Annual Review	02 – Until Superseded	03 – While Active	04 – Retain for Audit	05 – Tax Audit Requirements	06 – User Override
07 – Litigation	08 – Until Terminate	09 – Permanent	10 – Life of Corporation	11 – Life of Equipment/Facility	12 – Life of System
13 – Life of Project	14 – Until Expiration	Number of Years (Excluding the Current Year)		

Records Administration Approval (Print)	Date	Department Manager Approval (Print)	Date	Tax Representative Approval (Print)	Date	Law Representative Approval (Print)	Date
Signature		Signature		Signature		Signature	

(Source: *Sample Forms for Archival & Records Management Programs,* published by ARMA International and the Society of American Archivists)

Figure 3-3

Records Retention Schedule Approval Request

Internal Memorandum

DATE: _____

FROM: _____

TO: _____

Please review the attached revised Records Retention Schedule for the _____ Department.

If you agree with the information, please sign below in the space provided and forward to the Tax Department.

TAX DEPARTMENT – Please approve in the space provided. Please forward this RRS to the Law Department.

LAW DEPARTMENT – Please approve in the space provided. Please forward this RRS to the Corporate Secretary.

If any approver has an issue, please discuss it with the Records Coordinator or call _____ .

Thank you for your cooperation.

Approvals	Printed Name	Signature	Date
Records Manager			
Records Coordinator			
Department Head			
Tax Department			
Law Department			
Corporate Secretary			

(Source: Sample Forms for Archival & Records Management Programs, published by ARMA International and the Society of American Archivists)

To determine retention requirements, a program unit must first locate its records series among the many listed in a general schedule. In some cases, program units identify their records by titles different from those listed in the general schedule. An exact match is further complicated by slight variations in the scope and content of records series maintained by different program units. Offsetting these potential problems, proponents of functional retention schedules claim that they are easier and faster to create than program-specific schedules and that they promote consistent retention practices across organizational units. They also note that program-specific schedules can be difficult to update, given the frequency of reorganizations, mergers, divestitures, and other changes that realign or eliminate departments.

General schedules, by definition, present retention guidelines for multiple program units. The retention designations are based on input from some, but not necessarily all, program units that maintain a given records series. Presumably, the retention designations reflect the longest retention requirements for the listed series. For records that exist in multiple copies, however, a program unit may want to discard its copies of a given records series before the generalized retention period has elapsed. To address this requirement, a general schedule may designate an office of record responsible for retaining specific records series for the complete designated time period. Other program units can discard their copies of that series when local need has expired, but they must not retain them longer than the designated retention period.

General and program-specific schedules are not mutually exclusive options. They can, and often do, coexist in a given organization. General schedules are particularly useful for commonly encountered records, such as multipart business forms, correspondence and electronic mail, draft and final budgets, committee minutes, and records relating to personnel actions. An organization may issue general retention guidelines for its commonly held or enterprise-wide records series, and prepare customized program-specific schedules for records that are unique to particular departments, offices, or other program units. In the U.S. government, for example, general schedules prepared by the National Archives and Records Administration (NARA) cover records in over twenty major categories. Federal government agencies must prepare schedules for records not covered by the general schedules and submit those schedules to the NARA for approval.

Alternatively, program-specific schedules may be prepared where departmental retention requirements differ from retention periods specified in general schedules. In the United States and Canada, state and provincial archives have prepared general retention schedules for government agencies that are subject to their records management authority. The New York State Archives, for example, has issued general retention schedules for records maintained by state government agencies, counties, municipalities, school districts, and other governmental organizations. These agencies can either accept retention periods specified in general schedules issued by the State Archives or prepare their own schedules, which must be submitted to the State Archives for approval.

Whether a general or program-specific format is employed, a retention schedule must, at a minimum, list records series and indicate the period of time, usually in years, that each series is to be kept. Other useful information includes the physical storage media to be used, the location(s) where the records are to be stored, the date and method of records destruction where applicable, and the storage or records transfer instructions if destruction is not authorized. If this information is not contained in a retention schedule, a separate procedure or other supporting documentation must provide it. Some retention schedules also include citations to legal statutes or government regulations on which specific retention periods are based. Alternatively, such citations may be included in working papers associated with legal research relating to records retention.

A retention schedule may specify more than one physical storage medium and/or location for a records series. As an example, a municipal building department may store applications for building permits and zoning variances in paper form in the departmental office while the applications are under active review and for a short time thereafter. Periodically, records relating to approved applications may be microfilmed for long-term retention and the paper copies discarded. A security copy of the microfilm may be stored off-site. Similarly, a retention schedule may specify that records relating to withdrawn applications are to be kept in the departmental office for two years then transferred to off-site storage for five additional years, at the end of which time they will be discarded.

Retention Concepts

The preparation of retention schedules is a defining characteristic of records management work. No other information management discipline can properly claim responsibility for retention-related activities. Retention schedules are the core component in a systematic records management program. They provide a foundation upon which other records management activities discussed in this book are based. As explained in Chapter 1, recorded information is the property of the corporation, government agency, educational institution, or other organization that creates and maintains it. By preparing retention schedules, an organization acknowledges that systematic disposition of its records is a critical information management activity to be governed by formalized operating procedures rather than the discretion of individual employees.

In government, this concept often has the force of law. In the United States, 44 U.S. Code, Chapter 33, prohibits the destruction of federal government records without authorization from the Archivist of the United States. The National Archives of Canada Act prohibits the destruction of government and ministerial records without the consent of the Archivist of Canada. In the United Kingdom, the Public Records Act of 1958 authorizes the Public Records Office to work with government departments to determine retention requirements and identify records for permanent preservation. Under the Archives Act of 1983, the National Archives of Australia regulates the destruction of public records. Similar provisions limit the destruction of government records in other countries. In the United States, Canada, and elsewhere, state and provincial archives have retention authority over records created by government agencies within their jurisdictions.

A comprehensive inventory, as described in Chapter 2, will identify the records series to be included in retention schedules. The inventory collects information about the business purpose, characteristics, and quantity of records in each series, the ways in which the records are organized and used, and the relationship between a given records series and other records maintained by a given program unit or other parts of an organization.

Benefits of Using Records Retention Schedules

The business benefits of formalized retention schedules have been widely acknowledged for over half a century. When properly formulated, implemented, and enforced, retention schedules will minimize risks and reduce costs by:

- Ensuring the availability of specific records series for the appropriate period of time
- Ensuring compliance with **recordkeeping requirements** specified in legal statutes and government regulations
- Ensuring that records needed for evidentiary purposes will be available for and facilitate compliance with discovery requests and judicial orders
- Reducing labor requirements to locate records in response to audits, litigation, or government investigations
- Preventing unauthorized or arbitrary destruction of records, thereby avoiding potential legal problems associated with such actions
- Preventing unwarranted accumulation and inappropriate use of obsolete records
- Minimizing storage requirements by destroying records no longer needed
- Releasing file cabinets, filing supplies, and electronic recording media for reuse, thereby minimizing expenditures for new equipment, supplies, and media
- Making appropriate use of off-site storage and microfilming for inactive records
- Identifying records that merit permanent preservation for business or scholarly reasons

The records manager, in consultation with program-unit personnel and others, will use the inventory information, supplemented in some cases by additional research, to determine appropriate retention periods for specific records series.

A retention period places a value on a records series. The value is an estimate of the future usefulness or lack thereof of the series. Because retention periods are estimates, uncertainty and risk are unavoidable, but a careful analysis of retention requirements, based on an understanding of a given records series' purpose and characteristics, will increase the likelihood of a satisfactory determination.

Retention Criteria

Retention decisions are based on the content and purpose of records. Retention periods are determined by legal, administrative (operational), and scholarly (research) criteria. **Legal retention criteria** may be defined by laws or government regulations that mandate the retention of records for specific periods of time. A broader group of legal considerations is concerned with the admissibility of records as evidence in trials and other legal proceedings. Some records managers consider fiscal and tax-oriented retention criteria, which are concerned with the management and expenditure of public or corporate funds, to be distinct from legal parameters. Many fiscal and tax retention criteria, however, are embodied in laws and regulations. For purposes of this discussion, they are considered a subset of legal criteria.

Administrative retention criteria are based on the continued need for specific records series to support an organization's mission, the public interest (in the case of government records), and owners or stockholders' interest (for records of private or publicly held companies, including sole proprietorships and partnerships). Such criteria are concerned with the availability of records for long-term administrative consistency and continuity, as well as for the day-to-day operations of individual program units. Administrative criteria are the most important considerations when determining retention periods for many, if not most, records. This statement does not denigrate the importance of legal criteria; it merely recognizes that many records are not subject to legally mandated recordkeeping requirements and have no evidentiary significance.

Legal and administrative significance aside, electronic records maintained by corporations, government agencies, and other organizations may contain information of interest to historians, political scientists, sociologists, economists, demographers, or other scholars. Some records are also of interest to genealogists, private investigators, market trends analysts, and others who are not necessarily scholars but are nonetheless involved in research. Scholarly retention criteria are sometimes characterized as secondary value to distinguish them from the primary business purposes for which records are created and maintained.

This chapter discusses legal and administrative criteria for records retention. (Legal criteria include fiscal and tax considerations.) Scholarly retention criteria are beyond the scope of this book and of records management generally, although portions of the discussion of administrative criteria may be relevant for scholarly applications. As noted in Chapter 1, determination of scholarly value is principally the concern of archival administration. Such determination, sometimes described as *archival appraisal*, requires specialized knowledge about the scholarly disciplines and research activities for which particular records may be relevant. Many archivists have advanced academic degrees in a subject discipline, such as history or public administration, as well as training in archival management or library science. Archivists work closely with records managers to identify records of scholarly value and ensure that they are preserved. They often work together to identify these records at the time that retention schedules are prepared. In government agencies, academic institutions, and other organizations where preservation of records of scholarly value is required by law or institutional policy, the archivist typically has review and approval authority over retention schedules.

Official Copies

Much information maintained by corporations, government agencies, and other organizations exists in multiple copies and multiple formats. Accounting, purchasing, and other business transactions rely on multipart forms. Correspondence, reports, and other office documents are widely photocopied for distribution. Prints of engineering drawings, architectural renderings, and other large-format documents are routinely included in project files. Many office records and engineering drawings are micro-filmed and/or scanned, and the resulting microforms or digital images may themselves be duplicated for distribution or off-site storage. Increasingly, electronic records are the originating sources for paper documents, particularly with word processing files and computer-aided design files. Conversely, information from paper documents, such as invoices or employee time sheets, may be key-entered to create electronic records.

In the presence of multiple copies of a given record, the copy that will satisfy an organization's legal and administrative retention requirements is termed the *official copy* or the *record copy*. The program unit that maintains the official copy is designated the **office of record** for retention purposes, as previously noted. Copies maintained by other program units are considered *duplicate records*. Where information is unique to a given record, that record is necessarily an official copy. Where the same information exists in multiple copies, however, a corporation, government agency, or other organization may designate one of them as the official copy for retention purposes.

The official copy concept has a straightforward rationale: Not all copies of a given record need to be kept for the same amount of time. This principle is subject, however, to significant variations in application. Possibilities include, but are not necessarily limited to, the following:

- Retention schedules separately enumerate and specify retention periods for all copies of a given records series in all formats. Retention periods may differ among the copies, and, where legal or regulatory retention requirements exist, one copy is designated as the official copy. This approach can be effectively applied to multipart business forms and periodic reports with predefined distribution lists. With many business forms, distribution instructions are printed on the forms themselves. Separate identification of all copies is impractical, however, for records with unpredictable copying and distribution patterns.

- One copy of a record is designated as the official copy for retention purposes. Other copies can be kept as long as the official copy or discarded sooner if no longer needed.

- One copy of a record is designated as the official copy for retention purposes. A short retention period, perhaps one to three years, is mandated for all other copies.

- Retention periods and offices of record are designated for specific types of information, such as accounts receivable records or product specification sheets, without prescribing the specific copy or format in which the information is to be retained. The office of record determines which copy will be the official copy.

Official copy determinations are based on the assumption that all copies of a record are equivalent in content and functionality, which is not always the case. One copy may contain more information or be more useful than another copy. For example:

- Contracts, correspondence, and other documents generated from word processing files may be signed or amended after printing.

- A photocopy of a document may contain significant handwritten annotations absent from the original.

- Individual copies in multipart form sets may differ in color and legibility.

- Microfilm copies of engineering drawings may not satisfy all reproduction requirements for scaled documents.

- Electronic document images of deeds and mortgages may be easier to retrieve than the paper counterparts; but, in some localities, government regulations may prohibit their retention in lieu of paper records.

Legally Mandated Recordkeeping Requirements

Recorded information documents an organization's business operations, including hiring of employees, payment of taxes, and other activities subject to government regulation. Government auditors examine an organization's records to determine compliance with laws and regulations to which the records relate. To ensure the availability of adequate information for that purpose, various laws and government regulations include retention provisions for certain types of records. Such provisions are described as *legally mandated recordkeeping requirements*.

Avoidance of costly penalties for noncompliance with such recordkeeping requirements is an important benefit of systematically developed retention policies and procedures. When determining how long records are to be kept, legally mandated recordkeeping requirements are usually the first criteria to be considered. Where such requirements exist, they establish minimum retention periods for the recorded information to which they pertain. Retention periods determined by other criteria discussed in this chapter may be longer than those defined by legally mandated recordkeeping requirements, but they can never be shorter.

Recordkeeping laws and regulations apply to all private and public organizations that operate within a specific governmental jurisdiction. An organization's headquarters location or the governmental jurisdiction in which it is incorporated or chartered is not the determining factor. A corporation, government agency, educational institution, or other organization is considered to operate in a given location if it maintains an office, employees, or property there. Thus, a multinational manufacturing company headquartered in the United States must comply with applicable recordkeeping requirements in all countries where its products are sold, and records managers must consider those requirements when preparing retention policies and procedures. Similarly, a university, museum, or other cultural institution that has branch operations in multiple locations must comply with recordkeeping laws and regulations in every governmental jurisdiction where it maintains offices, has employees, or offers programs.

Identification of applicable laws and regulations is the essential first step toward compliance with legally mandated recordkeeping requirements. For organizations that operate in the United States, recordkeeping requirements can be found in the Code of Federal Regulations (CFR), which is updated by the Office of the Federal Register and published in the Federal Register, as well as in various state codes and local government statutes and regulations. In many other countries, recordkeeping requirements are contained in similar compilations of legal statutes and government regulations. Organizations that operate in Canada, for example, must comply with recordkeeping requirements in Canadian Consolidated Statutes and Regulations and with provincial and local laws and regulations that specify retention periods for certain records. Similarly, organizations that operate in Australia must comply with recordkeeping provisions in Commonwealth Consolidated Legislation and Commonwealth Consolidated Regulations as well as records retention requirements in various state laws and regulations.

Several publishers offer useful reference tools that identify, excerpt, categorize, and index legally mandated recordkeeping requirements in selected countries, thereby minimizing the need for time-consuming searches through legal books and databases. Even then, the examination of applicable laws and regulations is a formidable task requiring careful study, which must be repeated periodically to identify new legislation and government regulations. Consultation with attorneys is often required.

As a significant complication, recordkeeping requirements can be difficult to interpret. Some government regulations merely state that certain records must be kept without specifying a minimum retention period for them. In such situations, an organization may adopt long retention periods for the indicated records as a seemingly prudent precaution. However, unless a demonstrable business need for the records exists, that approach may not be necessary or advisable. Relatively short retention periods are legally acceptable for many records. In the U.S., for example, the Uniform Preservation of Private Business Records Act (UPPBRA), which has been adopted by many states,* specifies that records, with a few specified exceptions, can be destroyed after three years unless "express provision is made by law" for a longer retention period. The exceptions include minute books of corporations and sales records relating to

---

*   Uniform laws are developed by judges, attorneys, and other legal experts to promote uniformity in legal practice relating to commonly encountered matters. States may adopt or reject a given uniform law. In the latter case, a uniform law's provisions may be adequately covered by an existing state statute. The Uniform Preservation of Private Business Records Act is one of several uniform laws that play an important role in records management. Other uniform laws are cited elsewhere in this book.

weapons, explosives, or other dangerous substances. The UPPBRA interprets business records broadly to include records maintained by nongovernmental institutions, including private schools and universities, philanthropic foundations, professional associations, cultural institutions, and other not-for-profit organizations.

Legally mandated recordkeeping requirements apply to a subset of an organization's records, but, in some cases, the subset can be large. A widely publicized group of record-keeping requirements applies to specific industries or business activities regulated by one or more government agencies. Examples include banking, food processing, insurance, securities, public accounting, pharmaceuticals, communications, transportation, energy, healthcare, foreign trade, and waste management. In those industries, government regulations specify minimum retention requirements for many records.

Although they are most often associated with private businesses, some legally mandated recordkeeping requirements apply to government agencies and not-for-profit organizations. In many countries, government agencies are subject to laws that specify the retention authority of archival agencies over public records. The National Archives and Records Administration, as previously noted, has retention authority over records maintained by U.S. government agencies. State archival agencies have similar retention authority over state government records and, in many cases, records maintained by local governments, school districts, quasi-governmental authorities, public benefit corporations, and other entities. Many state archives have published general schedules that specify minimum retention requirements to which agencies within their jurisdiction must conform.

As a group, recordkeeping laws and regulations require the creation of information and its retention for designated time periods. In some cases, acceptable records storage formats and media—paper, microfilm, or electronic—are specified. With many recordkeeping laws and regulations, however, requirements for storage formats and media are omitted or implied rather than clearly stated. Recordkeeping laws and regulations that predate widespread computerization of business operations often omit or imply storage format and media information. Those laws and regulations are based on the assumption that required information is contained exclusively in paper documents; the acceptability of electronic media is not mentioned. Increasingly, however, recordkeeping laws and regulations are being revised to explicitly accept computer databases, word processing files, and other electronic records for retention of specified information. Many sections of the Code of Federal Regulations now permit the substitution of computer records for paper documents, provided that the computer records are appropriately indexed for retrieval, that complete descriptive documentation is available for the records and the computer systems that produce them, and that paper copies of the records can be printed on demand for audits or other purposes. Some other countries allow businesses to maintain accounting and tax-related records in electronic form. Unfortunately, generalization is impossible; the text of individual laws and regulations must be studied to determine the acceptability of electronic records for retention purposes in particular circumstances.

To illustrate the scope and characteristics of legally mandated recordkeeping requirements, the following discussion summarizes widely cited U.S. laws and government regulations that specify minimum retention periods for selected records related to three commonly encountered business operations: tax, accounting, and human resources. Tax auditors, compliance officers, and other government investigators require these records to determine compliance with laws or regulations to which the records pertain. The following discussion is illustrative rather than comprehensive and prescriptive. All applicable laws and regulations are not cited, nor are authoritative retention recommendations provided. It merely provides examples of laws and regulations that specify retention requirements. Retention periods for an organization's records are determined by statutory and regulatory requirements in combination with other factors discussed in this chapter. Readers are further cautioned that retention guidelines discussed here are subject to change.

Tax Records

As might be expected, government regulations specify minimum retention requirements for financial records pertaining to tax assessments. Such retention requirements ensure that government agencies will have sufficient information to determine taxes owed and paid. Section 6001 of the U.S. Internal Revenue Code requires that taxpayers keep sufficient records to determine their income tax liability. Section 7062 authorizes the Internal Revenue Service to examine these records to determine the accuracy of federal income tax returns. Similar provisions apply to state and local income tax records.

At a minimum, federal and state tax records—including tax returns and supporting documentation, such as income statements, canceled checks, and receipts—must be retained as long as the tax returns to which they pertain are subject to audit. In most cases, that time period is three years after the original due date of the return or the date the return is filed, whichever is later. The audit period increases to six years, however, for tax returns that understate income by more than 25 percent. Other factors warrant longer retention periods for certain tax returns and supporting documentation. For example, records relating to properties purchased and capital improvements made to those properties will be needed for tax basis adjustments if the properties are sold in the future. Similarly, certain depreciation deductions are subject to recapture if qualified business use falls below a certain percentage in future years. Records older than three years may be needed to substantiate business use in years subject to recapture. To address these issues, some authorities recommend that copies of tax returns and supporting documentation be retained permanently or at least for several decades. As a further complication, tax audits and any ensuing litigation may take years to resolve, forcing the retention of tax records while those matters are pending.

Corporate Audit Records

The Sarbanes-Oxley Act of 2002, which was passed in reaction to widely publicized corporate accounting irregularities, specifies a minimum retention period of seven years for accountants' work papers, correspondence, and other records that contain analyses, opinions, conclusions, financial data, or other information about corporate audits. The Act also specifies criminal penalties, including fines and imprisonment, for failure to comply with these retention requirements.

Employment Application Records

Federal and state laws prohibit hiring practices that discriminate against qualified job applicants on the basis of race, skin color, national origin, citizenship, gender, age, religion, union membership, or disability. Employment application records include application forms, correspondence, resumes, and other documents submitted by or pertaining to job applicants. U.S. law requires the retention of these records to confirm that an organization's hiring practices are not discriminatory, but the mandated retention periods are short. Under Title VII of the Civil Rights Act of 1964 and the Americans with Disabilities Act of 1990, employers must retain all hiring records, including application files, for one year from the date the records were made or the personnel action was taken, whichever is later. The Age Discrimination in Employment Act requires retention of hiring records, including job applications, inquiries, and resumes, for one year from the date of the personnel action.

Personnel Files

Corporations, government agencies, educational institutions, and other organizations maintain paper files and/or database records that contain information about permanent or temporary employees. Certain employee records are subject to legally mandated recordkeeping requirements, but the retention periods specified in laws and government regulations are typically shorter than the business need to retain such records. The Equal Pay Act of 1963 requires employers to retain job descriptions for two years. Such records may be filed separately or comingled with other documents in personnel files or employment application records. Under the Civil Rights Act of 1964, the Americans with Disabilities Act of 1990, and the Age Discrimination in Employment Act, records relating to employee promotion, demotion, layoffs, recalls, discharges, or selection for training must be retained for one year from the date of the personnel action. Records relating to leaves of absence under the Family and Medical Leave Act must be retained for three years. Under the Employee Polygraph Protection Act, employers must retain polygraph test results and the reasons for administering the test for three years.

Form I-9

All U.S. employers must complete and maintain INS Employment Eligibility Verification Form I-9 for each employee hired to work in the United States after November 6, 1986, whether the employee is a citizen or not. Form I-9 is not filed with the Immigration and Naturalization Service or other government agencies. It is kept by the employer and must be available for inspection by authorized government officials. Under the Immigration and Nationality Act of 1952, Form I-9 must be retained for three years following the date of hiring, or one year following termination of employment, whichever is later. Thus, Form I-9 must be retained for all current and recently terminated employees. Forms I-9 can be stored at an off-site location, but they must be available for inspection within three days when requested by government officials.

Employment Contracts

The Fair Labor Standards Act of 1938 and National Labor Relations Act specify a retention period of three years following termination for employment contracts, including collective bargaining agreements.

Employee Medical Records

Employers can maintain medical histories, test results, and other medical information about employees, but under the Americans with Disabilities Act such records must be filed separately from personnel records. Employee medical records, with the exception of first-aid records and experimental toxicological research records, must be retained for thirty years following termination of employment. Personal medical records of workers employed for less than one year need not be retained if they are provided to the worker on termination of employment. Records relating to employee testing for controlled substances or alcohol use must be retained for periods of one to five years, as specified by 49 CFR 382.401.

Certain government regulations mandate the creation and retention of certain work-related medical records. Under the Occupational Safety and Health Act, employers must keep a log and incident reports of work-related injuries and illnesses. The Occupational Safety and Health Administration provides forms for that purpose, although an equivalent insurance form or computer records may be substituted. The log and incident reports must be available within four hours when requested by an authorized government official. These records must be retained for five years following the year to which they relate. Records relating to employees' exposure to toxic substances or harmful physical agents must be retained for thirty years.

Workers' Compensation Records

Workers' compensation laws and their associated recordkeeping requirements vary from state to state. In New York State, for example, case files and other records for workers' compensation awards must be kept for eighteen years after the injury or illness or eight years after final payment of the award, whichever is longer. Records for claims that are disallowed or otherwise disposed of without an award must be kept for eighteen years after the injury or illness for the basic records of injuries or illnesses and seven years after the injury or illness for case files, excluding the basic records of injuries and illnesses. Records relating to injuries or illnesses that do not result in workers' compensation claims must be kept for eighteen years after the injury or illness

Payroll Records

Government regulations require the retention of certain payroll records to confirm that an organization's wage rates are not discriminatory. Under the Equal Pay Act of 1963 and Age Discrimination in Employment Act, payroll records that indicate employees' dates of birth, occupations, and rates of pay must be retained for three years. Such records may include time cards, information about wage rates, hours worked per pay period, total wages per pay period, and additions to or deductions from wages paid.

Under the Federal Insurance Contribution Act and the Federal Unemployment Tax Act, records relating to income taxes withheld from employees' wages, including W-4 withholding forms, must be retained for four years from the date the taxes are due or paid, whichever is later. As with personnel records, legally mandated retention requirements for payroll records may be shorter than the administrative value of such records. In government agencies and other organizations where pension eligibility is determined by employees' length of service, for example, payroll records may need to be retained for decades.

Employee Benefit Records

The Employee Retirement Income Security Act (ERISA) of 1974 defines responsibilities and recordkeeping requirements for organizations that offer pension plans, disability plans, health insurance, or other benefits to employees. Such organizations must maintain sufficient records to determine the benefits due to those employees, but the Act does not specify how long individual employee benefit files, where such files exist apart from personnel files, must be kept.

Most corporations, government agencies, and other organizations must file Form 5500 Annual Report/Return for Employee Benefit Plan for each pension or benefit plan offered to employees. Under the Employee Retirement Income Security Act, Form 5500 and supporting documentation must be kept for six years after the filing date.

Admissibility Into Evidence

Recordkeeping requirements specified in legal statutes and government regulations were examined in the preceding section. A different, much discussed group of legal considerations involves the retention of records for use as evidence in litigation, government investigations, or other legal proceedings. Broadly defined, *evidence* consists of testimony or physical items, such as records, that are submitted in relation to alleged facts in judicial or quasi-judicial proceedings. The purpose of evidence is to prove or clarify points at issue in such proceedings. Evidence that a judge or jury can properly consider is termed *admissible*.

Admissibility issues are important factors in retention decisions. Laws and government regulations that specify retention periods affect a subset of an organization's records. By contrast, any record might prove useful as evidence in litigation, and many organizations retain large quantities of records for their possible relevance to legal actions that may occur in the future. Although predicting which information will be involved in and relevant to lawsuits is difficult, obvious examples include records relating to the following:

- Contracts, including leases, loan agreements, insurance policies, and shareholder agreements
- Fair employment practices or their opposite—job discrimination, wrongful termination, and sexual harassment

- Intellectual property, including patents, copyrights, and trademarks
- Product quality and safety, including test results and quality assurance policies, procedures, and findings.

Healthcare providers, law firms, accounting firms, and other organizations that offer professional services must assume that any client matters with unsatisfactory outcomes are potential problems.

Although evidentiary issues are principally the concerns of corporate and institutional attorneys, records managers are responsible for planning and implementing recordkeeping systems that provide effective documentary support for possible future legal actions. In particular, records managers must be sure that evidentiary issues are considered when retention guidelines are formulated and that records are retained in a manner that will not imperil their admissibility in future legal proceedings. The following discussion provides a brief tutorial on selected evidentiary matters that records managers need to understand and consider when making retention decisions.

Authentication

In court trials, admissibility of records into evidence is determined by rules of evidence, which are embodied in legal statutes and court decisions (common law). In the United States, admissibility is guided by the Federal Rules of Evidence (FRE), which apply in federal courts; the Uniform Rules of Evidence (URE), which apply in those state courts where they have been adopted; and rules of evidence that apply in courts of other states. Similar rules of evidence apply in other countries. Examples can be found in the Canada Evidence Act (CEA), the Civil Evidence Act and Criminal Evidence Act in the United Kingdom, the Australian Evidence Act, and the New Zealand Evidence Act, with their various amendments.

To be admissible as evidence, a record must satisfy two foundation requirements that apply to all evidence: (1) The record's content must be relevant to the matter at issue; and (2) The record's authenticity must be firmly established—that is, the court must be convinced that the record is what its proponents claim it to be. Records managers are much more likely to be involved with authentication issues than with relevance determinations, which are case-specific and handled by attorneys.

The purpose of authentication is to demonstrate the reliability of records to a court's satisfaction. To be considered reliable, a paper, photographic, or electronic record must meet the following criteria:

1. The record must have been created at or near the time of the event that is the subject of litigation.
2. The record must have been created by a person with knowledge of the event.
3. The record must have been maintained in the regular course of an organization's business.

Under FRE, URE, and many state-specific rules of evidence, certain types of records are considered self-authenticating, meaning that extrinsic support for reliability is not required for them. Examples include public records bearing the official seal of a government entity or the signature of an authorized government official, certified copies of public records, and published documents such as newspapers and periodicals. Recent changes to FRE and URE have simplified authentication requirements for many business records. Correspondence, reports, or other records relating to regularly conducted business activity are considered authentic and admissible when accompanied by a written declaration by a custodian or other qualified person that the record satisfies the three criteria listed previously. A live witness is not required for authentication of such business records. In certain cases, as when a business record is maintained in a central file room or off-site storage facility operated by a records management unit, a records manager is the person best qualified to provide the required declaration. The party that offers business records in evidence must provide written notice of that intention to adverse parties and must make the record and declaration available to them for inspection and possible challenge.

Authentication principles apply to records in all formats: paper, photographic, and electronic. However, special concerns have been raised about the reliability of computer records. Those concerns relate to the ease with which records stored on magnetic disks, magnetic tapes, or rewritable optical disks can be erased, edited, or otherwise altered, possibly in an undetectable manner. Word processing documents and database records can be easily overwritten with new information. Recent advances in computer technology permit the undetected manipulation of electronic document images, digital photographs, computer-aided design files, video recordings, and audio recordings. In the case of electronic records maintained by networked computer systems, such alterations may be performed by a remote perpetrator, thereby circumventing physical accessibility requirements associated with the alteration of paper records. With nonelectronic recordkeeping systems, by contrast, modifications are often difficult to make and easy to detect. The alteration of an organization's paper-based accounting records, for example, may require tampering with various ledgers, balance sheets, invoices, and other source documents, some of which may be inaccessible to the perpetrator. As a further impediment, alterations to paper records involve physical changes, which may be detectable by specialists or even casual observers. Forensic scientists have decades of experience with the examination of suspect documents. Where records are stored on microfilm, undetectable alterations can prove particularly difficult to make.

To successfully address concerns about tampering, records managers may be expected to provide testimony and/or documentation pertaining to computer system administration, input procedures, equipment, software, security, and the competency of employees who operate the system. Computer hardware and software characteristics must be documented in a manner that fully describes the role of each component in the creation and maintenance of electronic records being submitted as evidence. The accuracy and trustworthiness of electronic records can be affirmed by thorough documentation of records creation procedures, as well as by descriptions of training given to data entry clerks, video camera operators, or other personnel responsible for creation of electronic records. Business processes that create electronic records must be documented through written procedures and workflow diagrams. Electronic records must be protected from physical damage or tampering that could impair their accuracy or raise questions about their trustworthiness. Media handling guidelines and access control procedures for electronic records and security provisions, such as password protection and privilege controls in computer-based systems, must be documented. All aspects of system operation should be audited regularly for compliance with established procedures. Audit findings and the implementation of corrective actions should be fully documented.

The foregoing discussion applies to the admissibility of records in federal and state courts. Certain legal and quasi-legal proceedings, however, are held before federal and state administrative agencies where court-oriented rules of evidence do not apply. Admissibility issues in such situations cannot be generalized. Federal administrative agencies are bound by the Administrative Procedures Act, which gives such agencies considerable discretion in determining the admissibility of records. At the state government level, the admissibility of evidence in administrative proceedings is typically governed by state administrative procedures acts and agency procedural rules. Significant variations in admissibility rules may be encountered from one state to another and, within a given state, from one agency to another.

Statutes of Limitations

Retention periods appropriate to the use of records in evidence are influenced by statutes of limitations that prescribe the time periods within which lawsuits or other legal actions must be initiated. **Statutes of limitations,** also known as *limitations of action,* define the time period during which a person or organization can sue or be sued for personal injury, breach of contract, or other reasons. **Limitations of assessment periods** are the fiscal counterparts of statutes of limitations. They prescribe the period of time that a government agency can determine taxes owed. Once the period defined by a given statute of limitations or limitation of assessment has elapsed, no legal action can be brought for a specific matter. If the statute of limitations on personal injury lawsuits is two years in a given locality, for example, the injured party loses the legal right to sue after that time.

In the United States, statutes of limitations vary from state to state. They also vary with the type of issue and the circumstances of the case. As a complicating factor for retention decisions, statutes of limitations begin when an event, such as a personal injury or breach of contract, occurs, not when records relating to that event are created. Recorded information about products being developed, tested, manufactured, or sold today may be relevant for legal actions several decades into the future.

Although they can have a significant impact on a given agency's records retention practices, statutes of limitations do not mandate retention periods. They simply define the maximum period of time during which records being retained in support of an actual or possible legal action can be used for that purpose. If records are being retained specifically and exclusively to support legal actions and they otherwise have no other business or scholarly value, retention periods longer than pertinent statutes of limitations serve no purpose.

Records can be destroyed in conformity with retention schedules while statutes of limitations are in effect, provided that no laws or government regulations mandate the retention of such records, as discussed previously. Destruction of pertinent records must stop, however, as soon as an organization becomes aware of a lawsuit, government investigation, or other actual or pending legal proceeding, even if retention periods for the records elapse while the legal proceeding is pending or ongoing.

An organization must have a plan to notify employees when litigation requires temporary suspension of destruction for certain records. Such litigation holds are usually handled by an organization's legal department, which identifies the pertinent records and notifies the affected departments where they are kept. In complex lawsuits or government investigations, litigation holds can remain in effect for years. Notification must be provided to employees when a litigation hold is released and destruction of records can resume.

Discovery

Recorded information is undeniably useful for litigation. Technical reports can show that products were properly designed and thoroughly tested. Contracts and related correspondence can prove that specific terms and conditions were not fulfilled. Employee evaluations and other personnel records can refute charges of wrongful dismissal or discriminatory employment practices. The obvious retention strategy is to keep records with helpful content for possible future litigation. However, making a conclusive identification of such records to the exclusion of others is difficult. As a result, attorneys have traditionally advised the retention of large quantities of records in the event that some of them may be needed for future litigation, but that practice may prove harmful rather than helpful.

In particular, retention of large quantities of records solely for their use in litigation poses risks for pretrial discovery, the investigative phase of litigation when the opposing party can obtain a subpoena (discovery order) for recorded information believed relevant to its case. Discovery orders can give the opposing party in a lawsuit access to information that it might not otherwise have. Few organizations exercise effective control over the content of recorded information associated with their business operations. Memoranda, e-mail messages, and other communications may contain ill-considered, inaccurate, and potentially damaging statements about an organization's employees, products, services, or activities. Recorded information obtained through discovery can be misinterpreted, cited out of context, or otherwise presented in court in a manner that proves damaging to an organization. The opposing party in a lawsuit can also make effective use of drafts, preliminary reports, notes taken at meetings, or other records that may not be complete or accurate.

Further, the identification, retrieval, duplication, and delivery of records in response to a discovery order are time-consuming and expensive activities. Studies indicate that pretrial discovery, including disclosure of records, accounts for as much as half the cost of civil litigation. The greater the volume of records retained or owned by an organization, the greater the number of records likely to fall within the scope of a discovery order, and the greater the effort and higher the cost to locate, reproduce, and deliver those records.

Failure to comply fully and conscientiously with a discovery order can have serious consequences, particularly if the requested records were destroyed without a satisfactory explanation. The obvious inference is that the records contained information harmful to the party that destroyed them. Depending on the nature of the records and the party's perceived intent, the possible corrective actions include adverse jury instructions, monetary sanctions, default judgments, or, at the extreme, criminal penalties for obstruction of justice.

Dozens of cases confirm these possibilities. In 1997, for example, a federal judge imposed a $1 million dollar fine on Prudential Insurance for its "haphazard and uncoordinated approach" to retention of documents subpoenaed in a class action lawsuit (*In Re Prudential Insurance Company Sales Practice Litigation*, 169 F.R.D. 598, D. N.J. 1997). In *Applied Telematics, Inc. v. Sprint Communications Co.*, WL539595, (E.D., Pa, 1996), the court ordered the defendant to pay the plaintiff's costs and attorney's fees for failure to retain records. In *Capellupo v. FMC Corporation*, 126 F.R.D., 545, 551 (D. Minn., 1989), the court ordered the defendant to pay twice the plaintiff's costs and attorney's fees for researching and presenting motions relating to document destruction. Widely cited cases in which the destruction of records led to default judgments include *Carlucci v. Piper Aircraft Corp.*, 102 F.R.D. 472, 475 (S.D. Fla. 1984), *William T. Thompson Company v. General Nutrition*, 593 F. Supp. 1443 (C.D. Cal. 1984), *Teletron Inc. v. Overhead Door Corp.*, 116 F.R.D. 107, 126-27 (S.D. Fla.1987), *Computer Associates International, Inc. v. American Fundware, Inc.*, 133 F.R.D. 166 (D. Colo. 1990), and *Baker by Cress v. General Motors Corp.*, 519 F.R.D. 519 (W.D. Mo. 1994).

U.S. v. Arthur Andersen, LLP, is the most widely publicized criminal case involving destruction of business records. In November 2001, the U.S. Securities and Exchange Commission (SEC) issued a subpoena to Arthur Andersen, a public accounting firm, requesting records related to work it performed for Enron Corporation, which at that time was the subject of a government investigation for possible violation of federal securities laws. That investigation began in October 2001, although the events leading up to it were widely reported during the preceding months. In January 2002, Andersen officials disclosed that the company had destroyed a number of records related to Enron audits. The officials said that the records were destroyed in conformity with company policy, which permitted the destruction of nonessential records relating to specific audits. Andersen officials further stated that the audit records were destroyed without criminal intent before the SEC investigation began and the subpoena was received. Federal prosecutors alleged, however, that Andersen destroyed the audit records after the SEC investigation had begun and that Andersen officials were fully aware that the company would be asked to produce the records. In March 2002, federal prosecutors charged Andersen with obstruction of justice for destroying records needed for the Enron investigation. The company was convicted of obstructing justice in June 2002, but considerable damage was done before the verdict was rendered. Many of Andersen's leading clients withdrew their business shortly after the criminal charges were announced, and the company drastically reduced its workforce and sold several of its operations to competitors.

The basic legal principal behind the cases discussed here is clear: Litigants have a duty to preserve evidence, including records that they know or reasonably should know are relevant to impending or ongoing litigation. Destruction of such records is considered **spoliation of evidence**, but organizations are not required to keep all records merely because some of them may be relevant to legal proceedings about which it has no current knowledge. The inability to comply with discovery orders is explainable if subpoenaed records were destroyed prior to the start of litigation in conformity with an organization's formalized retention policies and procedures. Widely cited cases that support this point include *Smith v. Uniroyal, Inc.*, 420 F.2d 438, 442-43 (Seventh Circuit, 1970), *Vick v. Texas Employment Commission*, 514 F.2d 734, 737 (Fifth Circuit, 1975), and *Moore v. General Motors*, 558 S.W. 2d 720 (Mo. Ct. App. 1977). In those cases, the courts found that spoliation inferences should not be drawn where records are destroyed in conformity with an organization's established retention policies and procedures. In other words, the records must have been discarded with the intention of destroying evidence to warrant adverse jury instructions, sanctions, or other penalties.

Merely having a retention policy is not an adequate defense against spoliation of evidence, however. In *Lewy v. Remington Arms Co.*, 836 F.2d 1104 (Eighth Circuit, 1988), an influential case in which the defendant was unable to produce customer complaint records that it had reportedly destroyed after three years, pursuant to the company's established retention practices, the court delineated guidelines for an acceptable retention policy. According to those guidelines, a retention policy must not be instituted in bad faith solely to dispose of potentially damaging evidence of possible relevance to future litigation. When determining retention periods, an organization must consider the frequency and magnitude of previous complaints and lawsuits that involved certain types of recorded information. The court found that a retention period of three years "may be sufficient for documents such as appointment books or telephone messages, but inadequate for documents such as customer complaints." Records that are likely to be the subject of future litigation should be retained for a longer period of time. For some records associated with certain industries or business activities, a possibility of relevance for future lawsuits always exists. That prospect warrants retention until all applicable statutes of limitations expire, which may be decades in some cases.

Once established, an organization's retention policies and procedures must be enforced. Systematic destruction must be carried out at prescribed periods to avoid any suspicion that records were discarded after a legal proceeding was initiated in order to avoid discovery of harmful evidence. Exceptions to an organization's established retention policies must be limited to special and infrequent situations where a demonstrable business need to retain certain records for an additional brief amount of time exists, after which the records will be destroyed. An example of such demonstrable need is to allow completion of auditing or analytical activities that require access to information uniquely available in the records to be destroyed. Even then, appropriate approvals should be obtained and the reason for the exception thoroughly documented.

Administrative Retention Requirements

Administrative retention criteria are variously described as *operational retention parameters* or *user retention parameters*. As their name suggests, they are determined by the administrative requirements of employees who rely on recorded information to support an organization's daily business operations or long-term goals. Administrative retention parameters should not be confused with the legal issues discussed previously. Even where recordkeeping regulations or evidentiary considerations warrant specific retention periods for particular records series, administrative requirements must also be considered. Often, such requirements exceed retention periods based on legal parameters. For each records series, administrative and legal requirements should be defined separately; the applicable retention period is determined by the longer of the two requirements. In some organizations, as previously noted, the scholarly value of records is also considered when making retention decisions. A subset of an organization's records may be of interest to historians, sociologists, public policy analysts, or other scholars. Such records are retained permanently for their research value, even though their business value has elapsed.

Determination

Like their legal counterparts, administrative retention periods are usually measured in years following the occurrence of a specified event such as the end of a fiscal year or calendar year, the completion of an audit, the fulfillment of a contract, the completion of a project, or the termination of employment. Administrative retention decisions are based on the content and business purpose of specific records series. Administrative retention periods are typically negotiated through meetings or other consultation with knowledgeable employees who rely on the records to fulfill their assigned work responsibilities.

A fundamental records management assumption is that users of records are qualified to determine their continuing value based on their experience with a given records series and their knowledge of specific business processes, operations, and objectives that the records support. Sometimes, however, users want to retain records longer than is necessary. Taking the view that long retention periods minimize the risk of discarding records that may be needed in the future, they may not recognize that retention of unneeded records entails its own risks. Through questions and discussion, records managers can help users clarify the relationship between business value and retention requirements for specific records series. As an aid to such clarification, comparing users' perceived retention requirements with prevailing practices as reflected in published discussions of records retention and in the retention schedules of government agencies, academic institutions, corporations, and other organizations with well-developed records management programs is often useful.

Meetings about administrative retention requirements are usually attended by one or more representatives of the departments or other program units that create and maintain specific records series. Often, the departmental records coordinator takes the lead in explaining the program unit's operational requirements at such meetings. Other interested parties, including administrative and managerial employees who maintain and use the records in question, may also be involved. Where records maintained by one program unit are referenced by others, employees in additional departments may also be consulted regarding retention decisions. Such consultation occurs, for example, with centralized paper files and with enterprise-wide databases, data warehouses, Web pages on organizational intranets, and other computer-based information resources.

Retention and the Information Life Cycle

As discussed in the preceding chapter, a thorough inventory includes questions about reference activity and retention practices associated with specific records series. A program unit's responses to such questions provide a useful starting point for the determination of administrative retention periods, which should be based on the reasonable probability that a given records series will be needed in the future to support specific business objectives or activities. Administrative retention designations are based on the information life cycle concept discussed in Chapter 1. The concept is important enough to bear repetition. Decades of records management theory and practice indicate that the business value of many, if not most, records varies inversely with the age of the records. Typically, records maintained by corporations, government agencies, and other organizations are most valuable and are consulted most frequently for a relatively brief period of time following their creation or receipt. As the records age, their business value and reference activity diminish, either gradually or abruptly. When, and if, their business value falls to or approaches zero, the records may be discarded, assuming that they have no other value such as for legal or scholarly use.

Operational retention periods are essentially estimates of life cycle duration for specific records series. Certain records, such as general administrative announcements sent to all employees in an organization or unsolicited product literature received from vendors, have very short life cycles—they are often discarded after an initial reading. Other records, such as computer-generated accounting reports, are updated by replacement at similarly brief intervals. Some office records, such as routine correspondence and budget preparation documents, may be retained for several years then discarded. Many transaction-oriented records, such as purchase orders, invoices, and insurance claims, are referenced frequently for several weeks or months following their creation or receipt, but only occasionally after the matters to which they pertain are resolved. Total retention periods for such records may range from six to ten years.

Certain records are useful for much longer periods. Their retention parameters may be determined by the life cycles of objects to which the records pertain. As an example, engineering drawings, specifications, and other technical records that pertain to facilities or equipment should be retained as long as the facilities or equipment remain in service. Test results, statistical data, quality assurance reports, and other records that relate to products are retained as long as the products are sold and often longer, because discontinued products may remain at customer sites for years after being withdrawn from the market. Finally, some records have continuing administrative value that warrants multidecade or permanent retention. Examples include patent files and other intellectual property records maintained by corporations; case files maintained by law firms; student transcripts maintained by academic institutions; and deeds, mortgages, birth and death certificates, marriage licenses, and court records maintained by government agencies.

In some cases, the time-dependent business value of a given records series can be established with confidence. Experience may confirm, for example, that mechanical and electrical drawings contain information essential to future building repairs and must be retained until an organization sells, demolishes, or otherwise disposes of the buildings to which they pertain. Similarly, closed contract files may have been used in the past to prepare new contracts or contract amendments. Consequently, they will likely prove useful in the future for that purpose. More often, however, the future need or lack of need for a specific records series is uncertain; therefore, some risk is inevitably associated with administrative retention decisions. Because destruction is irreversible, program units may be reluctant to discard older records on the off chance that they may need them. Long retention periods are consequently established by default to allow for improbable contingencies. Such conservative retention practices entail their own risks, however. When an organization is involved in litigation or government investigations, records are subject to time-consuming and costly discovery actions as discussed previously. Discovery actions aside, long-term storage of large quantities of unneeded records can prove expensive.

Special Considerations for Electronic Records

Long administrative retention periods for electronic records are complicated by the limited storage stability of certain electronic recordkeeping media and their dependence on specific configurations of computer, video, or audio hardware and/or software. Limited media stability and hardware/software dependence also have obvious and significant implications for scholarly retention criteria, which typically involve the permanent preservation of records.

In most records management applications, the useful lives of paper and photographic media equal or exceed the retention periods for information such media contain. With few exceptions, the useful lives of magnetic and optical media that store electronic records are much shorter than of paper and photographic films. In many cases, the stable life spans of electronic media are shorter than the retention periods for information recorded on such media.

Media stability, however, is rarely the limiting factor for long-term storage of computer-processable information, audio recordings, or video images. Even if the stability of electronic media were to improve to levels comparable to those of acid-free papers or photographic films, retention periods for electronic records would still be limited by the interdependence of media, recorded information, hardware, and software. The service lives of magnetic and optical storage devices is typically shorter than that of media intended for use in such devices. Magnetic tapes and optical disks may remain stable for several decades; however, few magnetic recording and playback devices are engineered for a useful life longer than ten years, and most will be removed from service within a shorter time. Computer storage peripherals are usually replaced with newer equipment within five years. Audio and video recorders may have longer service lives, but the enhanced capabilities and attractive cost-performance characteristics of new models provide a powerful motive for replacement at relatively short intervals. In computer applications, problems of hardware dependence are compounded by software considerations. Electronic records are intended for retrieval or other processing by specific application programs which, in turn, operate in a specific systems software environment. Even more than equipment, software is subject to changes that can render previously recorded information unusable. Successor versions of a given program may not be able to read data, text, or images recorded by earlier versions.

Data migration, the process of periodically converting electronic records to new file formats and/or new storage media, is necessary to satisfy long retention requirements for electronic records. Conversion of electronic records to new file formats will maintain the usability of recorded information when computer systems and/or software are upgraded or replaced. Conversion of electronic records to new storage media will maintain the usability of recorded information where the stable life span of a given storage medium is shorter than the retention period for recorded information or where product modifications or discontinuations render a given storage medium unusable. Data migration requirements should be determined when retention periods are defined for electronic records. The longer the retention period for recorded information, the greater the need for data migration to ensure the future usability of electronic records. A data migration plan is essential where the destruction date for electronic records is greater than five years from the implementation date of the computer system or software that maintains the records or where the total retention period for electronic records is ten years or longer.

Data migration requirements have no counterparts in nonelectronic record-keeping systems. They may prove impractical or impossible to implement in specific situations. Where electronic records must be retained for long periods of time, periodic recopying involves a future commitment of labor and economic resources of uncertain availability. Where electronic records are designated for permanent retention, the commitment is perpetual. Where the same information exists in electronic and nonelectronic formats, or where information can be converted easily and reliably to nonelectronic formats through printing or transcription, records managers may prefer paper or microfilm for information designated for long-term retention. Although conceptually unattractive, this method is easily implemented and minimizes the risk that required information will be unreadable in the future.

Implementation Issues

Retention schedules are initially prepared in draft form for review and approval by those who will be affected by and responsible for implementing them. Functional schedules are typically reviewed by a committee that represents key program units and organizational perspectives. Where it exists, a records management advisory committee, as described in Chapter 1, may play that role. Departmental retention schedules are reviewed by the program units for which they are prepared. All schedules are typically reviewed by other organizational officials or departments that have an interest in records retention. Such reviewers may include, but are not necessarily limited to, the legal department, the chief financial officer, the tax department, and an archival agency. The review process may lead to changes that will be incorporated into additional drafts, which may be subject to additional reviews. This process is repeated until agreement is reached.

Importance of Implementation

Once approved, an organization's records retention policies and procedures must be fully implemented by all program units. Records must be discarded when specified in the organization's retention schedules except where destruction of specific records has been suspended for litigation, government investigation, tax audits, or other reasons specified in the organization's records retention policies. If implementation is not done, the preparation of retention schedules is merely a time-consuming exercise. For an organization's retention practices to be considered legally acceptable, records must be discarded in the normal course of business when their retention periods elapse.

This point is confirmed by the previously cited case of *U.S. v. Arthur Andersen, LLP,* which involved the destruction of audit records relating to the government's investigation of Enron Corporation's accounting irregularities. Arthur Andersen had corporate retention guidelines that authorized the destruction of correspondence, e-mail messages, drafts, and other nonessential records when audits are completed, but apparently those guidelines were not strictly enforced. In October 2001, one of Andersen's attorneys sent an e-mail message to employees who worked on the Enron audit in the Houston office, reminding them about the policy, but federal prosecutors argued that the reminder was an instruction to destroy potentially damaging evidence relating to an impending government investigation. The reminder would not have been necessary, of course, had Andersen routinely monitored its business operations for routine compliance with retention policies. At trial, witnesses testified that after becoming aware that a government inquiry into Enron's financial irregularities had begun, Andersen executives discussed the need for its Enron auditing team to conform to the company's retention policy. Andersen's lead partner on the Enron account subsequently pled guilty to obstruction of justice, admitting that he had authorized the destruction of audit records after becoming aware that the government had begun investigating Enron's accounting practices.

Discretionary deviations from approved retention schedules are not acceptable. If, for any reason, a program unit cannot comply with an approved retention period for a given records series, it must notify the organization's records management program immediately to request a reevaluation of the retention period for the records series in question. The request must clearly state the reason that the prescribed retention period does not satisfy the organization's requirements. The program unit should suggest a more appropriate retention period if one can be determined. Destruction of the records series will be temporarily suspended while the retention period is reevaluated.

Implementation Actions

To implement retention schedules, program units must identify records series in their custody that are eligible for retention actions and apply the appropriate actions. Possible retention actions include but are not necessarily limited to the following:

- Destruction of records with elapsed retention periods
- Transfer of inactive paper or photographic records to off-site storage
- Transfer of inactive electronic records from hard drives to removable media for off-line or off-site storage
- Microfilming or scanning of records followed by destruction of paper copies
- Microfilming or scanning of records followed by transfer of paper copies to off-site storage

Records management coordinators are typically responsible for organizing and supervising retention initiatives in their program units. Prior to implementing retention schedules, records management coordinators must take the following actions and precautions:

- Conduct one or more training sessions to inform program unit employees about the organization's records retention policies and procedures

- Ensure that all program unit employees who will participate in retention initiatives have access to the latest version of the organization's retention schedules

- Determine that program unit employees who will participate in retention initiatives are able to accurately identify records series, correctly interpret retention periods for records in their custody, and take appropriate retention actions in conformity with the organization's retention schedules

- Consult with the organization's records management program to determine whether destruction of specific records has been suspended for litigation, government investigation, tax audits, or other reasons

Paper and photographic records eligible for retention actions must be located and removed from file cabinets or other containers. Electronic records must be located in hard drive directories and subdirectories. This process, which must be performed manually, is time-consuming. In some cases, folders or documents must be individually inspected to determine whether their retention periods have elapsed. To simplify the identification of records eligible for retention actions, records series should be subdivided chronologically whenever possible and practical. This practice is known as **breaking files**. It involves closing or cutting off a folder at the end of a calendar or fiscal year and establishing a new active folder. A file of purchase orders and supporting documentation, for example, might be arranged by year then by purchase order number. If the organization's retention schedule specifies that purchase orders are to be kept for two years in the program-unit office and five more years off-site, records eligible for disposal or transfer to off-site storage in a given year will be grouped together and easily identified.

Chronologic file breaks are best suited to accounting records, purchasing records, customer order records, and other transaction records. Case files, contract files, project files, and similar files can be cut off when the matters to which they pertain terminate or are resolved. At that time, they should be moved to a closed category that is subdivided by calendar or fiscal year.

Certificate of Destruction

A **certificate of destruction** documents the disposal of specific records in conformity with an organization's formally established retention policies and schedules. A certificate of destruction should be completed whenever official copies of an organization's records are destroyed. Depending on the format, a certificate of destruction may list multiple records series that are destroyed simultaneously. (See Figures 3-4a and 3-4b.) Alternatively, multiple certificates of destruction may be separately prepared for each

Records
Destruction
Authorization
and Certificate

Figure 3-4a

Records Destruction Authorization and Certificate			
Department, Unit, Name, Address		Department Manager	
		Date	

The records listed below are now eligible for destruction according to the approved records retention schedule. Please indicate your approval for the destruction unless reasons to delay exist. Your signature below attests that no unresolved (1) audit questions, (2) investigations, (3) civil suits or criminal prosecutions, or (4) other reasons for holding up the destruction exist. If the destruction is to be delayed, please give the reason in the space indicated and provide a revised destruction date.

Schedule Item No.	Series Title, Inclusive Dates, and Total Volume	Scheduled Destruction Date	Revised Destruction Date

Reason for Continued Retention

Security Destruction ☐ Yes ☐ No	Department Manager (Signature)	Date

Certificate of Destruction

This completed and signed form certifies that the records listed above have been destroyed on the date shown below.

If Security Destruction, Witnessed By (Signature)	Date
Records Center Manager (Signature)	Date

records series. In either case, the certificate of destruction must provide information about the records series that was destroyed, including the series titles or other description, the dates covered by the records, the date the records were destroyed, and the

Certificate of Destruction

Examples of forms to certify destruction of records in conformity with retention schedules.

Figure 3-4b

Certificate of Destruction	
Company:	
Department:	
Records Coordinator:	Phone:
FAX:	E-mail:
Schedule Issue Date:	

Records Disposed Of:

Records Code	Records Title	Date/Alpha Range

On _____, destruction of the above records was made by means of :
☐ Incineration   ☐ Shredding   ☐ Other _____

Total # Of Boxes Destroyed: _____

Name	
Signature	Date

(Source: *Sample Forms for Archival & Records Management Programs,* published by ARMA International and the Society of American Archivists)

destruction method. The form should be signed and dated by the department head and by the person who destroyed or supervised destruction of the records. A certificate of destruction is not typically required when duplicate records are discarded.

Secure Destruction

In most cases, records containing nonconfidential information may be discarded by any method consistent with an organization's waste management practices and with the waste removal requirements of the locality where the records will be discarded. Records with confidential or sensitive information about persons, organizations, research and development activities, strategic plans, products, prices, or other matters must be destroyed in an irreversible manner that obliterates their contents and renders them unreadable and unusable. Locked bins or other secure containers should be used to collect these records for disposal.

Shredding is the most common method of secure destruction for paper documents. Document shredders for paper documents vary in page capacity, speed, page sizes accepted, ease of operation, cost, reliability, and other performance characteristics. Based on their method of destroying documents, shredders are rated according to security levels defined in DIN 32757-1, *Office Machines—Destruction of Information Carriers—Part 1: Requirements and Testing Conditions for Equipment and Installations*, which is published by the Deutsches Institut fuer Normung. Level 2 shredders, which cut papers into strips that measure approximately one-quarter inch wide, is acceptable for some documents. In most cases, the strips are the same length as the page being shredded. Where greater security is required, Level 3 shredders provide cross-cut capabilities that produce small particles rather than strips. Level 4 and Level 5 shredders provide cross-cut capabilities that produce smaller fragments. To meet U.S. Department of Defense standards for secure destruction of highly confidential government and military documents, shredders must produce fragments that measure 1/32 by 7/16 inches. Such shredders are, in effect, pulverizers. In addition to paper documents, some shredders can destroy microfilm, X-rays, and other photographic media.

Incineration and chemical disintegration are possible alternatives to shredding for secure destruction of paper documents and photographic media, but they may be prohibited by local ordinances. Recycling is not an acceptable method of secure destruction because recycling contractors may store records in unsupervised areas before they are recycled.

Although file deletion may permit the recovery of information, it is the only practical method of destroying confidential electronic records stored on hard drives that will remain in service following destruction of the information. A hard drive that previously contained confidential information should be reformatted then physically destroyed when it is taken out of service. Secure methods of destroying confidential electronic records stored on magnetic tapes, floppy disks, or other removable magnetic media include degaussing (bulk erasure) or reformatting, followed by physical destruction of the media. Special shredders are available for that purpose. Secure methods of destroying confidential electronic records stored on optical disks, including compact disks and DVDs, include cutting, crushing, pulverizing, and chemical disintegration.

Organizations may have adequate in-house facilities to shred small quantities of confidential records, but secure disposal of a large volume of records will often require the services of a contractor that specializes in records destruction. A number of companies offer plant-based and mobile services of this type. If an organization contracts with a commercial provider for destruction of records, the contractor must:

- Specify the destruction method to be used for confidential and nonconfidential records

- Specify the amount of time that will elapse between pickup of records from an organization's location and their destruction

- Allow the organization's representatives to observe all stages of the destruction process from pickup of records to disposal of remnant material following destruction of records

- Demonstrate safeguards for confidential information at all stages in the destruction process

- Complete a certificate of destruction as specified by the organization

- Provide proof of destruction of records in the manner specified by the organization

- Assume full liability for breaches of confidentiality involving records while they are in the contractor's custody

The National Association for Information Destruction (NAID), a not-for-profit trade association with over 250 members, has developed a third-party security certification program that specifies minimum standards for employee hiring and screening, operations, the destruction process, insurance, and other factors relating to the secure destruction of records. It provides annual audits to certify records destruction contractors and facilities.

Compliance

In most organizations, individual program units are responsible for implementing retention schedules for records in their possession. The records management staff should provide training for that purpose and be available to interpret retention guidelines as needed. Departmental records coordinators play a key role in the implementation process. Some organizations designate annual review periods or cleanup days for destruction of records with elapsed retention periods or transfer of inactive records to off-site storage in conformity with retention schedules. Department managers may be required to sign a certificate of compliance attesting that the annual review has been completed and that retention guidelines have been properly implemented.

Regular or unscheduled physical audits of selected departments are recommended to confirm these self-assessments. The authority to conduct or commission such audits should be clearly established when a records management program is established. Records retention audits, which involve a sampling of records in one or more series, may be performed by the records management department itself or by a compliance-oriented organizational unit such as an internal audit or quality assurance department. In the latter case, the records management department typically provides a checklist of recordkeeping characteristics to be examined for compliance with organizational policies and procedures. In addition to conformity with retention schedules, an audit may consider the security of records, appropriate methods for destroying confidential information, backup protection for vital records, efficient use of available storage space, or other matters.

To be effective, of course, audit findings must be taken seriously. In most organizations, audit reports that indicate compliance problems and present recommendations for corrective action are initially discussed with line management in the departments involved. A return visit is then scheduled to confirm that appropriate corrective actions have been taken. Continuing problems are referred to executive management for resolution.

Revision of Retention Schedules

Retention schedules require periodic revisions to add or delete records series or to change retention periods. Program units should be instructed to notify the organization's records management program when any of the following occurs:

- A new records series is created
- A records series was overlooked when the organization's retention schedules were initially prepared or last revised
- The organization obtains one or more records series through a merger or acquisition
- The retention schedules do not conclusively identify an existing records series
- The title or form number for an existing records series changes
- An existing records series has been divided into multiple series, each having different retention requirements
- An existing records series has been combined with another records series that has a different retention period
- A records series listed in the organization's retention schedules has been discontinued
- The retention period prescribed for a given records series is not clear
- Legal or regulatory developments warrant reconsideration of retention periods for specific records series

Revisions to retention schedules typically apply retroactively. If a revision decreases the retention period for a given records series, records that would have been kept under the old retention schedule are to be destroyed at the earliest opportunity in conformity with the new retention period.

Chapter 4

Managing Inactive Records I: Records Centers

A **records center** is a specially designed, warehouse-type facility that provides safe, economical, high-density storage for records that are consulted infrequently but must be retained for legal or administrative reasons. Properly organized and operated, a records center is an important component in a systematic records management program and a critical resource for cost-effective storage of records in the inactive portion of the information life cycle.

A records center may be operated by a corporation, government agency, or other organization for its own use. Such in-house records centers are an important component of some records management programs. Alternatively, many organizations contract with commercial records centers that charge predetermined fees for storage and related recordkeeping services. These two approaches are not mutually exclusive. Some organizations use commercial providers to supplement their in-house records centers for specific types of records or in specific geographic locations.

Whether in-house or outsourced, records center operations are typically integrated with and provide essential support for an organization's retention initiatives. Retention guidelines specify which records are to be transferred to a records center by specific program units and when the transfer should occur. These instructions may be included in retention schedules or presented in separate procedural documents. Preparing records for transfer by removing them from file cabinets, packing them in appropriate containers, and inventorying their contents is an important aspect of retention schedule implementation. A records transfer list (See Figure 4-1) is prepared for and accompanies the containers transferred to a records center. These activities are typically considered when program units are audited for compliance with retention policies and procedures.

Completing the retention cycle, most records centers will destroy records when their retention periods elapse, subject to required approvals, in conformity with an organization's policies and procedures. Some organizations limit records center storage to inactive records that have a specified destruction date, usually within 10 or 15 years

Records Transfer List

A container inventory form for records transferred to off-site storage.

Figure 4-1

Records Transfer List			
			Date Prepared:
Dept. Name	Dept. No.	RRS No.	Location: ☐ _____ ☐ _____
Bar Code Label Number (6 Middle Digits):		Contact Name/Tel No. / E-mail Address:	

Records Title & Description From Records Retention Schedule	Records Dates From – To	Destruction Year

Affix Bar Code Label Here: ☞

1. Contact Records Coordinator to arrange pickup.
2. Make 4 Copies of Form: Place Bar Code Label on Copy 1.
                                Give Copies 1 & 2 to Driver.   Copy 3 to Records Coordinator.
                                Copy 4 Retained by User.

(Source: Sample Forms for Archival & Records Management Programs, published by ARMA International and the Society of American Archivists)

from the date of transfer. Records center storage, where conveniently available and compatible with users' access requirements, is almost invariably the best practice for cost-effective management of such records. As discussed in Chapter 5, microfilming may be a more economical alternative for large quantities of inactive records with longer retention periods, although microfilming and records center costs must be carefully compared on a case-by-case basis.

The business case for records centers is straightforward: Expensive office space and filing equipment should be reserved for records that will be consulted frequently and that must be available immediately when needed. Inactive records should be stored elsewhere, provided that they can be retrieved on demand within a reasonable period of time. In office areas, where records are stored in conventional file cabinets, wide aisles are required to accommodate extended file drawers and the air space above cabinets is wasted. The resulting cubic-foot-to-square-foot ratio, an important indicator of storage efficiency and economy, rarely exceeds 1:1. A moderately full four-drawer letter-size filing cabinet, for example, contains about six cubic feet of records but requires about eight square feet of installation space, including floor space that must be allocated for the extended drawer and for a user to stand while inserting or removing files. Assuming that the cabinet costs $350 and has a 10-year useful life and that office space rents for $20 per square foot per year, the annual cost of records storage is $32.50 per cubic foot, calculated as follows:

- The cost of the cabinet ($350) is divided by a ten-year useful life, which equals an effective annual cost of $35 per year.
- The file cabinet occupies eight square feet times $20 per square foot, which equals $160 per year.
- The total filing cabinet and floor space cost is $195 per year.
- That amount divided by six cubic feet of records equals $32.50 per cubic foot.

In a records center, by contrast, storage density is maximized by combining floor-to-ceiling shelving with standardized containers designed specifically for records storage. Cubic-foot-to-square-foot ratios routinely exceed 4:1 within records storage areas (as opposed to administrative areas) and are often substantially higher. Based on rates charged by commercial records centers, the resulting annual storage costs range from about $1.50 to $3 per cubic foot, which is a fraction of the cost of in-office storage.

A records center thus functions as a less costly extension of an organization's office space. Individual departments or other program units retain full authority over the records they transfer to a records center, which merely serves as a physical custodian for such records. In this respect, records centers differ from archival agencies, which usually assume full responsibility for records transferred to their custody. More significantly, records centers and archives differ in their missions. Archival agencies are principally concerned with the preservation of records of scholarly value or long-term policy or administrative value, while records centers support an organization's business objectives through safe, economical recordkeeping. In practice, the relationship between records centers and archives is complementary rather than competitive. In government and academic institutions, in-house records centers are often operated by archival agencies. The National Archives and Records Administration's Records Center Program, for example, is a network of geographically dispersed facilities that store over 20 million cubic feet of federal government records. Similarly, the National Archives of Canada operates a coast-to-coast network of storage facilities for records transferred from federal government offices. In some cases, a records center provides intermediate storage for permanent records that will eventually be transferred to an archival agency.

Although records centers were originally developed for paper documents, they can and do store recorded information in any format. Many records centers provide vault areas for environmentally controlled storage of microforms as well as for computer tapes, videotapes, optical disks, or other electronic media. Regardless of media, records centers are intended for inactive records or, in the case of electronic media and microforms, backup copies that require secure storage. Records center storage is not suitable for **active records**, which are subject to urgent retrieval demands to support ongoing business operations. Depending on a records center's location, retrieval requests may take a day or longer to fulfill. Frequent retrieval demands also increase staffing requirements for records center operations with a resulting increase in costs. Where commercial records centers are used or where in-house records centers charge back their services to individual program units, retrieval charges can mount up quickly.

Although records centers provide economical storage space, they are not mere warehouses. They are designed and equipped specifically for records storage and related services. Records centers should not be used for library books, undistributed inventories of publications, product samples, or other nonrecord materials discussed in Chapter 1.

This chapter surveys records center characteristics and components, including records storage containers, shelving, fire-protection requirements, and environmental controls. It also describes retrieval operations and other services that support records storage. The chapter concludes with a discussion of commercial records centers. The discussion emphasizes factors that records managers must consider when planning, implementing, and operating in-house records centers and when evaluating the facilities and capabilities of commercial storage providers. It draws on requirements and recommendations presented in standards and related documents, including ANSI/ARMA TR-01, *Records Center Operations*, Second Edition; *Standards for Physical Storage of Commonwealth Records*, published by the National Archives of Australia; FC311(M), *Standard for Records Storage*, published by the Fire Commissioner of Canada; *Records Management Standard: Storage of Semi-Current Records*, published by the United Kingdom Public Record Office; and 36 CFR part 1228, *Disposition of Federal Records, Subpart K, Facility Standards for Records Storage Facilities.*

Features and Functions of Records Centers

As previously discussed, records centers offer economical storage for records that need to be retained but are seldom referenced. A records center's economic advantages over office storage are based on a combination of location and storage density. Records centers seldom occupy prime real estate. In cities and well-developed suburbs where office space is costly, records centers may be located in semi-industrial areas away from major business districts, on the perimeters of office parks or academic campuses, or in other relatively inexpensive, subprime locations that are safe for records storage but generally unacceptable for office use. Some commercial records centers, for example, are located in former warehouses or factory buildings, which, admittedly, have been extensively refurbished for secure records storage but are not suitable for other business purposes. Alternatively, a records center may be located in outer suburbs or rural areas at some distance from the offices where active records are maintained, hence the designation *off-site storage* as a synonym for records centers. The distance must be compatible with responsive service, however.

General Characteristics

Whether in an urban or rural area, a records center must occupy a safe location above flood plains and away from known, avoidable hazards such as chemical factories, oil refineries, and utility plants. A records center's location should be served by nearby police and fire services. The perimeter of the records center should be well lighted and free of landscaping or large objects that obscure the building.

A records center is a utilitarian structure. It may be built specifically to house records or adapted for records storage from a structure originally intended for other purposes. In either case, a records center building must be ruggedly constructed, preferably of brick or concrete. It must be well insulated, preferably windowless but well ventilated with high ceilings, adequate lighting, and, where necessary, firewalls to separate records storage areas from hazardous substances in adjacent rooms or buildings. Some archival agencies have published guidelines for the location and construction of records storage facilities to be used by government agencies subject to their authority. Such guidelines typically prohibit or strongly discourage self-service storage in basements, closets, or other unsupervised areas.

A records center building must comply with local building, electrical, plumbing, and other codes. Its structural characteristics must be appropriate for records storage. In particular, floors above ground level must be engineered to bear the substantial weight of large quantities of records, shelving, and related equipment. Floor loads of 300 to 500 pounds per square foot are typical in records storage areas as compared with about 150 pounds per square foot in office areas. Refurbished structures will often require floor reinforcement. The records center building must be able to withstand strong storms, lightning strikes, or other extreme weather conditions. Because weather can affect electrical systems, emergency power systems should be installed.

A records center must be kept clean and in good repair. Storage areas and shelving should be inspected regularly. Because insects and rodents are a threat to records, building maintenance plans should include pest management measures. Building entrances should be well controlled and supervised during operating hours. Intruder alarms linked to a local law enforcement agency should be installed on all doors and windows to protect records while the building is unoccupied. If a records center shares a building with other organizations or business functions, access to records storage areas must be restricted to records center personnel.

Within a records center, a small percentage of the interior space is reserved for administrative offices and work areas where records are received, prepared for shelving, and housed temporarily while awaiting destruction or delivery in response to retrieval requests. Some records centers also provide a reference room where records may be examined by authorized persons. Most of the interior space, however, is dedicated to and optimized for records storage. As previously explained, a combination of floor-to-ceiling shelving and standardized containers yields high cubic-foot-to-square-foot storage ratios. As a general guideline that is subject to some local variation, the amount of floor space required for records storage will be one-fourth to one-fifth the number of cubic feet of records to be stored. Thus, 4,000 to 5,000 square feet of floor space will be required to store 20,000 cubic feet of records, which is equivalent to about 13,000 letter-size file drawers.

Records Center Containers

Records centers store records in cardboard containers rather than in metal cabinets. The containers must be an appropriate size for the records to be stored. The most widely used records center container has interior dimensions of 10 inches high by 12 inches wide by 15 inches deep. Its external measurements, which affect shelving configurations and capacity, are 10.5 inches high by 12.5 inches wide by 16.5 inches deep. This container is routinely available from a number of manufacturers and office supply companies. Widely described as a *cubic-foot container* or *records center box*, it can store approximately one cubic foot of records. (The container requires about 1.25 cubic feet of shelf space, but its interior space is just slightly greater than one cubic foot.) (See Figure 4-2a.) More importantly, a cubic-foot container can accommodate the three most commonly encountered sizes of office records:

- Letter-size folders and pages packed along the 12-inch side
- Legal-size folders and pages packed along the 15-inch side
- Unbound computer printouts stacked from top to bottom

Larger containers, sometimes described as *transfer cases*, measure 10 inches high by 12 inches wide by 24 inches deep. (See Figure 4-2b.) They can store the entire contents

Cubic-Foot Storage Container

(Courtesy: Fellowes)

File Transfer Box

Figure 4-2b

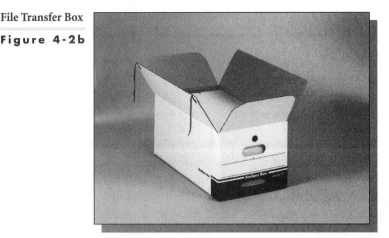

(Courtesy: Fellowes)

of a letter-size file drawer, but they are heavier than cubic foot containers, require deeper shelves, and often prove less durable when handled frequently. Their use is consequently discouraged.

Properly packed, a records center box can also store index cards and other small documents, as well as microforms and certain electronic media such as computer tape cartridges, videotape cassettes, audiocassettes, and optical disks. Containers that are densely packed with such media may be heavier than comparably sized containers that store paper documents. Special containers are available for other records, including bank checks, X-rays, bound computer printouts, engineering drawings, architectural plans, and maps. Whenever possible, large documents should be stored flat rather than rolled. If flat storage is not possible, the document should be rolled around the outside of a paper tube to provide support then inserted into a tube-shaped container for protection.

When filled with paper documents, a cubic-foot container weighs 25 to 35 pounds. Side openings serve as handles for easy portability. Containers must be strong enough to protect records during handling and multiyear storage. In the event of sprinkler activation, they must also be able to absorb moisture without collapsing. Products with double-wall (two-ply) construction on the sides and bottom are recommended, particularly where several containers will be stacked in staging or storage areas. Some shelving arrangements stack containers to reduce costs. Because double-wall containers are durable, they can often be reused when their contents are destroyed in conformity with retention schedules.

Conventional records center containers are constructed of wood pulp. They are adequate for business records with medium-term retention periods. For permanent records, so-called archival containers conform to requirements presented in ANSI/NISO Z39.48, *Permanence of Paper for Publications and Documents in Libraries and Archives*, and in ISO 9706, *Information and Documentation—Paper for Documents—Requirements for Permanence*. Available in cubic foot and other sizes, archival containers are constructed of acid-free materials buffered with calcium or magnesium carbonate as an alkaline reserve to protect valuable records. As might be expected, these containers are several times more expensive than conventional records center boxes. Before they are packed into acid-free containers, records should be transferred into acid-free folders or envelopes. Folder specifications are covered in ANSI/ASTM D3301, *File Folders for Permanent Records.*

Shelving

Shelving characteristics are covered in ANSI MH281, *Specifications for the Design, Testing, Utilization and Application of Industrial Grade Steel Shelving,* and in ANSI/NISO, Z39.73, *Single-Tier, Steel Bracket Library Shelving.* Most records centers employ steel shelving or pallet rack units with open backs and sides that are braced for stability and lateral rigidity. Conventional shelving units are suitable for low-volume in-house records centers operated by corporations, government agencies, and other organizations. They resemble their library counterparts, but shelf widths are designed specifically for cubic-foot containers. A 42-inch shelf, for example, provides a clear opening for easy insertion and removal of three cubic-foot containers along their 12-inch sides.

In commercial records centers and other high-volume installations, pallet racks are preferred to conventional shelving for cost and capacity. Pallet racks feature steel uprights and beams that create a frame for decking on which records storage containers are placed. Steel is the preferred decking material for strength and fire safety. Rack units with particleboard or plywood decking are less expensive than all-steel units, but they are not recommended for records storage.

Shelving units must be strong enough to bear the weight of wet records and containers in case fire sprinklers are activated. Wet paper weighs about 2.5 times as much as dry paper. *Gauge* is a measure of the thickness of steel shelving—the lower the gauge, the heavier and stronger the shelving, but the higher the cost. Most manufacturers recommend 18- or 20-gauge steel for records center shelving, but well-constructed 22-gauge shelving units are often suitable for records storage.

The storage capacity of a records center depends on the shelving layout, which is determined and constrained by the dimensions of the storage area. Shelving configurations and storage density are obviously affected by ceiling height. As previously noted, records centers employ floor-to-ceiling shelving for maximum density, although bottom shelves are usually about three inches off the floor to allow for flooding, and the top shelves must provide sufficient space between containers and sprinklers as specified in local building codes. Very high ceilings permit multilevel storage with mezzanines and catwalks supported by the shelving units themselves. These structures must comply with regulations established by the Occupational Safety and Health Administration.

Aisles between rows of shelving must be wide enough to allow easy passage of wheeled carts, platform ladders, and other equipment but not so wide as to compromise storage density. Typical aisle widths range from 30 to 36 inches, although main corridors are usually wider. To increase storage density by minimizing the number of aisles between shelving units, containers may be stored two or three rows deep on shelves or rack decking. To reduce cost by minimizing the number of required shelves, containers may be stacked two or three high as well as two or three deep. Such multicontainer stacking is typical in pallet rack installations. Because multiple boxes must be moved, however, additional time and labor will be required to retrieve and replace containers located in interior rows or bottom layers. This effort can be reduced by reserving the top layers and outermost rows for records likely to be retrieved, but future reference activity for inactive records is difficult to predict.

Mobile shelving units that roll along a floor-mounted track can maximize storage density by drastically reducing the amount of floor space required for aisles, but such units are much more expensive to purchase and install than their static counterparts. As discussed in Chapter 7, mobile shelving units are usually installed in offices rather than records centers. Within a records center, mobile shelving is more likely to be installed in vault areas than in open warehouse space.

Material Handling Equipment

Records centers must have material handling equipment to transport containers of records to and from shelves when they are initially acquired, requested by authorized persons, or removed for destruction. Examples of useful devices include, but are not limited to, the following:

- A *platform ladder* is designed like a movable stairway with handrails, a platform at the top is used for placing cartons, and it has spring wheels that make the ladder stationary when in use. It is rolled from aisle to aisle within a records storage area to access containers stored on upper shelf levels. Platform ladders are well suited to ceiling heights up to 15 feet. If boxes are stacked 14-feet high, the ladders will need to be a little over 11 feet from the floor to the top platform rail, and about 8.5 feet from the floor to the top step. A ten-step platform ladder will satisfy this requirement. As with shelving, metal construction is recommended for sturdiness and fire resistance. Platform ladders must conform to Occupational Safety and Health Standard 1910.29, which specifies rules and requirements for the design, construction, and use of manually propelled mobile ladder stands and scaffolds. Pneumatic tires are required in catwalk installations.

- *Forklifts or other motorized lifting equipment* may be required for heavy loads or very high shelving units. These devices are covered by Occupational Safety and Health Standard 1910.178 and ANSI/ASME B56.1, *Safety Standard for Low Lift and High Lift Trucks.*

- *Pallet jacks* are wheeled devices that can move single pallets of records storage cartons from place to place within a records center. To avoid the risk of water damage, records should never be stored on the floor. While awaiting shelving, delivery, or reshelving, containers should be placed onto raised pallets or other platforms.

- *Dollies* can be used to move a small quantity of cartons from place to place within a records center or to and from delivery vehicles for pickup and retrieval service.

- *Four-wheel, nonmotorized platform trucks* can move loads of records cartons from loading docks and processing areas to and from storage areas or within the storage area itself. A useful size for these units is 30 by 72 inches, with sides

4 feet high. This size and type of platform truck can transport up to 40 cubic-foot containers.

- *Table-top carts* are used for retrieval and interfiling tasks in records storage areas. They must be small enough to maneuver between rows of shelving.

- *Cargo vans,* one or more, are operated by some in-house records centers for pick-up and delivery of records. Alternatively, a records center may rely on *transport services* provided by other departments within their organizations such as general services or facilities management that operate fleets of vehicles.

Environmental Controls

Heat accelerates chemical reactions that can damage paper and nonpaper media. High humidity, in combination with heat, promotes the growth of mold, fungi, and other contaminants. The temperature and relative humidity in records storage areas must consequently be controlled, but the nature and extent of required control depends on the retention periods for records to be stored. Generally, the shorter the retention period, the less stringent the environmental controls need to be. Records centers store many records that will be retained for 15 years or less. Such records are typically stored in open warehouse areas, which should be well ventilated to prevent stagnant air; air conditioning is not required. The temperature should be less than 81 degrees Fahrenheit (27 degrees Celsius) with a relative humidity below 60 percent.

Many records centers provide one or more storage vaults for permanent paper records, photographic films, or electronic media that require special environmental controls, security, or fire protection. All authorities advocate cool, dry storage conditions for permanent records, but specific recommendations vary with the physical composition of the records media. For combined storage and user areas, NISO TR-01, *Environmental Guidelines for Storage of Paper Records,* recommends a maximum temperature of 70 degrees Fahrenheit (21 degrees Celsius) with relative humidity ranging from 30 to 50 percent. For storage areas where users are excluded, the recommended maximum temperature is 65 degrees Fahrenheit (19 degrees Celsius). Daily fluctuations must not exceed two degrees Fahrenheit for temperature and three percent for relative humidity. Air within vault areas should be filtered to remove dust and other particulate matter as well as gaseous pollutants such as sulfur dioxide and ozones that can promote acid formation.

ANSI/NAPM IT9.11, *Imaging Materials—Processed Safety Photographic Film—Storage,* standard specifies maximum temperatures and acceptable relative humidity for extended-term (permanent) and medium-term storage of microforms. For black-and-white microforms that contain permanent records, the extended-term storage recommendations specify three combinations of temperature and relative humidity:

- A maximum temperature of 70 degrees Fahrenheit (21 degrees Celsius) with relative humidity of 20 to 30 percent

- A maximum temperature of 60 degrees Fahrenheit (15 degrees Celsius) with relative humidity of 20 to 40 percent

- A maximum temperature of 50 degrees Fahrenheit (10 degrees Celsius) with relative humidity of 20 to 50 percent

These recommendations apply to all types of microfilm, including camera original and duplicating films as discussed in Chapter 5. They also apply to other black-and-white photographic films. As with paper records, low temperature and low humidity promote stable storage of photographic films. Lower temperatures can compensate for high humidity, but the relative humidity cannot exceed 50 percent in microform storage areas. Relative humidity below 20 percent is not recommended because low humidity extracts moisture from photographic emulsions, which can lead to brittleness and curling of microfilms. Humidity must be controlled within the specified ranges; variations must not exceed 5 percent in 24 hours. The recommended environmental conditions may be maintained within individual microform housings or within the storage area that contains such housings.

For extended storage of color microforms and other color photographic films, the ANSI/NAPM IT9.11 standard recommends a maximum temperature of two degrees Celsius (36 degrees Fahrenheit) with relative humidity of 20 to 30 percent. At lower temperatures, a broader range of relative humidity is permissible. Color films should be stored in two heat-sealed foil bags for moisture protection and to limit exposure to air.

The ANSI/NAPM IT9.11 standard defines medium-term storage conditions as suitable for preservation of microforms and other photographic films for at least ten years. For medium-term storage, environmental requirements are much less stringent than previously cited requirements. The maximum temperature should not exceed 77 degrees Fahrenheit (25 degrees Celsius). Storage temperatures below 70 degrees Fahrenheit (21 degrees Celsius) are preferable. The peak temperature for short periods in medium-term storage areas can reach 90 degrees Fahrenheit (32 degrees Celsius), but short-term fluctuations in temperature must be avoided. Depending on the records center, these conditions may be satisfied outside of a vault environment. Relative humidity for medium-term storage can range from 20 to 50 percent. Humidity variations must not exceed 10 percent per day. Prolonged exposure to higher humidity conditions promotes bacterial growths and accelerates the harmful effects of residual processing chemicals.

Temperature and humidity conditions recommended in the ANSI/NAPM IT9.11 standard are similar to those specified in ANSI/NAPM IT9.23, *Imaging Materials—Polyester Base Magnetic Tape—Storage.* The IT9.23 standard specifies medium-term storage conditions, which are suitable for the preservation of recorded information for a minimum of ten years, and extended-term storage conditions, which are suitable for the preservation of recorded information of permanent value. The standard does not state or imply, however, that magnetic tapes have permanent keeping properties. For medium-term storage of magnetic tapes, the maximum temperature is 73 degrees Fahrenheit (23 degrees Celsius) with a relative humidity of 20 to 50 percent. Temperature variations in the storage area must not exceed four degrees Fahrenheit (two degrees Celsius) over a 24-hour period. Humidity variations must not exceed 10 percent over a 24-hour period. Rapid cycling of temperature and humidity can damage binder materials and media substrates.

For extended-term storage of magnetic tapes, the ANSI/NAPM IT9.23 standard, like its IT9.11 counterpart, specifies three combinations of temperature and relative humidity:

- A maximum temperature of 68 degrees Fahrenheit (20 degrees Celsius) with relative humidity ranging from 20 to 30 percent
- A maximum temperature of 59 degrees Fahrenheit (15 degrees Celsius) with relative humidity ranging from 20 to 40 percent
- A maximum temperature of 50 degrees Fahrenheit (10 degrees Celsius) with relative humidity ranging from 20 to 50 percent

For both medium- and extended-term storage, the ANSI/NAPM IT9.23 standard notes that an air-conditioned facility is usually necessary to maintain temperature and humidity within approved limits. A vault environment may be required to maintain low temperatures within the specified humidity ranges. Where air conditioning is not practical or required, as in underground storage areas with naturally low temperatures, dehumidification is often necessary.

Fire Protection

NFPA 232, *Protection of Records*, published by the National Fire Protection Association (NFPA), provides the most thorough and informative review of fire-protection principles, issues, and requirements for records storage. Several destructive fires in commercial records centers underscore the importance of fire protection in the design and operation of records storage facilities. Paper ignites at 451 degrees Fahrenheit (230 degrees Celsius). That temperature is quickly reached in a fire, which may originate in the records center building or spread from neighboring structures. Large quantities of paper documents stored at high density in cardboard containers are a powerful source of fuel for any fire; high ceilings and catwalks provide open space for the uninterrupted upward flow of flames, heat, and smoke. Steel shelving can collapse during prolonged exposure to temperatures encountered in uncontrolled fires. Once started, records center fires can be long burning. Total burnouts have occurred.

Fire control depends on rapid detection and suppression. At a minimum, records center buildings must conform to local fire codes and ordinances, which typically mandate heat and smoke detectors, fire alarms connected to a local fire department, portable fire extinguishers, standpipes and hoses, and automatic sprinkler systems or other fire-suppression systems in storage and work areas. To limit the spread and destructive potential of fires, a much debated section of the NFPA 232 standard recommends that a records center's open-storage area be divided into two or more compartments separated by fire walls with a four-hour fire-resistance rating. Most fire walls are masonry structures faced on each side with brick or reinforced concrete. The fire-resistance rating is the time in hours that a structure will remain in place and stop the passage of flames after a fire begins. Fire resistance is influenced by wall thickness. Solid fire walls without doors are preferred. Unavoidable wall openings should be fitted with two-hour fire doors on each side of the wall.

Properly constructed fire-resistant vaults and safes provide additional protection against total burnout in one or more records storage compartments. Although their names are often used interchangeably, vaults and safes have different characteristics:

- A *vault* is a sealed room-size storage enclosure incorporated into a structure, either at ground level or on one of the upper floors. Walls, roof, and doors of a vault should have a minimum fire-resistance rating of four hours. To limit the quantity of records exposed to fire and to reduce the possibility of fire originating within the vault itself, the NFPA 232 standard recommends that vault size be limited to 5,000 cubic feet with a ceiling height of 12 feet.

- A *safe* is a fire-resistant, theft-resistant container for valuable items. A safe may be a freestanding chest or installed into a wall. Safes vary in size, capacity, and construction. Fire-resistant safes for paper records are rated by Underwriters Laboratories for the period of time, in hours, that the interior temperature will remain below 350 degrees Fahrenheit (175 degrees Celsius) when exposed to fire temperatures up to 1,700 degrees Fahrenheit (920 degrees Celsius). Safes that pass the test are described as Class 350 products. Underwriters Laboratories' impact test confirms that a safe will remain intact and protect its contents when exposed to high temperatures for 30 minutes then dropped onto concrete rubble from a height of 30 feet. Safes are also placed into an oven at 2,000 degrees Fahrenheit (1,085 degrees Celsius) to confirm that they will not explode. Underwriters Laboratories imposes more stringent fire-resistance requirements for safes that store electronic media. Described as *Class 125 products*, such safes must maintain an interior temperature below 125 degrees Fahrenheit (53 degrees Celsius) with a relative humidity below 85 percent.

Automated sprinkler systems can help confine a fire to a limited area, but records in a much wider area will become wet and possibly damaged in the process. As might be expected, water exposure is greatest for containers on high shelves, which are closest to sprinkler heads. High-quality records center containers can absorb some water. In some cases, the fire will be extinguished before wet containers collapse.

Alternative fire-suppression technologies prevent water damage and simplify salvage operations. Examples include high-compression foam, which fills an entire storage space with bubbles that contain a small quantity of water; and carbon dioxide systems, which deprive a fire of oxygen. Because these technologies are more expensive than conventional sprinkler systems, they are often limited to vault installations that house microfilm, electronic media, and vital paper records. Bromotrifluoromethane (halon) extinguishes flames through chemical interaction, but it is toxic and depletes the earth's ozone layer. Halon products are no longer manufactured in the United States, Canada, and some other countries.

Pest Control

Large quantities of paper records can be damaged by rodents and insects, including termites, cockroaches, crickets, and silverfish, which are attracted to dark spaces and feed upon cellulose, starches, adhesives, and other organic substances found in paper.

Exclusion and extermination of vermin is the most effective way to prevent such damage. Storage and work areas should be inspected periodically for pest infestation, which may indicate possible openings under doors, around windows and service ducts, or in the records center structure itself. Good housekeeping procedures are essential. Records storage and work areas must be kept clean to remove dust, which provides a breeding ground for vermin. Food and potted plants should be prohibited in storage areas. Traps and gaseous or chemical pest extermination should be employed when necessary, but care must be taken to avoid damage to records or cardboard containers. Trash should be removed promptly from storage and office areas, and trash containers should be located away from the entrance to the records center building.

Services

A records center provides safe, economical storage for inactive records that must be retained for legal or administrative reasons. Records centers also provide a variety of related services. Such services include, but are not necessarily limited to, the following:

1. Picking up records from program units or client sites
2. Entering data and indexing for newly acquired containers
3. Retrieving records requested by authorized persons
4. Delivering requested records to program units or clients
5. Reshelving previously retrieved records when returned to storage
6. Destroying records when their retention periods elapse

All records center operations depend on accurate packing, labeling, and inventorying containers. A records center must provide clear, detailed instructions for these tasks, which are usually performed by personnel in the program units where the records reside. Records centers operated by corporations, government agencies, and other organizations typically supply cubic-foot containers to program units or make arrangements for program units to purchase approved containers from authorized suppliers. Commercial records centers usually sell containers, but clients can obtain them from other sources provided they meet the records center's specifications.

In either case, a container inventory lists the contents of each container in a given shipment in sufficient detail to identify the records when they need to be retrieved. Depending on the nature of the records and anticipated retrieval requirements, the inventory may provide a summary description of the contents of each container or a detailed listing of individual folder titles, reports, microforms, electronic media, or other items in each container. Depending on records center procedures, inventory information may be prepared on a special transmittal form or entered online. Records centers increasingly support the latter option. When packing, inventorying, and labeling are completed, the program unit notifies the records center, which will arrange to pick up the records. Some records centers support electronic vaulting in which computer-generated records are transmitted to the records center's computer via telecommunication arrangements. The records center then copies the transferred information onto magnetic tapes or other media for storage.

At the records center, transmittal forms are matched against containers, and information about newly received records is logged into a computer database or other index. Depending on records center procedures, the computer database may contain detailed inventory information or a summary description of each container. Control numbers, assigned by the records center when shipments are received, identify each container to the exclusion of others, including containers in previous shipments from a given program unit or client. Containers may be bar-coded to simplify tracking. Some records centers provide bar code labels to program units to affix to containers when records are being prepared for transfer.

Shelf locations are determined based on space availability. All containers in a given shipment or from a given program unit may be stored contiguously, but this practice becomes increasingly difficult to achieve as a records center fills up. Large shipments may consequently be dispersed for storage. Increasingly, records centers rely on software to assign control numbers, store inventory information, determine space availability, and keep track of container locations. The software, which may be custom-developed or purchased from a company that specializes in such products, also supports retrieval operations, container tracking, and other services.

Records sent to a records center are presumably inactive and, if properly scheduled, should experience little retrieval activity, but some items must occasionally be consulted. A records center is a custodial facility not a reference library. As previously explained, individual program units retain full authority over the records they transfer to a records center, which merely serves as the physical custodian for such records. All retrieval requests must be authorized by the program unit that transmitted the records. Depending on records center procedures, requests may be submitted by telephone, by e-mail, by fax, by interoffice or conventional mail, or in person. Often a specific request form, similar to the one shown in Figure 4-3, is required. Records center personnel are not reference librarians. They are not familiar with the contents of records in their custody and are not qualified to interpret retrieval requests or otherwise assist customers in determining which records they need. Consequently, requests for records must be unambiguous. The requestor must accurately identify desired container(s), which he or she may do by consulting the descriptive information in container inventory forms or online inventory lists associated with specific shipments.

When a retrieval request is received, records center staff consult a database or other index to determine the shelf location(s) for the requested container(s). Inventory details determine the types of retrieval requests a records center can accommodate. Where inventory information is limited to container summaries, the most common retrieval requests involve temporary removal of entire containers for return to program units or clients that transmitted them to the records center. If inventory information is sufficiently detailed, some records centers will retrieve individual file folders, documents, or other items from within containers. In either case, software keeps track of containers or individual items charged out to specific clients and will check them back in when they are returned to storage. In this respect, a records center operates much like a circulating library.

In some records centers, returned containers are replaced into their original shelf locations and placeholders may reserve the empty spaces for that purpose.

Sample Reference Request Form

A form for requesting records from off-site storage

Figure 4-3

Reference Request				
			Request Number	
Date Requested	Date Answered	Dates Followed Up		Date Returned

Requester	Requested By ☐ E-mail ☐ Mail ☐ Phone ☐ Visit	Answer By ☐ ☐ ☐ ☐ ☐ ☐	Loan of Item Phone Inspection Copy Letter E-mail	Answered By ☐ ☐ ☐ ☐ ☐ ☐
Building and Room Number or Location	Phone No. / E-mail		Reason, If Not Answered	
Department	Records Series Title			

Identification Detail	Years	Location

(Source: Sample Forms for Archival & Records Management Programs, published by ARMA International and the Society of American Archivists)

Some records centers, however, allocate shelf space dynamically. Newly acquired records may be assigned to spaces previously occupied by charged-out containers, which will be assigned new shelf locations on their return. Where large numbers of records are charged out at any given time, dynamic allocation makes productive use of shelf space that would otherwise sit empty. As in library circulation control systems, some records center software will generate periodic reminder notices for charged-out containers or items.

Most records centers will deliver requested records within a reasonable period of time—one or two days in most cases—although some records centers offer same day delivery for urgently needed records. Pickup by authorized persons is also an option. Where inventory information includes detailed item lists, specified pages may be photocopied for or faxed to requestors. Some records centers offer a scan-on-demand service by which specified pages are digitized and the resulting images transmitted to requestors as e-mail attachments. For financial audits, litigation support, or other activities that require lengthy examination of large quantities of information, some records centers provide workrooms where authorized persons can examine records. In-person examination may also be necessary to locate specific records where container contents cannot be verified by consulting inventory information.

Among other services, some records centers will add records to previously transmitted containers. Most records centers will also destroy records when their retention periods elapse, subject to client approval. They may be equipped with shredders, incinerators, or other equipment for destruction of confidential records. Some records centers have paper recycling arrangements for discarded documents, but recycling is not suitable for destruction of confidential information. Recycling facilities manually examine records to remove unacceptable papers or other materials. Acceptable papers may be stored under unsecured conditions for long periods of time while they wait to be recycled.

Commercial Records Centers

A **commercial records center** is a for-profit company that provides fee-based storage and related services for records of multiple clients. The membership of PRISM International, a not-for-profit trade association for the records storage industry, ranges from relatively small, privately owned warehouse installations in a single location to large publicly traded companies with hundreds of storage facilities throughout the world. Commercial records centers obviously compete with off-site storage facilities operated by corporations, government agencies, and other organizations. However, many organizations lack secure, economical in-house storage arrangements for their inactive records. Rather than constructing warehouses or refurbishing inadequate facilities, purchasing shelving and material handling equipment, and hiring records center employees, such organizations may find that outsourcing its records storage requirements is cheaper and more convenient. (See Figure 4-4.) Only a detailed cost analysis can determine whether outsourcing is the better choice.

Even where in-house records storage facilities are effective and economical, commercial records centers can provide complementary or supplementary services. Some large corporations, for example, have in-house storage facilities for records generated at a headquarters location but rely on local commercial records centers to serve branch

Commercial Records Center

Figure 4-4

(Courtesy: Iron Mountain)

offices, manufacturing facilities, and other geographically dispersed operations. Similarly, a company, government agency, or other organization may limit its in-house records center to warehouse-type storage of paper documents and use commercial providers for electronic media or confidential records requiring vault storage.

Commercial records centers are subject to the same evaluative criteria as in-house storage facilities. The records center building must be appropriately construct-ed, fire-resistant, and secure, with shelving and environmental controls appropriate to the types of records stored. Access to the building should be limited to employees and other authorized persons. Provisions for fire protection must conform to local building codes and to the NFPA 232 standard previously discussed. Vault space must be available if needed. The records center's staff must be large enough and appropri-ately skilled for the services to be provided. Operating procedures must be well organized and effectively administered. Computer systems, including any software provided to clients, must be reliable, efficient, and capable of tracking shelf locations for containers transferred by a given client, the movement of records within the records center, charge-out activity, destruction of specific containers, and other oper-ations. A growing number of commercial records centers support Web-based access for entry and searching of inventory information, as well as for online initiation of records retrieval requests.

A commercial records center's services and fee structure depend on several factors, including geographic location and clientele served. As a defining characteristic, all commercial records centers provide fee-based storage, usually for a specified monthly rate per cubic-foot container for paper documents. Per-item storage charges may be imposed for microforms, X-ray films, electronic media, or large-format paper records such as engineering drawings and maps. Storage charges vary inversely with the quantity of records stored by a given customer; i.e., storing a larger quantity of records at the commercial records center results in lower cost per cubic foot.

Typically, records containers of different customers are commingled in a commercial records center's open warehouse area. Customers who consider commingling to be unacceptable may be offered reserved shelving areas or dedicated storage rooms at extra cost. Some commercial records centers also offer shelf-type filing cabinets, of the type described in Chapter 7, for semi-active folders that are not packed in containers. Vault storage, where available, commands a premium price.

Commercial records centers also charge for the following services on a per-incident basis:

- Pickup of records, including new shipments and previously retrieved records being returned to storage

- Entry of inventory data for newly acquired records, including key-entry as well as conversion of computer-processible inventory data provided by clients

- Retrieval of records, including entire containers or individual files, when requested by authorized persons

- Delivery services for retrieved records, including normal and rush delivery where available

- Photocopying of records requested by authorized persons

- Faxing or scan-on-demand services for records requested by authorized persons

- Reshelving or refiling of records returned to the records center

- Interfiling of records into containers previously sent to the records center

- Destruction of records when authorized, including confidential destruction when requested by the client

- Preparation of periodic or special reports about records storage and retrieval activity

Basic records center charges typically apply to services provided during normal business hours, as defined by the commercial records center. After-hours retrieval and delivery services may be available at a higher rate. Some records centers will provide these services around the clock, 365 days a year.

Terms, conditions, and per-incident charges for records center services are specified in customer contracts, to which rate schedules are customarily appended. Generally, clients can expect to incur a charge any time their records are handled, whether they are being acquired, retrieved, transported, reshelved, or destroyed. Although costs usually depend on the volume of records affected by a particular service, minimum charges may apply to certain services such as pickup and delivery of records.

Commercial records centers produce a variety of periodic and customized reports for clients that may be printed or delivered to clients via e-mail or on electronic media. Report possibilities include, but are not limited to, the following:

- Inventory proof lists
- Lists and statistical tabulations of records in storage by media type
- Lists and statistical tabulations of records in storage by the transmitting program unit, which can be used for charge back or other cost control measures
- Lists of records scheduled for destruction on specific dates
- Lists and statistical tabulations of records destroyed as authorized by the client
- Transaction histories by date or program unit
- Lists of records removed from storage and not yet returned
- Lists of records permanently removed from storage
- Billing summaries by activity and period
- Lists and statistical tabulations of per-incident charges

In some cases, commercial records centers impose per-container charges for the permanent removal of records from storage, whether through destruction of records in conformity with a client's retention schedules, or because the records will be moved to a competitor or to an in-house records storage facility. These termination charges are commonly described as *exit fees* or *out charges*. Where present, they are usually equal to about one year's storage fee for the container being removed. Some customers refuse to accept contracts that include termination charges. In such cases, the customer may be charged slightly higher monthly storage fees to offset the loss of revenue when service is terminated.

Safekeeping for valuable information resources is an often claimed and much advertised advantage of commercial records centers, but fire and other calamities can and have occurred. Records center contracts indicate insurance coverage and normal reimbursement amounts for records lost, damaged, or destroyed by fire, natural disaster, or accident while in the records center's custody. Such reimbursements are typically nominal. Often based simply on the replacement value of cubic-foot containers, they do not reflect the adverse consequences that an organization may incur if needed records are unavailable. A commercial records center may offer additional insurance coverage at extra cost. Depending on contract provisions, customers may seek additional remedies, such as litigation, for records that are lost as a result of a records center's negligence.

Chapter 5

Managing Inactive Records II: Micrographics

As described in Chapter 4, records centers minimize storage requirements for inactive records by transferring them from expensive office space to more economical off-site locations. Micrographics technology, the subject of this chapter, takes a different approach. It miniaturizes inactive records for compact storage in offices or elsewhere.

Micrographics is a document imaging technology concerned with the creation and use of microforms as storage media for recorded information.* A **microform** is a photographic information carrier that contains highly miniaturized document images. The images, which are termed **microimages**, require magnification for eye-legible viewing or printing. That requirement distinguishes microforms from optically reduced photocopies, which are smaller than the documents from which they were made but can be read with the unaided eye. Microimages, by contrast, are drastically reduced—their defining characteristic.

Microforms can be produced from paper documents, called *source documents*, or from computer-processable information that would otherwise be printed on paper. **Source document microfilming** or microphotography is the oldest and most easily understood method of microform production. Cameras equipped with reducing lenses take pictures of paper documents, recording them as microimages onto high-resolution photographic film designed specifically for that purpose. Typical steps in microfilming source documents are shown in Figure 5-1. Depending on the application, the source documents may be office correspondence, financial records, technical reports, legal case files, patient records, insurance claim files, customer service

---

*   The term *micrographics* was introduced in the 1970s as a broader, more meaningful alternative to the then-current term *microfilm*, which is just one of several types of microforms. Used as a singular noun, *micrographics* denotes the technology itself as well as the professional specialty that applies micrographics technology to records management problems. Used as an adjective, *micrographics*— or, less commonly, *micrographic*—describes products and services offered by equipment manufacturers, media suppliers, service bureaus, consultants, and others. In recent years, the micrographics industry has adopted the alternative phrase *film-based imaging* to obtain a closer identification with electronic document imaging technology, which is discussed in Chapter 8.

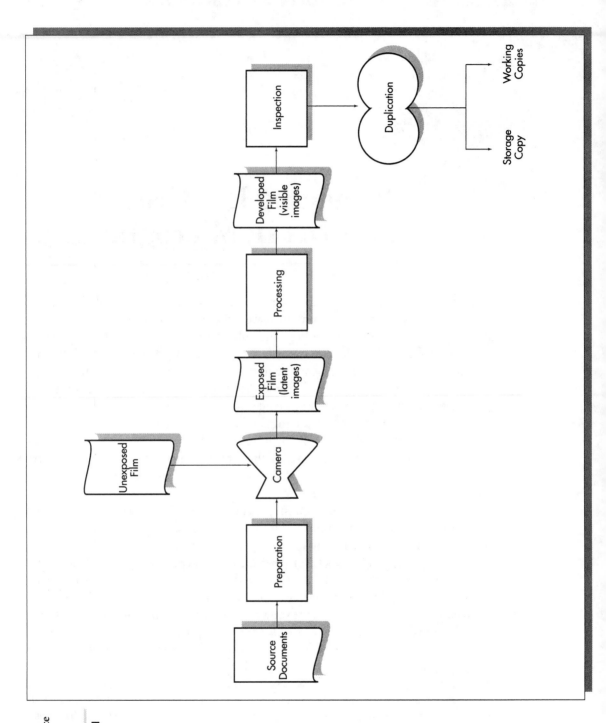

Typical Work
Steps for Source
Document
Microfilming

Figure 5-1

records, student records, engineering drawings, maps, or library research materials. These and other records are microfilmed every day by government agencies, corporations, banks, insurance companies, law firms, hospitals, schools, libraries, and other organizations. **Computer-output microfilm (COM)**, the other method of microform production, is a variant form of computer printing technology that records computer-generated information in human-readable form directly onto microfilm. COM differs from other computer printing technologies in two important respects: (1) the printouts are miniaturized, and (2) they are recorded on film rather than paper. Computer-output microfilm is compatible with any computer program that produces printed output. COM images look like microfilmed versions of printout pages or other computer-generated documents, but no paper documents are involved in COM production.

Micrographics technology has been an important component of records management practice for decades. Among their professional responsibilities, records managers identify candidate applications for micrographics technology, plan and implement micrographics storage and retrieval systems, and prepare cost estimates and cost justifications for micrographics projects. Some records management departments operate microform production capabilities. Where microfilming is outsourced, records managers typically prepare specifications for the work to be done and evaluate the qualifications and capabilities of microfilm service bureaus.

This chapter examines the role of micrographics technology, products, and services in records management. It begins with a discussion of the distinctive characteristics and advantages of micrographics technology for managing recorded information, particularly inactive records. Subsequent sections describe microfilm production and retrieval concepts and practices, emphasizing equipment and methods for records management applications.

Advantages for Records Management

Long associated with compact storage of records that must be kept for long periods of time, micrographics technology offers significant advantages for the inactive stages of the information life cycle. In addition to compact storage, it provides superior stability, minimal system dependence, and legal acceptability. Micrographics is also a useful technology for vital records protection.

Although these advantages are significant, micrographics technology must be judiciously implemented in the context of a formal records retention program that identifies appropriate applications and storage solutions. A comprehensive, systematically implemented records management program will combine micrographics with selective destruction and off-site storage of inactive records. Destruction rather than microfilming is obviously recommended for obsolete records that have no continuing value for business or other purposes. Off-site storage, where available and appropriate, will usually prove more economical than microfilming for inactive records that are retained for less than 10 years and in some cases as long as 15 years. After that time, accumulated annual charges for off-site storage will exceed microfilming costs.

Compact Storage

As previously described, micrographics technology miniaturizes recorded information, with a corresponding reduction in storage space requirements for a given quantity of paper documents. Compact storage is particularly important where large quantities of documents must be retained for long periods of time. Micrographics technology has a long-standing and well-deserved reputation for efficiency and effectiveness in such situations. Business applications involving microfilming of inactive records for long-term storage date from the 1930s. When compared to paper filing methods, micrographics can reduce storage space requirements by 95 percent or more.

As an example, a reasonably full four-drawer vertical filing cabinet, of the type described in Chapter 7, contains about 10,000 letter-size pages. Assuming that filed pages contain information on one side only, the contents of a four-drawer cabinet can be reduced to two reels of 16mm microfilm of the type described in Chapter 6. Put another way, a typical six-drawer cabinet for 16mm microfilm can store as many pages as 350 four-drawer cabinets filled with paper documents, yet it occupies the same amount of floor space as one 4-drawer cabinet. The space-saving potential of micrographics is not limited to source document microfilming. Computer-output microfilm can eliminate bulky computer printouts. A single COM-generated microfiche can store 270 computer printout-size (11-by-14-inch) pages. A desktop microfiche tray can store the equivalent of a 100-foot stack of computer printouts.

Media Stability

As applied to recorded information, **stability** denotes the extent to which a given storage medium retains physical characteristics and chemical properties appropriate to its intended purpose. Put another way, *stability* is the period of time that a given medium will remain useful for its intended purpose. The stability period is equivalent to the useful life, lifetime estimate, or life span of a given medium. Decades of scientific research confirm that microfilm offers excellent physical and chemical stability for long-term retention and archival preservation of valuable documents. Microfilm offers superior stability attributes when compared to many types of paper and electronic media. These attributes are important enough to warrant a more detailed explanation.

Microfilms can be divided, by their intended purpose, into two types: camera films and duplicating films. **Camera films**, as their name suggests, are intended for original microphotography in source document cameras and **COM recorders**. Microfilms used in source document cameras are of the silver gelatin type. Depending on the device, COM recorders may utilize silver gelatin or thermally processed silver (TPS) microfilms, also known as *dry silver microfilms*. **Duplicating films**, variously termed *copy films* or *print films*, are designed to produce copies of other microforms; they are not suitable for use in microfilm cameras or COM recorders. Duplicating films may employ silver gelatin, diazo, or vesicular photographic technologies.

In the United States, standards that specify the stability characteristics of photographic films, including microfilms, are published by the American National Standards Institute (ANSI). Comparable standards have been developed by national standard-setting organizations in other countries. The scope and content of standards that specify the stability characteristics of silver gelatin microfilms have changed significantly since the 1970s. Earliest versions emphasized the preservation of information of permanent value. They specified the conditions under which silver gelatin microfilms must be manufactured, processed, and stored for permanent stability. Silver gelatin microfilms that conformed to those standards were characterized as *archival quality*. Films that did not meet archival specifications were often categorized as *commercial quality*. American national standards developed in the early 1980s retained the archival specifications for permanent preservation of information, while recognizing two shorter periods of microfilm stability: long-term (100 years) and medium-term (10 years).

Since 1991, the American National Standards Institute has replaced the archival, long-term, and medium-term categories with **life expectancy (LE) designations** for specific media under recommended storage conditions. The LE designation is a prediction of the minimum life expectancy, in years, for a given medium. For example, a life expectancy of LE-100 represents a stability period of at least 100 years. Among its principal objectives, the ANSI stability nomenclature is designed to minimize confusion resulting from differing uses of the term *archival* in information management. In records management, for example, the term implies permanence. In computing, however, the archival designation is broadly applied to magnetic tape and other removable media suitable for offline storage of inactive information, an activity termed **data archiving**. Implications of media stability are not associated with such data archiving.

Under the ANSI designations, the life expectancy is 100 years (LE-100) for silver gelatin microfilms with cellulose triacetate base material and 500 years (LE-500) for silver gelatin microfilms with polyester base materials. In each case, the assumption is that the media are manufactured, processed, and stored in conformity with pertinent American national standards cited later in this chapter. ANSI standards specify a life expectancy of 100 years (LE-100) for thermally processed silver microfilms, which are utilized by some COM recorders, and for diazo and vesicular microfilms, which are utilized for microform duplication. As with silver gelatin microfilms, the assumption is that appropriate storage conditions are utilized.

Where microforms will be used for long-term retention or permanent preservation of recorded information, a distinction must be made between **storage copies**, which are used to produce one or more working copies and seldom handled thereafter, and **working copies**, which are intended for display, printing, distribution, or other purposes. The standard life expectancies discussed previously apply to microform storage copies only. Microform working copies, which may be referenced frequently, are imperiled by use, and their life expectancies are invariably compromised. Typically stored in office locations rather than in controlled environments, working copies may be exposed to high temperatures and relative humidities. They may be scratched during viewing, printing, duplication, filing, or distribution. Working copies may also be contaminated by airborne particles, smoke residues, skin oils, fingerprints, and spilled liquids.

Minimal System Dependence

System dependence denotes the need for specific hardware or software components to access information recorded on a given medium. Because a risk exists that required components may not be available in the future, system dependence complicates the long-term retention or permanent preservation of recorded information. System independence is consequently preferred in such circumstances.

Paper documents, which require no special hardware or software to access recorded information, offer superior system independence. Micrographics implementations have minimal hardware dependencies. Microimages, like paper documents, contain human-readable information, but they require magnification for eye-legible display or printing of recorded information. The system components needed for that purpose are straightforward, however. Microform display and printing devices have been widely available for decades from multiple suppliers. Given the large installed base of microforms in corporations, government agencies, and other organizations throughout the world, future discontinuation of such products is unlikely. Unless computer databases are used to index microimages, micrographics implementations have no software dependencies.

Micrographics technology has a long history of standardization, which offers exceptional compatibility and interchangeability of recorded information among the products of different vendors. Users can exchange microforms worldwide with confidence that recorded information will be viewable and printable by available equipment. Similarly, micrographics equipment offers superior backward compatibility. Assuming appropriate magnification, newly manufactured micrographics equipment can display or print microimages created in the past. Similarly, micrographics users can have a high degree of confidence that microimages created today will be compatible with display and printing equipment introduced in the future. In this respect, micrographics enjoys an important competitive advantage over computer technologies, such as electronic document imaging, for long-term retention or permanent preservation of recorded information. As discussed in preceding chapters, electronic records are subject to significant hardware and software dependencies that can adversely affect the future retrievability of such information.

Legal Acceptability

The legal acceptability of microforms is well established for both admissibility of documents as evidence in court trials and other judicial proceedings and to satisfy recordkeeping (records retention) requirements imposed by laws and government regulations. The legal acceptability of microimages is based on their status as duplicate records—that is, true copies of the documents from which they are made, a **true copy** being one that accurately reproduces an original document. An existing body of laws and legal cases addresses the legal acceptability of copies. In the United States, pertinent statutory provisions include the Uniform Photographic Copies of Business and Public Records as Evidence Act (Title 28, Section 1732 of the U.S. Code), as well as the Uniform Rules of Evidence (URE) and its counterpart, the Federal Rules of Evidence (FRE).

The Uniform Photographic Copies of Business and Public Records as Evidence Act, commonly known as the Uniform Photographic Copies Act (UPA), permits the substitution of photographic copies for original documents for all judicial or administrative purposes. It consequently addresses both legal issues mentioned previously: admissibility of microforms as evidence and the use of microforms to satisfy legally mandated recordkeeping requirements discussed in preceding chapters. The UPA specifically mentions microfilming as an acceptable method of document reproduction.

As its title indicates, the UPA applies to copies of public records maintained by federal, state, and local government agencies. It also applies to business records maintained by corporations, partnerships, sole proprietorships, nonprofit institutions, and other nongovernmental organizations. In every case, the copies must be accurate reproductions of original documents, and they must have been produced in the regular course of business as part of an organization's established operating procedures. Similar provisions are contained in the Preservation of Private Business Records Act, which allows records retention requirements to be satisfied by copies.

The UPA permits, but does not mandate, the destruction of original documents, allowing organizations to rely solely on copies. Destruction is prohibited, however, where retention of the original documents is specifically required by law. Applicable statutes and regulations must be examined individually to determine whether such restrictions apply. Some states have added a clause to the UPA that prohibits destruction of original documents held in a custodial or fiduciary capacity; in such situations, their owners' permission is required for destruction of the original documents following microfilming. In any case, destruction of the original records must be performed in the regular course of business.

Rule 1003 of the URE and FRE permits the admission of duplicate records in evidence as substitutes for original documents unless serious questions are raised about the authenticity of the original records or, in specific circumstances, admitting a copy in lieu of an original is judged unfair. Rule 1001(4) of the URE and FRE defines a *duplicate record* as a "counterpart produced by the same impression as the original, or from the same matrix, or by means of photography, including enlargements and miniatures, or by mechanical or electronic re-recording, or by chemical reproduction, or by other equivalent techniques which accurately reproduces the original." Unlike the UPA, Rule 1003 of the URE and FRE does not require that duplicate records be produced in the regular course of business. The URE and FRE do not authorize destruction of original records, nor do they prohibit it.

The Uniform Photographic Copies Act and Uniform Rules of Evidence are examples of uniform laws developed by legal commissioners of the various states to reconcile differences in legal practice among the states. Uniform laws apply only in those legal jurisdictions where they have been adopted. Both the UPA and URE apply in federal courts. One or both of the laws have been adopted by 88 percent of the states. In other situations, state-specific statutes may permit or restrict the admissibility of microform copies or their suitability for retention in specific circumstances. As an additional limitation, the foregoing discussion applies only to source document microfilming.

Microforms produced by COM recorders are considered original rather than duplicate records, although duplicates of COM-generated microforms are considered copies.

Vital Records Protection

Vital records, as defined in Chapter 6, contain information essential to an organization's mission. If a vital record is lost, damaged, destroyed, or otherwise rendered unavailable or unusable, critical business operations will be discontinued or severely curtailed, with a resulting adverse impact on the organization. The time-honored approach to protection of vital records involves microfilming them to create security copies for off-site storage, usually at a sufficient distance from the original records so as to be unaffected by the same destructive events. If vital records are lost, the security copies can be used to recover documents needed for essential business operations. If desired, paper files can be reconstructed by printing microimages.

Often, commercial records centers are used for off-site storage of vital records. Such facilities charge customers by the amount of storage space consumed. Microfilm's compactness is a valuable attribute in such situations. As a further advantage, microforms created for other business purposes can be easily and economically duplicated to make additional copies for vital records protection.

Micrographics for Active Records

Although compact storage, media stability, and other characteristics outlined previously confirm the advantages of microforms for records requiring long-term retention, permanent preservation, or backup protection, micrographics technology can also enhance business operations through improved retrieval and control of records during the active phase of the information life cycle.

Certain micrographics products and methods were developed specifically for applications involving frequently referenced documents. Self-threading cartridges, for example, automate and simplify loading and viewing of 16mm microfilm, the most common micrographics medium for office documents. Since the 1960s, microfilm jacket systems have miniaturized files that are subject to updating through periodic interfiling of new documents; examples include insurance claims, student records, and medical records. A **microfilm jacket** is a transparent carrier with sleeves or channels for insertion of strips of 16mm or 35mm microfilm. Because microfilm jackets are compact, they are often easier to handle than their paper file counterparts. Aperture cards similarly facilitate the handling, reproduction, and distribution of engineering

---

Advantages of Using Active Micrographic Records

- Time-consuming trips to remote file areas to obtain needed information are eliminated when documents are miniaturized because large quantities of records can be stored in close proximity to office workers who must reference them. Once a given microform is loaded into a retrieval device, hundreds or thousands of pages are available for convenient browsing, displaying, and printing.
- Micrographics technology can simplify file maintenance requirements by minimizing or eliminating filing and refiling operations associated with paper documents. Microforms also enhance file integrity. Once documents are microfilmed, their sequence is fixed. Removal or misfiling of individual pages is difficult or impossible, although individual microforms can be misfiled or misplaced. As a related advantage, documents recorded on microfilm cannot be altered or deleted.
- Micrographics technology facilitates dissemination of information. Microforms are easily duplicated for distribution to geographically dispersed departments, branch offices, or other locations. Document miniaturization reduces mailing costs; an ordinary business envelope can contain thousands of pages. Microforms also simplify the relocation of records from one work area to another—when office locations are changed, for example, or where large quantities of documents must be taken to construction sites, satellite offices, or other field locations. Available technology also permits the electronic transmission of microimages to remote locations.

drawings, maps, and other large documents that are cumbersome in their original form. An **aperture card** is a tabulating-size card with an opening that contains one frame of 35mm microfilm. Compared to paper printouts, computer-output microfilm can simplify the production, distribution, and handling of accounting reports, tabular listings, and other computer-generated documents. For the most demanding applications, **computer-assisted retrieval (CAR)** systems use computer databases to index microfilm images for rapid retrieval.

Microforms and Reductions

Microforms can be categorized by their physical shape into two broad groups: roll microforms and flat microforms. *Roll microforms* are ribbons or strips of microfilm that measure 16mm or 35mm wide. Roll microfilm may be wound onto a plastic or metal reel or loaded into a self-threading cartridge. *Flat microforms,* by contrast, consist of sheets or pieces of film that contain one or more microimages. Flat microforms include microfiche, microfilm jackets, and aperture cards.

Whether roll or flat, microforms store images that are greatly reduced in size when compared with the paper documents from which the images were produced. **Reduction** is a measure of the number of times a given linear dimension (one of the sides) of a document is reduced through microphotography. This measure is expressed as 15×, 24×, 48×, and so on, where the reduced linear dimension is 1/15, 1/24, or 1/48 the length of its full-size counterpart. Alternatively, reduction can be expressed as a ratio that represents the relationship between a given linear dimension of a source document and the corresponding linear dimension of a microimage made from that document—for example, 15:1, 24:1, or 48:1. In most cases, these measurements are nominal rather than exact. Actual reductions may vary as much as plus or minus 1× from the amounts stated in product specifications. Thus, the actual reduction will range between 23× and 25× for a microfilm camera that is advertised as having a 24× lens. These slight variations are rarely significant.

In any micrographics application, the choice of reduction is based on several factors, including the characteristics of the source documents being microfilmed, the type of microform used, and the capabilities of available equipment for microform production, display, and printing. Higher reductions are attractive because they increase the number of images that can be recorded on a given microform and correspondingly reduce the number of microforms necessary to store a given document collection, thereby simplifying filing, duplicating, and other handling of microforms. The reduction selected, however, must be suitable for microfilming a given group of source documents without loss of information. The reduction must also support the production of legible duplicate microforms through the required number of generations. Some quality is lost in duplication, hence the need for very high-quality camera original microfilms. Further, legibility is important where camera original microfilms or duplicates will be scanned for conversion to digital formats.

Following long-standing industry practice, reductions below 15× are termed *low.* They are most often utilized in library and archival applications that involve historical manuscripts, newspapers, and books of marginal legibility. Office records and engineering drawings are typically microfilmed at medium reductions, which range from 15× to 30×. Common examples are 24× for U.S. letter-size (8.5 by 11 inches) and international A4-size pages and 27× to 29× for U.S. legal-size and international B5-size pages. Reductions of 30× to 32×, which fall just outside the medium range, are used to microfilm U.S. computer printout-size (11 by 14 inches) pages and their international B4-size counterparts. Engineering drawings, architectural renderings, maps, and other large-format documents up to D-size (24 by 36 inches) or international A1-size can be microfilmed at 24×. E-size (36 by 48 inches) and international A0-size drawings are usually microfilmed at 30×.

High reductions, which range from 30× to 60×, are possible but rarely advisable for highly legible source documents in uniformly excellent physical condition. They are typically reserved for computer-output microfilm, which is produced from computer-processable information rather than source documents. With COM technology, type fonts, character sizes, image density, and other factors that affect legibility can be optimized for microreproduction. The most widely encountered reduction in COM applications is 48×. Some long-standing applications continue to utilize 42×, which was popular in the 1970s before 48× COM recorders became widely available. Very high reductions (60× to 90×) and ultra high reductions (90× and above) play no role in records management applications.

Roll Microforms

Like motion picture film, most unexposed microfilm is supplied in roll formats for use in the source document camera and COM recorders. Available microfilm widths are 16mm, 35mm, and 105mm. Film lengths range from 50 feet to more than 1,000 feet, with 100 and 215 feet being most widely encountered. Following exposure and development, microfilm rolls may be converted to other formats. Microfilm in 105mm width is usually cut into 148mm lengths to create microfiche. Individual frames, cut from developed rolls of 35mm microfilm, may be inserted into aperture cards. Strips of developed 16mm or 35mm film may be inserted into microfilm jackets. Often, however, processed 16mm and 35mm microfilm is simply wound onto plastic or metal reels for viewing, printing, or storage. Physical characteristics of microfilm reels are specified in the ANSI/AIIM MS34 standard, *Dimensions for Reels Used with Processed 16mm and 35mm Microfilm Not for Use in Automatic Threading Equipment*, and in the ISO 1116 standard, *Microcopying—16mm and 35mm Microfilms, Spools and Reels*. Image layouts are discussed in ANSI/AIIM MS14, *Specifications for 16 and 35mm Roll Microfilm*.

Although 16mm microfilm and 35mm microfilm share certain attributes, they are intended for different purposes:

- Since the inception of commercial microphotography, 16mm has been the preferred microfilm width for office records measuring up to 11 by 17 inches in size. The image capacity of a given reel of 16mm microfilm depends on several factors, including document size, reduction, image positioning, film length, and camera characteristics. For letter-size documents reduced 24×, a 100-foot reel of 16mm microfilm can store about 2,500 pages, which is the approximate contents of one file cabinet drawer. A 215-foot reel can store about 5,400 pages. The 215-foot length is the more economical choice for storage-oriented records management applications. Compared to 100-foot film, it provides more than twice the image capacity but does not cost twice as much to purchase. It also reduces the number of reels that must be stored in a given application. Thus, a one-million-page collection of paper documents that occupies 400 reels of 100-foot microfilm would require just 185 reels of 215-foot microfilm.

- With its larger image area, 35mm microfilm permits the legible reproduction of engineering drawings, architectural plans, maps, and other large documents at medium reductions. Storing large documents is the principal records management application for 35mm microfilm. Microfilm in 35mm width is commonly supplied in 100-foot lengths. Because they store large documents or pages recorded at low reductions, 35mm microfilm reels have lower image capacities than their 16mm counterparts. A 100-foot reel can store about 700 D-size engineering drawings reduced 24×. Microfilm in 35mm width is also used for preservation microfilming by libraries, archives, historical agencies, and other cultural organizations. As noted previously, research materials are often microfilmed at low reductions. With its large image area, 35mm microfilm facilitates the legible recording of manuscripts, books, newspapers, and other documents with problematic physical or typographic characteristics.

Regardless of width, microfilm reels are usually the least expensive microforms to create from a given collection of source documents. They are consequently preferred for inactive records that are microfilmed for long-term retention and compact storage. Microfilm reels are also well suited to vital records protection, where microform copies of mission-critical documents will be stored in off-site locations that charge by the amount of space consumed. For maximum flexibility in adapting to changing information management requirements, microfilm on reels can be converted to other microforms as circumstances warrant. Microfilm in 16mm width stored on reels can be converted to cartridges, microfilm jackets, or microfiche. Microfilm in 35mm width stored on reels can be converted to microfilm jackets or aperture cards. Other microforms cannot be altered as easily.

As their principal disadvantage, microfilm reels require cumbersome film handling for display or printing. They are consequently recommended for storage copies only. For working copies, 16mm microfilm should be loaded into self-threading cartridges, which offer the economy and capacity of microfilm reels but are much easier to use. When a cartridge is inserted into an appropriate display or printing device, a motorized mechanism loads the film and advances it at high speed to locate specific microimages. A standard cartridge format, introduced in the mid-1970s, is described in ANSI/AIIM MS15, *Dimensions and Operational Constraints for Single Core Cartridge for 16mm Processed Microfilm.*

Microfiche

A **microfiche** is a sheet of film that contains multiple microimages in a two-dimensional grid of rows and columns. In the United States, the term is considered both a single and plural noun. In other countries, the plural form is sometimes spelled with an *s*. The term *microfiche* is often shortened to *fiche*, a French word that translates approximately as an index card or slip of note paper. (The French word *fichier* denotes a file for index cards.)

Microfiche characteristics are specified in the ANSI/AIIM MS05 standard, *Microfiche*, in the ISO 9923 standard, *Micrographics—Transparent A6 Microfiche—Image Arrangements*, and in the comparable publications of other standard-setting organizations. Although microfiche have been produced in several different sizes over the years, American and international standards specify external dimensions of 105mm by 148mm (the international A6-size), which is approximately 4 by 6 inches. Microfiche are created by special cameras that expose 105mm microfilm. The film may be supplied as precut fiche-size sheets or in rolls that are cut into 148mm segments following development.

Within a given microfiche, individual images are arranged in a grid of rows and columns. A fixed amount of space is allotted to each film frame. Source documents or COM-generated information must be reduced sufficiently to fit into the available space. An area at the top of each fiche, equivalent to one row of frames, is reserved for eye-legible title information. Within the image grid, rows are identified by letters, and columns are identified by numbers. Any given microimage can be identified by its row and column coordinates. Microfiche produced from source documents are usually paginated horizontally; successive pages are recorded across individual rows from left to right. COM-generated microfiche are usually paginated vertically; successive pages are recorded down individual columns from top to bottom.

The standards cited previously define several microfiche formats that differ in their image layouts, reductions, and intended applications. Microfiche formats are customarily identified by numeric designations that indicate the reduction utilized and the number of images each fiche contains:

- The 24/98 format, the most common format for microfiche made from source documents, provides 7 rows and 14 columns for a total of 98 images. The recommended reduction is 24× for letter-size pages. Lower reductions are possible for smaller documents. Book pages in the 5-inch-by-7-inch size, for example, can be microfilmed at 16×, while 7-inch-by-9-inch book pages can be reduced 19×. If desired, several small documents may be combined in a single frame. Larger pages must be microfilmed at higher reductions or, less desirably, in sections that occupy several frames. The recommended reduction for A4-size pages, for example, is 26×. Legal-size pages are typically filmed at 29×.

- The 48/270 format, the most common format for microfiche produced from computer output, provides 15 rows and 18 columns for a total of 270 images. Based on 11-by-14-inch computer printouts, the 48/270 format is intended for landscape-mode pages that are wider than they are tall. The recommended reduction is 48×. An older microfiche format, designated 42/208, predated the commercial availability of 48× COM technology. It provides 13 rows and 16 columns for a total of 208 images based on 11-by-14-inch pages. The recommended reduction is 42×.

- Other microfiche formats, though covered by national and international standards, are rarely encountered in records management applications. The *48/420 for-*

mat, for example, provides 15 rows and 28 columns for a total of 420 pages with a preferred reduction of 48× for letter-size pages. A related microfiche format, designated *42/325*, provides 13 rows and 25 columns with a preferred reduction of 42× for letter-size pages. The *20/60 format* dates from the 1960s and is now considered obsolete. Better known as the *COSATI format*, it was developed by the U.S. government's Committee on Scientific and Technical Information for reproduction and distribution of research reports. The *24/63 format* provides 7 rows and 9 columns for a total of 63 images. The preferred reduction is 24×. It can be used for microfiche recording of computer printouts and other landscape-mode source documents, but 16mm microfilm is often a better choice for such applications.

Format variations aside, a microfiche is a highly functional unit record for relatively small groups of related documents. With their high image capacities, microfilm on reels and 16mm microfilm cartridges are characterized as *nonunitized microforms*. In many applications, unrelated documents are grouped on a single microfilm reel or cartridge. If client files contain 50 pages each, for example, a 100-foot reel of 16mm microfilm can store 50 such files, each pertaining to a different client. A user interested in one client's file must consult a microform that includes the records of 49 other clients. Obvious confidentiality issues arise where users may not be authorized to view all documents recorded on a given microfilm reel or cartridge. In addition, desired documents may be difficult to locate among the many others recorded on the same reel.

With their lower image capacities, microfiche and other flat microforms are considered *unitized media*. They establish a one-to-one correspondence between a physical record (a microform) and a logical record (a client file, student file, patient file, technical manual, laboratory notebook, or computer-generated report, for example). For the example cited previously, each client file would be recorded onto a separate microfiche. If space remains within a given fiche, it is left blank. Because their contents are limited to related documents, unitized microforms address the confidentiality and retrieval concerns noted previously. Because they preserve familiar document groupings, unitized microforms permit miniaturization of documents without disruptive changes in filing methods or other records management procedures.

Among their other advantages, microfiche can be quickly and easily duplicated for distribution or security. Prevalent standardization permits the exchange of microfiche worldwide with reasonable assurance of size and format compatibility. Given their compact, uniform dimensions, microfiche are easy to handle. Microfiche display and printing devices are less complex and expensive than comparable devices for roll microforms. Portable microfiche readers are also available. As their principal disadvantage, microfiche of source documents can be more expensive to create than roll microforms. The higher cost is attributable to the high prices and limited availability of microfiche cameras. In COM applications, however, microfiche are less expensive to produce than roll microforms.

Microfilm Jackets

In active paper-based filing systems, new documents are routinely added to and removed from individual folders. Microfilm jackets were developed for such situations. They permit the addition of new microimages to previously filmed files and the removal of microimages no longer needed. Microfilm jackets can also be used as alternatives to microfiche for miniaturization of closed files.

A *microfilm jacket* is a transparent acetate or polyester carrier with one or more sleeves, channels, or chambers designed to hold flat strips of 16mm or 35mm microfilm. The strips are cut from microfilm rolls. In most implementations, camera original microfilm rolls are duplicated, and the copies are cut into strips for insertion into jackets. The original rolls are retained as storage copies for retention or security purposes. Although microfilm strips can be inserted into jackets by hand, a motorized device called a *viewer-inserter* is customarily used. Most microfilm jackets include a translucent, matte-finished heading area—sometimes described as an *index strip*—for eye-legible title information, which may be handwritten, typewritten, or computer-printed. Alternatively, adhesive labels with eye-legible titling may be affixed to the heading area.

Jacket dimensions and other basic characteristics are described in the ANSI/AIIM MS11 standard, *Microfilm Jackets*, the ISO 8127-1 standard, *Micrographics—A6 Size Microfilm Jackets—Part 1: Five Channel Jacket for 16 mm Microfilm*, and the ISO 8127-2 standard, *Micrographics—A6 Size Microfilm Jackets—Part 2: Other Types of Jacket for 16mm and 35mm Microfilm*. The most commonly encountered jackets are designed for 16mm microfilm strips. In the United States, the most popular jacket configuration measures 4 1/8 inches high by 6 inches wide (approximately 103mm by 152mm). It features five channels for the insertion of 16mm microfilm strips. A heading area can hold one line of identifying information. Image capacity depends on several factors, including the size of documents being microfilmed, the reduction, the image orientation, and the amount of space between frames within a film strip. For letter-size pages reduced 24×, a six-inch strip of 16mm microfilm will contain 12 or 14 images, which yields a maximum capacity of 60 or 70 pages per five-sleeve jacket.

Jackets for 35mm microfilm strips are intended for engineering drawings, architectural plans, maps, medical X-rays, and other large documents. A jacket that measures 4 1/8 inches high by 6 inches wide (103 by 152mm) provides two sleeves for 35mm film strips and a one-inch (26mm) heading area. It can store up to six D-size drawings or eight X-rays filmed at 24×. Jackets that feature both 16mm and 35mm sleeves can combine drawings recorded on 35mm microfilm with reports, correspondence, technical specifications, and other project documentation recorded on 16mm microfilm. In medical applications, patient histories and treatment information recorded on 16mm microfilm and X-rays recorded on 35mm microfilm can be unitized in a single carrier.

Like microfiche, with which they are often confused, microfilm jackets are unitized microforms that store related documents. Unlike microfiche, however, jackets are updateable microforms. If space is available in one of the sleeves, new images can be added to a given jacket. Similarly, obsolete images can be removed. Given this updateability, microfilm jackets are well-suited to active records management applications where current filing methods are satisfactory but space constraints warrant document miniaturization. Jackets are easily integrated into existing file arrangements and reference patterns. Users simply treat them as miniaturized substitutes for paper files. As their principal disadvantage, microfilm jackets are time-consuming and labor-intensive to create, especially in high-volume file conversions. Multiple work steps involving several pieces of equipment are required.

Aperture Cards

As previously defined, an *aperture card* is a tabulating-size card with an opening (aperture) that contains one frame of 35mm microfilm. As with microfilm jackets, the frame is usually cut from a roll of microfilm. In most cases, a duplicate roll is created from the camera original film. The duplicate is cut into frames, and the camera original roll is retained as a storage copy. A special device, called a *viewer-mounter*, is used to insert 35mm microfilm frames into aperture cards. Alternatively, certain cameras and COM recorders accept aperture cards with premounted frames of unexposed 35mm microfilm.

Aperture card characteristics are specified in several standards, including ANSI/AIIM MS41, *Dimensions of Unitized Microfilm Carriers and Apertures (Aperture, Camera, Copy and Image Cards)*, and ISO 3272-3, *Microfilming of Technical Drawings and Other Drawings Office Documents—Part 3: Unitized Aperture Card for 35mm Microfilm*. The standard aperture card measures 3.25 inches high by 7 3/8 inches wide (86 by 187 mm), which is identical in size to the 80-column punched cards used in early computer configurations and tabulating equipment.

The aperture card is an excellent microform for large single-page documents. Since the 1960s, it has been the most widely used microform for engineering drawings, architectural plans, and maps. Typically, each aperture card contains one drawing. Aperture cards provide ample paper space for eye-legible information that identifies and describes the microfilmed material. This information may be handwritten, typed, or computer printed. The front and back of an aperture card can be custom printed to accommodate special application requirements. Cards can be ordered in various colors or with color striping to differentiate portions of a document collection. During the 1960s and 1970s, aperture cards were often keypunched with drawing numbers or other identifying information for machine sorting and selection, but keypunching is seldom done today because card sorting equipment is obsolete.

Microfilming Source Documents

As noted previously, microforms can be created by microfilming source documents or from computer-processible information that would otherwise be printed on paper. In source document microphotography, the oldest and best-known approach to microform creation, specially designed cameras reproduce office records, engineering drawings, library books, and other documents as highly miniaturized images on rolls of 16mm or 35mm microfilm, on microfiche, or on aperture cards. Following exposure and development, camera original microforms are usually duplicated to produce additional storage or working copies. Following duplication, 16mm microfilm rolls may be loaded into cartridges or cut up to produce microfilm jackets. Rolls of 35mm microfilm may be cut up for insertion into microfilm jackets or aperture cards.

Document Preparation

Preparation is the essential first step in source document microphotography. Its purpose is to make source documents camera-ready—that is, to put documents into a condition and sequence appropriate for microfilming. Well-prepared source documents are critical to efficient use of microfilm cameras and to the production of usable microforms. In most cases, source documents are prepared for microfilming in batches. In 16mm and 35mm microfilm applications, for example, sufficient documents to fill an entire roll are usually prepared before filming begins. In high-volume microfilming installations, preparation of source documents is a continuous activity. Multiple workers may be dedicated to document preparation, while others operate microfilm cameras or perform other production-related tasks.

All source documents require some preparation. Specific work steps, however, depend on application characteristics, file organization, the physical condition, and other attributes of the documents to be filmed, the type of microfilm camera to be used, and other factors. At a minimum, correspondence, memoranda, project reports, case files, and other office records must be removed from file cabinets, folders, or other containers; unfolded if necessary; and stacked neatly in the correct sequence for microfilming. Torn pages must be mended or photocopied prior to filming. Most microfilm cameras require removal of staples and paper clips from source documents. Even when not required, removal of fasteners improves the productivity of camera operators and enhances the appearance of microimages. In some applications, specially prepared divider sheets called *targets* must be inserted between groups of records. Targets contain identifying information that is microfilmed before the pages to which they pertain. In some cases, targets that contain large characters to be read without magnification are microfilmed between groups of records to simplify retrieval.

Document preparation is time-consuming and labor-intensive. Sustainable preparation rates rarely exceed 1,000 pages per hour for office records in good condition. The contents of a file cabinet drawer will consequently require at least 2.5 hours of preparation time. This estimate is based on the assumption that source documents will be microfilmed as they are currently filed without misfile detection, rearrangement, purging of unneeded records, or other evaluation of the records for correctness or completeness. If the sequence of pages within a file must be changed, if certain records must be purged, or if files must be checked for misplaced or missing pages prior to filming, preparation time will escalate dramatically. Further, note that older source documents, which may be in poor condition, usually take longer to prepare, as do large documents such as engineering drawings, architectural plans, and maps.

Microfilm Cameras

Microfilm cameras, also known as *microfilmers*, are special-purpose photographic devices that produce highly miniaturized reproductions of source documents. Although early models required many operator decisions that could be made only by specially trained technicians, most new microfilm cameras are designed for operation in an office environment by nontechnical personnel with little or no knowledge of photography. Focus and film advance mechanisms are invariably automat-

Microfilm Cameras for Source Document Microfilming

- *Rotary cameras* – designed for high-volume microfilming applications where productivity is a paramount consideration. Also known as *flow-type cameras*, rotary cameras take their name from their document feeding mechanisms. Source documents inserted into a narrow opening are quickly transported past a lens and a light source where they are recorded onto 16mm microfilm. Input is limited to single sheets of paper with all staples, paper clips, and other fasteners removed. (See Figure 5-2.) Depending on the model, rotary cameras can accept documents that measure 12 to 14 inches wide by any reasonable length. To avoid double-feeding, skewing, and jamming, letter-size pages and other office documents are usually inserted into the rotary camera's transport mechanism by hand. A moderately skilled operator can sustain filming rates of 800 to 1,000 letter-size pages per hour, assuming that the pages are properly prepared. Automatic page feeders permit rapid microfilming of stacks of bank checks and other small documents. Their mechanical operating speeds can exceed 500 checks per minute.
- *Planetary* or *flatbed microfilmers* – combine a camera unit, a flat exposure surface, a light source, and various operator controls in a tabletop or free-standing device. The camera unit contains a lens system, film supply, and film advance mechanism. With an overhead planetary microfilmer, the most common type, source documents are individually positioned, face-up, on a flat copyboard for microfilming by a camera unit mounted on a vertical column. (See Figure 5-3.)
- *Planetary microfilmers* – the camera unit and light source are located below or behind a glass exposure surface on which source documents are positioned face-down for microfilming. Depending on the model, planetary cameras produce 16mm or 35mm microfilm. Special models are available for engineering drawings, architectural plans, and other large documents. Rotary cameras, as described previously, microfilm

continued on page 114

ic. Simplified control panels, push-button operation, informative operator displays, and attention to ergonomics are the rule. Warning lights and audible alarms alert the operator to the approaching end of a roll of film, improper film loading, burned-out lamps, and other problems. Automatic exposure controls compensate for variations in color, texture, contrast, and other document characteristics. With some models, unexposed microfilm is supplied in cartridges to simplify camera loading. Cameras for source document microfilms are typically categorized by the types of microforms they produce and their mode of operation.

Microfilm Processing and Inspection

Following exposure, camera original microfilms contain latent (invisible) photographic images that require development. Microfilm processing equipment applies physical and chemical treatments that make latent images visible and stable. Exposed microfilm is removed from a camera and carried to a processor in a light-tight canister. Microfilm processors are available in tabletop and floor-standing models that vary in capability and complexity. The most flexible devices can process 16mm, 35mm, and

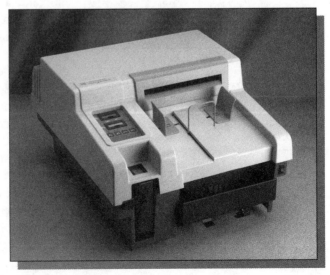

Rotary Microfilm Camera

Figure 5-2   (Courtesy: Eastman Kodak)

Planetary Microfilm Camera

Figure 5-3

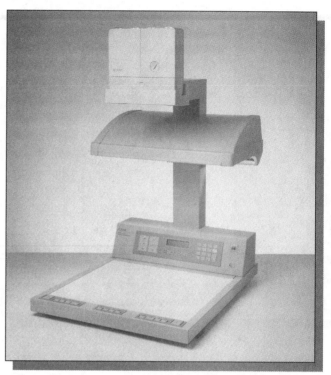

(Courtesy: Eastman Kodak)

documents while they are moving, which can degrade image quality. Planetary cameras, by contrast, film stationary documents, which yields excellent image quality but compromises productivity. When source documents are properly prepared, an experienced planetary camera operator can sustain filming rates up to 500 letter-size pages per hour. However, large pages, fragile documents, or bound volumes can take much longer to film. Engineering drawings, for example, may take several minutes each to position, expose, and remove. To enhance productivity while maintaining high image quality, some planetary cameras feature automatic page feeders, which transport documents to an exposure surface where they are stopped momentarily for microfilming.

- *Step-and-repeat cameras* – create microfiche by recording source documents onto 105mm microfilm in a predetermined format of rows and columns. Depending on the model, a step-and-repeat camera may accept 105mm film in 50- or 100-foot rolls, with individual fiche being cut to size following exposure or development of a full or partial roll. Alternatively, a step-and-repeat camera may accept unexposed microfilm in precut 105-by-148mm sheets. Step-and-repeat cameras resemble planetary microfilmers in design and operation. With manually fed models, each page is positioned on a flat copyboard where it remains stationary during microfilming. Following exposure, the page is removed, the camera automatically steps over to the next image position on the film, another page is placed onto the exposure surface, and the process is repeated. Filming rates are comparable to those for manually fed planetary cameras. Automatic-feed step-and-repeat cameras enhance throughput by eliminating manual placement of individual pages. Whether source documents are manually positioned or automatically fed, step-and-repeat cameras can also record one or more lines of eye-legible title information in the microfiche heading area. Newer models incorporate character-generators and computer controllers for that purpose.

continued on page 115

105mm microfilm at speeds up to 250 feet per minute. Simpler tabletop models are designed for operation by nontechnical personnel in an office environment. They can process up to 10 feet of microfilm per minute. Less commonly, a processing unit may be integrated into a microfilm camera. The resulting device, called a *camera/processor*, exposes and develops microimages in a continuous series of operations. Camera/processors are intended for applications where microimages will be viewed or printed immediately after exposure.

Processed microforms must be inspected for image quality and stability. Recommended inspection procedures described in ANSI/AIIM MS23, *Practice for Operational Procedures/Inspection and Quality Control of First-Generation Silver-Gelatin Microfilm of Documents,* and in ISO 6200, *Micrographics—First Generation Silver-Gelatin Microforms of Source Documents—Density Specifications and Method of Measurement.* ISO 3272-2, *Microfilming of Technical Drawings and Other Drawing Office Documents—Part 2: Quality Criteria and Control of 35mm Silver Gelatin Microfilms,* covers quality control procedures for engineering applications.

- *Aperture card cameras* – record miniaturized images of engineering drawings or other large source documents onto 35mm microfilm frames that are premounted into tabulating-size cards. The cards, called *camera cards*, contain unexposed film. As a potentially more convenient alternative to manual cutting and mounting of individual frames from developed rolls of 35mm microfilm, aperture card cameras are planetary in design and operation. The source document to be microfilmed is positioned face-up on a flat copyboard, and the aperture card camera takes a picture of it. Aperture card cameras are actually camera/processors; following exposure, camera cards pass through a processing chamber and are delivered, fully developed, in about a minute.

- *Filmer/scanners*, variously described as *camera/scanners* or *scanner/filmers* – are microfilm cameras that can also operate as electronic document scanners. A filmer/scanner produces a microfilm image and a digital image of a page in a single exposure. Intended for applications where both microform and electronic copies are desired, it offers a labor-saving alternative to microfilming and scanning source documents in separate operations with different equipment. Alternatively, a filmer/scanner can be used as a microfilm camera only or as a document scanner only for applications that do not require both types of images. Depending on the model, a filmer/scanner may be rotary or planetary in design and operation. Most scanner/filmers are high-speed, heavy-duty devices intended for large-scale imaging projects, centralized document conversion departments, or commercial service bureaus. Rotary filmer/scanners, the most common configuration, produce 16mm microfilm, like their camera-only counterparts.

The purpose of image quality inspections is to ensure that microforms are sufficiently legible for their intended purposes, which may include viewing microimages, printing paper copies of all or selected microimages within a given microform, duplicating microforms to create working or storage copies, or scanning of microimages for facsimile transmission or input to an electronic document imaging system. Determinations of image quality are usually based on resolution and density measurements, which compare microimages to predetermined values for images of acceptable quality. **Resolution**, which roughly equates to image sharpness, measures the ability of microfilm equipment and photographic materials to render fine detail visible within a microimage. Resolution is tested by examining a microimage of a specially designed chart, which is recorded onto a roll of microfilm or microfiche. *Image density tests* measure the contrast between information and noninformation areas within microimages. This test is done with a device called a *densitometer*. High contrast between line and background densities is desirable for microimages that contain textual information or line art.

With silver gelatin microfilms, the type used in the cameras described previously, latent images are developed by a chemical agent that converts exposed silver grains to black metallic silver. Development is followed by the application of a fixing bath that converts unexposed silver grains to silver thiosulfate compounds, making them water-soluble so that they can be washed out of the film. If left on the film, thiosulfate will darken on exposure to light. Adequate film washing is consequently essential for microforms that contain permanent records. Guidelines are presented in ANSI/NAPM IT9.1, *Imaging Materials— Processed Silver-Gelatin Type Black-and-White Film— Specifications for Stability.* The *methylene blue test* is the best known and most widely applied of several methods of confirming adequate removal of thiosulfate during microfilm processing. It should be performed each time film, chemicals, or the microfilm processor are changed.

Microform Duplication

Microform duplication is the production of single or multiple microform copies from a master microform, which may be a roll of 16mm or 35mm microfilm, a microfiche, a microfilm jacket, or an aperture card. The master microform may be a camera original microform produced directly from source documents or a copy one or more gen-

Print Films: Technical Characteristics and Records Management Applications

- *Diazo microfilms* are intended exclusively for duplication; they are not suitable for use in cameras. Diazo print films are exposed to ultraviolet light and developed with ammonia fumes. The resulting copies have excellent viewing properties and are scratch-resistant. Diazo technology produces a negative-appearing copy of a negative-appearing master microform and a positive-appearing copy of a positive-appearing master microform. As a result, diazo duplication is most widely used in source document microfilm applications where master microforms are usually negative-appearing and negative-appearing working copies are desired.* When properly stored, diazo microfilms will remain stable for 100 years as specified in ANSI/NAPM IT9.5, *Imaging Materials—Ammonia Processed Diazo Photographic Film—Specifications for Stability.*
- *Vesicular microfilms* are exposed to ultraviolet light and developed by heat, without chemicals or fluids. As its principal advantages, vesicular technology is convenient, fast, odorless, and completely dry. It produces a positive-appearing copy of a negative-appearing master and a negative-appearing copy of a positive-appearing master. As a result, vesicular duplication is most widely used in computer-output microfilm applications where master microforms are often positive-appearing and negative-appearing working copies are desired. Vesicular copies are easily identified by their distinctive beige, gray, or light blue color. When properly stored, vesicular microfilms will remain stable for 100 years as specified in ANSI/NAPM IT9.12 standard, *Processed Vesicular Photographic Film—Specifications for Stability.*
- *Silver gelatin print films* are typically reserved for applications that require permanent microform storage copies. When properly processed and stored, silver gelatin print films have the same stability characteristics as silver gelatin camera films. Copies made from silver gelatin print films may be either positive- or negative-appearing, depending on the type of print film used.

* Microform users often prefer negative-appearing working copies, which hide scratches and mask uneven illumination in certain microform display devices. Sometimes, a specific polarity is required to produce a meaningful microimage. For example, microimages of X-rays must be negative-appearing, and microimages of photographs must be positive-appearing.

erations removed from the camera original microform. Microform duplication is used to make additional microform copies for storage or reference. A **microfilm duplicator** is used to produce copies of microforms. Microform working copies may be intended for distribution or used as printing intermediates, from which additional microform copies will be produced. When a large number of microform copies is required, preparation of one or more printing intermediates is recommended to prevent damage to the master microform.

Unlike original microphotography, which is an optical process, microform duplication relies on contact printing methodologies. Microfilms intended for duplication are called *print films* or *copy films* to distinguish them from camera films. Print films are available in three types: silver gelatin, diazo, and vesicular. The films differ in their technical characteristics, which determine the records management applications for which they are suitable.

Computer-Output Microfilm (COM)

Just as source-document microfilm can miniaturize voluminous collections of office documents, engineering drawings, or records, COM offers a compact, easily managed alternative to the unwieldy paper printouts produced by many computer programs. Particularly troublesome are long printouts—such as customer lists, account status reports, and budget tabulations—that are printed at frequent intervals for distribution to multiple users within a corporation, government agency, or other organization. General ledgers and other accounting reports, for example, may be printed weekly or monthly in continuously cumulating versions that become larger and larger as the fiscal year progresses. Each time the reports are printed, copies are distributed to multiple departments, where they are typically bound and stored on shelves or in filing cabinets. Such printouts are time-consuming to produce and package for distribution. They consume large amounts of paper, require substantial storage space in multiple office locations, and are cumbersome to file, reference, and photocopy. Like any other documents, paper printouts can, of course be microfilmed to save space, but COM addresses these problems at their source: It records computer-processible information onto micro-forms instead of, rather than after, printing it.

COM Recorders

A **COM recorder**, the device that produces computer-output microfilm, combines the functionality of a computer printer and a microfilm camera. Like a computer printer, a COM recorder converts the results of computer processing to human-read-able form. Like a microfilm camera, a COM recorder produces page images that require magnification for viewing or printing. Depending on data characteristics and equipment capabilities, COM-generated microimages may contain textual or graph-ic information. The information may be recorded onto microfiche, roll microfilm, or aperture cards. Following exposure and development, COM-generated microforms are usually duplicated to produce additional storage or working copies.

COM production begins with computer-processible information that would oth-erwise be printed onto paper. The information, appropriately formatted, is trans-ferred, manually or electronically, to a COM recorder, which creates microimages that resemble miniaturized versions of printed pages. Like conventional printers, COM recorders belong to the category of computer support devices that are collectively termed *output peripherals*. As peripheral devices, COM recorders can operate online or offline. An online COM recorder, like most conventional printers, is directly con-nected to a host computer, usually through a channel interface. Programs operating on the host computer transfer information electronically to the online COM recorder, just as they do to online printers. Typically, the host computer recognizes the COM recorder as a specific type of online printer. Offline COM recorders, by contrast, are standalone devices. A program operating on a separate computer initially records information onto a magnetic tape, which must be physically transported from the computer to the offline COM recorder. Depending on the circumstances, an offline COM recorder may be located in the same facility as the computer that generated the information to be recorded, in another department within the same facility, or at a remote site. Many offline COM recorders are operated by service bureaus.

Output Characteristics

Most COM recorders produce microfiche, although devices that produce 16mm or 35mm roll microfilm are also available. COM recorders are categorized as alphanu-meric or graphic devices, depending on the type of information they can print. *Alphanumeric COM recorders* can print alphabetic characters, numeric digits, punc-tuation marks, and other symbols commonly encountered in textual documents. They are suitable for accounting reports, customer lists, and other straightforward business applications. Alphanumeric COM recorders were originally developed as alternatives to line printers in mainframe and minicomputer installations. The most prevalent COM page format emulates an 11-by-14-inch computer printout sheet that contains 60 to 64 lines of information with up to 132 characters per line. The 48/270 microfiche format described previously can store 270 images of that page type.

Graphic COM recorders have full alphanumeric capabilities. They can also print engineering drawings, charts, graphs, plots, circuit diagrams, maps, and medical imagery, as well as digitized images created by document scanners and digital cameras. As such, graphic COM recorders are the micrographics counterparts of computer plotters. Microrecording of CAD-generated engineering drawings and related graphic documents is their most important use. Rather than using plotters to print CAD-generated engineering drawings onto paper for subsequent microfilming by planetary cameras, graphics COM devices permit direct recording of such drawings onto 35mm roll microfilm or aperture cards. Microreproduction of electronic document images produced by document scanners is one of the newest uses for graphic COM recorders. It is intended for records management applications that rely on digitized images for reference, as discussed in Chapter 8, but require a highly stable microform copy for long-term retention or other purposes.

Microfilm Storage

When properly stored, microforms offer superior stability for recorded information requiring long-term retention or permanent preservation. Authoritative storage recommendations are presented, in considerable detail, in ANSI/NAPM IT9.11, *Imaging Media—Processed Safety Film: Storage*. For extended-term (permanent) storage of microfilm, the standard specifies three combinations of temperature and relative humidity:

- 70 degrees Fahrenheit (21 degrees Celsius) with relative humidity of 20 to 30 percent

- 60 degrees Fahrenheit (15 degrees Celsius) with relative humidity of 20 to 40 percent

- 50 degrees Fahrenheit (10 degrees Celsius) with relative humidity of 20 to 50 percent

Low temperatures and low humidity promote image stability. Lower temperatures can compensate for high humidity, but the relative humidity cannot exceed 50 percent in microform storage areas. Relative humidity below 20 percent is not recommended because low humidity extracts moisture from photographic emulsions, which can lead to brittleness and curling of microfilms. In most cases, air conditioning will be required to maintain storage area temperatures and relative humidity within specified limits. Where properly air-conditioned facilities cannot be established within a given building, extended-term storage requirements can often be met by renting space in an environmentally controlled commercial storage vault.

The ANSI/NAPM IT9.11 standard also specifies medium-term storage conditions for preservation of microfilm for at least ten years. For medium-term storage, the maximum temperature should not exceed 77 degrees Fahrenheit (25 degrees Celsius). Storage temperatures below 21 degrees Celsius (70 degrees Fahrenheit) are preferable. Humidity for medium-term storage can range from 20 to 50 percent. Although these medium-term environmental requirements are less stringent than those cited previously, they may prove difficult or impossible to implement in older buildings that lack reliable heating and air-conditioning systems.

As specified in ANSI/NAPM IT9.2, *Imaging Media—Photographic Processed Films, Plates, and Papers—Filing Enclosures and Storage Containers*, boxes, envelopes, folders, sleeves, or other microform enclosures must be chemically stable and free of acids or peroxides that can cause blemishes or other chemical decomposition of microimages.

Microform Viewing and Scanning Equipment

Most micrographics applications involve storage copies and working copies. Storage copies are kept in a safe, environmentally controlled location to satisfy retention or backup requirements. Working copies, by contrast, are designed to be used. As replacements for paper records, they contain useful information that will be consulted for business or other purposes. User acceptance of microforms in such situations depends on the convenient and reliable ability to display, print, or otherwise process microimages when needed. Several types of devices are available for those purposes.

Microform Readers

A **microform reader** projects magnified microimages onto an integral screen. When evaluating microform readers for specific records management applications, the main considerations include the type of microforms accepted, the availability of appropriate magnifications, and the size and orientation of the reader's screen. Important technical and operational considerations involve the image projection method, the quality of displayed images, the film transport mechanism, equipment design and construction, and ease of use. ANSI/AIIM MS20, *Readers for Transparent Microforms—Performance Characteristics*, defines essential attributes and minimum performance expectations.

Most microform readers support interchangeable drop-in lenses that can be inserted and removed to address specific application requirements. Common screen sizes and orientations include 8.5 by 11 inches, portrait mode for full-size display of letter-size source documents and partial-size display of legal-size pages; 8.5 by 11 inches, landscape mode for partial-size display of COM-generated images and print-out-size source documents; 11 inches square for full-size display of letter-size source documents and partial-size display of COM-generated images, legal-size pages, or printout-size source documents; and 11 by 14 inches, landscape mode for full-size display of source documents and COM-generated images. Readers with larger screens are available for partial- or full-size display of engineering drawings, maps, newspaper pages, and other large documents.

Two related devices, microform viewers and microform projectors, have limited records management applications. A *microform viewer* is a handheld, usually monocular magnifier for microfiche, microfilm jackets, and aperture cards. Viewers are suitable only for brief reference to microimages. As display devices of last resort, they can be used by field engineers, surveyors, equipment maintenance personnel, and other workers at construction sites, in vehicles, or in other locations where technical documentation or other information recorded on microfiche must be consulted but microform readers cannot be utilized. *Microform projectors* magnify microimages for display onto a wall or wall-mounted screen. They permit the use of microforms as presentation aids in situations where source documents or computer-generated printouts must be examined and discussed.

Reader/Printers

Although micrographics is often depicted as a paperless information technology, most users want or need paper copies of microimages for reference, distribution, or other purposes. **Microform reader/printers** can display magnified microimages onto a screen and make paper copies of displayed images on demand. In effect, a reader/printer is a microform reader with an integral photocopier.

ANSI/AIIM MS36, *Reader-Printers*, delineates essential equipment attributes. Reader/printers are more accurately characterized as *locator/printers*. Unlike readers, they are rarely used for prolonged microform viewing. Typically, users display microimages briefly onto a reader/printer's screen to confirm their identity and properly align them to make paper copies. (See Figure 5-4.) All newly manufactured reader/printers employ xerographic technology, which prints enlarged microimages on plain (uncoated) paper. They can produce legible, high-contrast enlargements that are well accepted by microform users.

Related devices, called *enlarger/printers*, make enlarged paper copies of microimages but are not designed for microform viewing. If they have a screen at all, it is intended for image identification and alignment prior to printing. If reader/printers are the micrographics counterparts of low-volume photocopiers, enlarger/printers are analogous to high-speed duplicators. Compared to reader/printers, enlarger/printers are more automated and much faster. They are intended for organizations that maintain large microform collections and have high-volume printing requirements. Engineering

**Microform
Reader/Printer**

Figure 5-4

(Courtesy: Konica Minolta)

contractors and large government agencies, for example, use enlarger/printers to assemble bid packets that incorporate drawings recorded onto aperture cards.

Microform Scanners

Microform scanners digitize microimages for computer processing, storage, retrieval, printing, or distribution. A microform scanner combines the attributes of a microfilm densitometer and a document scanner. The scanning component operates much like scanners for paper documents, which are described in Chapter 8, but the pages they scan are highly miniaturized film images.

Microfilm scanners are available in production-level and low-volume versions. Production-level devices can scan large quantities of microimages at relatively high speed with little or no operator intervention. (See Figure 5-5.) Their principal role in records management is scanning of microform backfiles for input to electronic document imaging systems, computer-aided design software, or other computer applications. Depending on the model, a production-level microform scanner may be able to digitize microimages recorded onto 16mm or 35mm microfilm reels, 16mm microfilm cartridges, microfiche in various formats, and aperture cards.

For low-volume scanning requirements, reader/scanners, sometimes described as *digital microimage workstations*, combine the capabilities of microform reader and document scanners. A reader/scanner produces electronic document images from magnified microimages that are displayed onto a screen. Significant operator involvement is required because microimages must be individually located, displayed,

**Microform
Scanner**

Figure 5-5

(Courtesy: Eastman Kodak)

focused, and positioned for scanning. Reader/scanners are best suited to selective scanning of microimages for printing or electronic transmission. When connected to a laser printer, a reader/scanner can operate as a digital reader/printer. Reader/scanners can also digitize microimages for input to electronic document imaging systems, for distribution over computer networks as attachments to e-mail messages, for optical character recognition, for input to desktop publishing programs, or for other purposes. Alternatively, a reader/scanner can be equipped with a fax modem for facsimile transmission of digitized images.

Microfilm Service Bureaus

Any or all microform production work steps can be performed in-house or by a service bureau. A **micrographics service bureau** is a business that performs one or more micrographics services to customer specifications using the customer's own documents, computer data, or other source material. A service bureau may offer any combination of microform production and support services, including consulting for application selection and systems design, document preparation, source document microfilming, COM data preparation and recording, microfilm processing, microimage inspections, stability testing of processed microfilm, microform duplication, microform reformatting, cartridge loading and labeling, and preparation of microfilm jackets and aperture cards. Increasingly, micrographics service bureaus offer microform scanning and related services for integration of micrographics and electronic document imaging technologies.

Depending on the service bureau and customer requirements, micrographics services may be performed at the service bureau's facilities or at the customer's location, although on-site implementations are more costly and may limit the types of services to be offered. Some service bureaus also sell readers, reader/printers, and other micrographics equipment or supplies.

Outsourcing arrangements are increasingly popular in records management operations. Some organizations use service bureaus for their entire source document microfilming requirements, and many in-house micrographics departments contract with service bureaus for at least one phase of microform production. For example, service bureaus often process, inspect, and duplicate microfilm exposed by an in-house micrographics department. Micrographics service bureaus are particularly useful for high-volume work that must be completed in a short time or for tasks, such as microform reformatting, that require special equipment or technical expertise that are unavailable in-house.

Service bureau capabilities and rates vary. The nature and acceptability of services to be rendered must be negotiated between the customer and the service bureau's management. Critical criteria for service bureau selection include a demonstrated understanding of the customer's requirements, micrographics equipment, and technical expertise appropriate to the tasks to be performed, the ability to provide high-quality service within customer-specified deadlines, and a record of satisfactory performance in similar applications. A tour of the service bureau's facilities prior to contract award is strongly recommended.

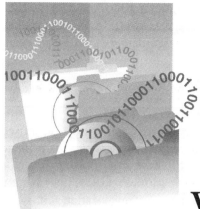

Chapter 6

Vital Records

Vital records, as briefly defined in preceding chapters, contain information that is essential to an organization's mission. All organizations have certain business operations that they must perform. Such business operations are characterized as *mission-critical*. Vital records contain information needed for **mission-critical operations**. If vital records are lost, damaged, destroyed, or otherwise rendered unavailable or unusable, mission-critical operations will be curtailed or discontinued, with a resulting adverse impact on the organization. This impact may not occur immediately, but it will occur inevitably.

Vital records protection is one of the most important components of a systematic records management program. Recognizing the importance of vital records, the previously cited ISO 15489-1 standard includes risk assessment and protection of records among the requirements for records management operations. The importance of protecting vital records is treated in ANSI/ARMA 5, *Vital Records Programs: Identifying, Managing, and Recovering Business-Critical Records*. Properly conceived and administered, a vital records program can make an indispensable contribution to business effectiveness. For many organizations, information contained in vital records is their most important asset. Without vital records:

- Equipment manufacturers would be unable to build, market, deliver, or repair their products.
- Pharmaceutical companies would be unable to develop, test, or prove the safety and efficacy of chemical compounds.
- Utility companies would be unable to operate and maintain their facilities.
- Local government agencies would be unable to document property ownership, determine tax assessments, evaluate zoning applications, or issue building permits.
- Hospitals and clinics would be unable to render effective medical care.
- Social services agencies would be unable to help families and individuals in need.
- Schools and colleges would be unable to document the attendance or academic achievements of students.

- Insurance companies would be unable to determine policy coverage or collect premiums.
- Financial institutions would be unable to document customer account balances or collect debt.
- Lawyers, engineers, architects, social workers, and other professionals would be unable to serve their clients.

In many cases, the loss of recorded information can have more devastating consequences for continuation of an organization's operations than the loss of physical plant or inventory, which are often replaceable and insured.

Vital records are considered vital specifically and exclusively for the information they contain and the relationship of that information to an organization's mission-critical operations. Vital record status is not necessarily related to other record attributes. Physical format is immaterial; vital records may be paper documents, photographic films, or electronic media. Vital records may be active or inactive, originals or copies. Vital record status is similarly independent of retention designations. Vital records need not be permanent records; some vital records may, in fact, be retained for brief periods of time and replaced at frequent intervals. Furthermore, some records may be considered vital for only a portion of their designated retention periods. Invoices, billing documentation, and other accounts receivable records, for example, are vital until the matters to which they pertain are paid, although they are usually retained for several years following receipt of payment for legal reasons, internal audits, or other purposes.

Specific record attributes aside, a **vital records management program** is a set of policies and procedures for the systematic, comprehensive, and economical control of adverse consequences attributable to the loss of mission-critical information. Many businesses, government agencies, and other organizations have developed contingency plans for the protection of personnel, buildings, machinery, inventory, and other assets in the event of fire, weather-related disasters, or other emergencies. Protection of recorded information essential to mission-critical business operations has long been recognized as an indispensable aspect of such emergency preparedness and disaster recovery initiatives. Since the 1950s, for example, U.S. laws have mandated the identification and protection of vital operating records of federal government agencies. Management of vital records must be part of each agency's plan for continuity of business operations in the event of emergencies, as stated in 36 CFR 1236. Similar regulations apply to protection of government records in other countries.

Traditionally, records management has emphasized the protection of vital records against accidental or willful damage, destruction, or misplacement. Misplacement encompasses a spectrum of inadvertent or malicious events ranging from misfiling to theft of records. An organization may also be harmed, however, by misuse of, alteration of, or unauthorized access to vital records. In the case of computer records, these considerations have been widely discussed by public policy analysts and legal scholars, but they also apply to paper and photographic records.

Whatever the threat, a vital records program provides formalized procedures to help an organization withstand and limit the impact of adverse events, enabling it to

Vital Records Protection Program Components

- Formal endorsement of the program by a directive from an organization's senior management with responsibility and authority for protection of vital records assigned to the records management activity, to be coordinated, where appropriate, with related contingency planning activities;
- Identification and enumeration of vital records;
- Risk analysis to determine the extent to which specific vital records are threatened by hazards and to calculate exposures;
- The selection of appropriate loss prevention and records protection methods; and
- Employee training, implementation, and compliance auditing.

continue information-dependent business operations—though possibly at a reduced level—following a disaster.

The vital records protection program components conform closely to the multistep process defined in ISO/IEC 17799 standard, *Information Technology—Code of Practice for Information Security Management*. That standard, which was published in 2000, emphasizes security measures to protect computer-based information assets, including databases and their associated software, but its principles and practices are broadly applicable to recorded information in all formats. The following sections will explain and discuss vital records protection requirements and program work steps in greater detail.

Establishing the Vital Records Program

Citizens have a reasonable expectation that government agencies will safeguard essential records. Similar expectations apply to corporate shareholders, to clients of professional services firms, to medical patients, to students in academic institutions, and to any other persons or organizations that may be affected by the recordkeeping practices of others. These expectations are based on the legal concept of "standard of care," which is the degree of care that a reasonable person would exercise to prevent injury to another.

Responsibility of Senior Management

As discussed in Chapter 1, recorded information is an asset. In any organization, senior management has ultimate responsibility for protection of assets, including the formulation of effective plans for loss control and disaster recovery. Senior management is, therefore, ultimately responsible for the protection of vital information assets. Effective leadership and decisive action by senior management can mitigate the impact of adverse events. If the loss, destruction, or misuse of vital records results in the interruption of critical business operations, senior management must accept responsibility for the ensuing financial losses or other adverse consequences. According to *Corpus Juris Secundum*, volume 19, section 491, corporate officers "have a duty to be vigilant and to exercise ordinary or reasonable care and diligence and the utmost good faith and fidelity to conserve the corporate property; and, if a loss or depletion of assets results from their willful or negligent failure to perform their duties, or to a willful or fraudulent abuse of their trust, they are liable, provided such losses were the natural and necessary consequences of omission on their part."

Senior management's responsibility for protecting vital records is explicitly stated or implied in several laws and government regulations:

- Within the U.S. government, for example, 36 CFR 1236.12 makes agency heads responsible for protecting vital records, which are defined as records needed to meet operational responsibilities under emergency conditions or to protect the legal and financial rights of the government and those affected by government activities.

- For public companies and privately owned businesses, the Foreign Corrupt Practices Act (FCPA) of 1977 (as amended in 1988 and 1998), which was originally intended to prevent the destruction of records in order to conceal bribery or other crimes, makes corporate executives personally liable for the failure to keep accounting records and other information pertaining to certain assets. Similarly, the Sarbanes-Oxley Act of 2002 makes corporate executives responsible for the accuracy of accounting statements and imposes criminal penalties, including imprisonment, for failure to retain certain auditing records. Accidental destruction of irreplaceable records is not an adequate excuse for failure to comply with these and other statutory retention requirements. Indeed, an obligation to protect records until legally mandated retention periods elapse is implicit in all record-keeping laws and regulations.

- Organizations in specific industries are subject to records protection and computer security requirements enforced by regulating agencies. The Health Insurance Portability and Accountability Act (HIPAA) of 1996, for example, specifies security and disaster recovery requirements for medical records maintained by healthcare providers, insurance companies, and others. Guidelines enforced by the Federal Financial Institutions Examination Council (FFIEC), the Office of the Controller of the Currency (OCC), the Federal Home Loan Bank Board, and other agencies present disaster preparedness requirements for banks, thrifts, and other financial institutions.

Vital Records Protection as Insurance

A vital records protection program is, in effect, an insurance policy for essential information. Like any insurance policy, vital records protection can be difficult to sell to decision makers. Vital records protection is costly but makes no direct contribution to revenues, product development, or improvement of services. It provides no benefits unless and until a disaster occurs.

Many threats to vital records have a low probability of occurrence. Senior management may consequently ignore them in favor of more pressing business concerns. The very nature of insurance is to provide protection against the adverse impact of improbable events; insurance protection is usually unavailable for probable events. Like all insurance policies, vital records protection must be justified by the intolerable consequences that follow an improbable but adverse event.

Senior management must be made to appreciate the potential for tangible and intangible damages associated with the loss, destruction, or misuse of vital records however unlikely that loss, destruction, or misuse may seem. Examples of such damages include, but are by no means limited to:

- Loss of customers because of the inability to fulfill orders and contracts, support products, or provide services

- Loss of revenue or disruption of cash flow because of a lack of accounts receivable records and resulting inability to reconstruct amounts to be billed

- Loss of opportunity because information needed for contracts, partnerships, or other business agreements is unavailable

- Fines or other penalties for failure to provide records needed for government investigation

- Penalties for late payment of payroll or other taxes for which records are unavailable

- Increased assessments, plus penalties and interest, following tax audits because of inadequate documentation of business expenses, depreciation, and other deductions, allowances, and tax credits

- Delayed compliance with governmental reporting requirements for public companies

- Lawsuits resulting from an inability to pay employees and document pension benefits to retirees

- Lack of records needed for litigation or government investigations

- Inability to document insurance claims with resulting delay or reduction in settlements

- Longer completion times for product development, design, testing, marketing, support, and other information-dependent business operations

- High costs to reconstruct recorded information when needed

- Tarnished reputation and loss of customer goodwill

Further, an organization may be sued for damages resulting from its failure to protect essential operating records from accidental or willful loss or destruction. A hospital's failure to protect medical records, for example, could complicate treatment and damage a patient's health. A university's failure to protect academic transcripts could place its graduates at a disadvantage when competing for employment or seeking further education. A corporation's failure to protect its personnel records could make determining retirement eligibility or accurately calculating pension benefits impossible. Loss of revenue resulting from a public company's failure to protect essential business records could lower the value of the company's stock, provoking shareholder lawsuits. Destruction of birth, death, marital, or property records maintained by state or local government agencies can have actionable consequences for individuals and organizations.

Legal actions related to an organization's failure to protect recorded information may have occurred but have gone unreported because they were settled out of court. Arguments in favor of liability for failure to protect records are based on the previously discussed concept of standard of care. Arguments that vital records protection plans are not required by law or not pervasive in a given industry are no defense. The Hooper Doctrine, which dates from a 1928 case in which a company was held liable for the sinking of barges because it did not equip its tugboats with radio receivers, established the principle that an organization can be held liable for failing to take reasonable precautionary measures, even where such measures may be widely ignored by others.

An organization's senior management bears ultimate responsibility for safeguarding mission-critical information assets; however, its involvement is typically and properly limited to delegating authority for the creation, implementation, and operation of a systematic vital records program. To formalize a protection program for vital records maintained by a business, government agency, or other organization, senior management should issue a written directive that:

- Acknowledges the value of recorded information as an organizational asset essential to mission-critical operations
- Emphasizes the importance of protecting vital records as an integral component of the organization's security policies and contingency planning initiatives
- Establishes a program for systematic, comprehensive, and economical protection of vital records
- Identifies records management as the business function responsible for implementing the program
- Solicits the cooperation of personnel in all program units where vital records are maintained

As with other records management activities discussed in this book, the development and implementation of a successful vital records program depends on the knowledge and active participation of program unit personnel who are familiar with the nature and use of recorded information in specific work environments. An advisory committee of program unit representatives can provide a formal structure for such participation. Such a committee can support the records management unit in planning, implementing, and operating a program to protect vital records.

Identifying Vital Records

As previously defined, vital records contain information indispensable to an organization's mission-critical business operations. Identifying vital records is a two-step process. First, mission-critical operations must be determined, then records essential to those operations must be identified.

Some mission-critical operations are easily identified and widely encountered. All organizations, for example, must pay their employees, withhold payroll taxes for periodic submission to government agencies, account for pensions and other benefits, collect receivables, and maintain office buildings, factories, warehouses, or other facilities that they own or occupy. Other mission-critical operations are associated with particular types of organizations or industries. A municipal government, for example, must maintain public safety, assess and collect taxes, issue building permits, enforce building codes, and process zoning applications. A charitable institution must process applications for aid, dispense payments, and otherwise assist those in need. An automobile manufacturer must develop, test, produce, sell, and support cars, trucks, or other vehicles. A law firm must represent its clients. An insurance company must sell policies and process claims. A bank must process deposits, withdrawals, and other transactions; make loans and collect payments; and safeguard and transfer funds.

With the assistance of knowledgeable persons in individual program units, records managers can identify information essential for successful performance of these and other mission-critical operations. The end product of this process is a descriptive list of vital records series. The following data elements should be included for each series:

- Series title

- Brief description of the records' purpose, scope, and operational and physical characteristics

- Mission-critical operation(s) the records support

- Adverse consequences to the organization if the records are lost, destroyed, or otherwise unavailable

- Name of the program unit responsible for protecting the vital records series

- Method of protection to be implemented

When determining that a given records series is vital, a records manager must be able to clearly and convincingly state which mission-critical operations would be prevented by the loss, destruction, or other unavailability of the indicated records series. The effect on mission-critical operations is the ultimate test of a vital record.

Vital Records vs. Important Records

Although all vital records are associated with mission-critical operations, nonvital records may be employed in those operations as well. When asked to identify vital records, program unit personnel often include most, if not all, of the records they routinely utilize. Employees place a high value on useful information and would not want to lose any of it. However, the contents of a given records series may be helpful yet not truly essential to mission-critical operations. Records managers must help program unit employees distinguish vital records from important ones.

Important records support a program unit's business operations and help it fulfill its assigned responsibilities. The loss of such records may cause delays or confusion that impede a program unit's work, but it will not bring mission-critical business operations to a halt. Some important records are replaceable; their contents may be reconstructed from other records, although such reconstruction may involve considerable time, inconvenience, and expense. In some computer applications, for example, operations supported by important electronic records may be performed—though, admittedly, less quickly or efficiently—by reversion to manual procedures. Truly vital records, by contrast, are essential and irreplaceable. Unless appropriate protection is provided, their contents cannot be reconstructed, and the business operations they support cannot be performed without them.

As a complicating factor, a records manager must differentiate records that are vital to a corporation, government agency, or other organization as a whole from those that are vital to a specific program unit within that organization. Records series in the former category support operations that are truly mission-critical, while those in the latter group support valuable but not essential activities. In many organizations, certain program units perform useful functions that are not critical to the organization's mission. Loss or destruction of recorded information may cause a temporary or permanent disruption of business operations in such program units, but the organization's mission will not be imperiled. Such records cannot be considered vital, because the activities they support are not vital to the organization as a whole. As an example, a bank's community relations department may maintain records about local charitable institutions, community activists, housing preservation associations, or other groups with which it interacts. If those records are lost, the department's work will be impeded or possibly discontinued, but the bank's mission-critical business operations, such as processing cash transactions or making loans, will not be curtailed.

Vital Records Survey

As noted in Chapter 2, a vital records survey can be integrated with inventories conducted for purposes of preparing retention schedules. That approach is recommended where practical. A combined records inventory/vital records survey will minimize duplication of effort; vital record status can be discussed with knowledgeable employees and evaluated as each series is identified during the inventory. Vital records protection can also be coordinated with retention-oriented management actions such as off-site storage or microfilming of specific records series.

When a separate vital records survey must be conducted, the procedures are similar to those employed in a retention-oriented records inventory. Based on interviews with program unit personnel, a records manager prepares a tentative list of vital records for consideration and comment by interested parties, both within and outside the program unit, that maintain the records. A series of meetings or other consultations will resolve concerns and disagreements, leading eventually to a final approved list of vital records. (See Figure 6-1.) Several drafts may be required before a final version is obtained, however.

As with retention scheduling, the records manager coordinates the meetings, directs the discussion, redrafts the vital records lists, and provides a broad perspective on information management issues that transcend the responsibilities and requirements of specific program units. Vital records surveys prepared for individual program units may be combined to form a master list (See Figure 6-2) of vital records maintained by an entire organization or by a specific administrative entity such as a division or subsidiary.

Although many records series are undeniably useful, vital record status should not be conferred indiscriminately. In most organizations, a small percentage of nonelectronic records are properly considered vital. A somewhat greater, but not necessarily large, percentage of an organization's electronic records may be essential to mission-critical operations. In corporations, government agencies, and other organizations, the

Sample Vital Records Index

A worksheet for listing and describing vital records

Figure 6-1

Vital Records Index

Organization Unit With Original	No.

Records Name | Schedule No.

Classification
☐ Vital
☐ Important

Physical Description	Distribution of Copies			
	Unit	No.	Location	Media

Purpose of Record	Impact if Destroyed

Suggested Method of Protection
☐ Duplication   ☐ Dispersal
☐ Extra Copies   ☐ Protected Storage
☐ Fast Copies   ☐ Remote Storage
☐ Microfilm   ☐ Reduction Ratio
(___ mm   ___ : ___)

	Explain Method

Other Protection Details

Method of Recovery

Comments

Requested By	Date	☐ Approved ☐ Not Approved	Corp. Records Mgmt.	Date

(*Source: Sample Forms for Archival & Records Management Programs, published by ARMA International and the Society of American Archivists*)

**Sample Vital
Records Master
List Form**

Figure 6-2

Vital Records Master List		
Records Title	**Responsible Department**	**Method of Protection**

Example:

Records Title	**Responsible Department**	**Method of Protection**
Accounts Receivable Invoices	Accounts Receivable	COM – Original stored off-site
Corporate Documents	Legal	Microfilm – Original stored off-site
Inspection Reports	Quality Assurance	Dispersal
Journal Entries and Register	Controller	Microfilm – Original stored off-site
Payroll Reports	Payroll	Microfilm – Original stored off-site
Personnel File – Terminated	Human Resources	Microfilm one year after termination & shred paper
Standard Operating Procedures	Compliance	Dispersal

(Source: Sample Forms for Archival & Records Management Programs, published by ARMA International and the Society of American Archivists)

most important business operations have historically been priority candidates for computerization. Certain mission-critical operations, such as accounts receivable and payroll processing, are encountered in a broad range of work environments. Information that supports those activities has been computerized for decades. Other widely computerized records are associated with mission-critical operations in specific types of organizations or industries. Examples include policy and claim files in an insurance company; customer account records in a bank or other financial institution; inventory control data in a retail organization; customer files and order fulfillment records in a catalog sales company; records related to development and testing of drugs in a pharmaceutical company; patient records in a hospital; and academic transcripts and course scheduling information in a school, college, or university.

As with retention schedules, electronic and nonelectronic vital records may be integrated in a single listing, and that approach is often advisable. At a minimum, vital record designations for electronic and nonelectronic records series should be coordinated. If exactly the same information exists in electronic and nonelectronic records, one of the formats should be selected for vital records protection. If purposeful duplication and off-site storage will be used, it will usually prove faster and more economical to protect electronic records than paper or photographic records that contain the same information. Compared to their nonelectronic counterparts, electronic records are more compact and easier to duplicate.

Risk Analysis

The purpose of **risk analysis**, sometimes termed *risk assessment,* is to determine and evaluate the exposure of vital records to specific risks. Its outcome provides the basis for protection planning and other records management decisions. A thorough risk analysis begins with the identification of threats and vulnerabilities to which vital records are exposed. Once identified, threats and vulnerabilities can be evaluated using qualitative or quantitative approaches.

Identifying Risks

Threats to vital records are customarily divided into three broad categories: (1) destruction, (2) loss, and (3) corruption. A fourth category—threats associated with the improper disclosure of recorded information—has been widely discussed by computer security specialists, lawyers, public policy analysts, civil rights advocates, and other interested parties. Although such threats pose important security problems for corporations, government agencies, and other organizations, they are typically outside the scope of records management responsibility and, consequently, of this discussion.

Protection of essential information against malicious or accidental destruction is a well-established component of vital records planning. Malicious destruction of recorded information may result from warfare or warfare-related activities such as terrorist attacks, civil insurrections, purposeful sabotage, or seemingly aimless vandalism. Potentially catastrophic agents of accidental destruction include natural disasters such as violent weather, floods, and earthquakes. Vital records can also be damaged or destroyed by human-induced accidents such as fire or explosions that result from carelessness, negligence, or lack of knowledge about the consequences of specific actions.

More likely causes of accidental records destruction are less dramatic and more localized but no less catastrophic in their consequences for mission-critical operations. Records in all formats can be damaged by careless handling. Paper documents, for example, are easily torn, damaged by spilled fluids, or otherwise mutilated. Microforms, X-rays, and other photographic films can be scratched. With very active records, the potential for such damage is intensified by use. In many work environments, for example, valuable engineering drawings subject to frequent retrieval are characteristically frayed and dog-eared.

Information recorded on magnetic media and certain types of optical disks can be erased by exposure to strong magnetic fields. Careless work procedures, such as mounting magnetic tapes or diskettes without write protection, can expose vital electronic records to accidental erasure by overwriting. Mislabeled rewritable media may be inadvertently marked for reuse, their contents being inappropriately replaced by new information. Computer hardware and software failures can damage valuable information. Electronic records may be accidentally deleted during database reorganizations or by utility programs that consolidate disk space.

Records in all formats can be misfiled, misplaced, or stolen. Like many business tasks, filing of paper records is subject to errors. Documents can be placed into the wrong folders, and folders can be placed into the wrong drawers or cabinets. Widely quoted sources claim misfile rates ranging from one to ten percent for documents in office files, but such claims are typically substantiated by anecdotal reports rather than scientific studies that present detailed statistical data about filing activity in specific work environments. Nonetheless, even a very low misfiling rate can pose significant problems in large filing installations. In a central filing area with 25 four-drawer cabinets, for example, a misfiling rate of just one-half of one percent means that over 1,000 records are filed incorrectly. Of course, even a single misfiled document can have serious consequences if it contains information needed for an important business purpose.

Color-coded folders, as discussed in Chapter 7, can simplify detection of misplaced folders, but they are not applicable to every filing situation nor can they identify individual documents filed in the wrong folder. Microfilm's advocates claim that it will eliminate misfiles associated with refiling activity. However, unless misfile detection is performed during document preparation, pages can be microfilmed in the wrong sequence, in which case misfiles are irreversible. Further, individual microfiche, microfilm jackets, and aperture cards can themselves be misfiled within cabinets or trays. With electronic records, data entry errors are the counterparts of misfiles. Although effective methods, such as double-keying of information, are available for error detection and correction, they are not incorporated into all data entry operations.

Like any valued asset, recorded information can be stolen for financial gain or other motives, by intelligence operatives or by disgruntled, compromised, or coerced employees. Traditionally, espionage-related concerns have been most closely associated with government and military records, but they apply to other work environments as well. Commercial information brokers, for example, are interested in names, addresses, telephone numbers, and other information about an organization's employees, a company's customers, a hospital's patients, an academic institution's students, and a professional association's members. Trade secrets, product specifications, manufacturing methods, marketing plans, pricing strategies, and customer information are of great interest to a company's competitors. Burglars, confidence artists, and other criminals are interested in financial and asset information contained in donor and patron records maintained by charitable and cultural institutions. A museum's records, for example, indicate the owners and locations of valuable artworks. Files in a university development office contain addresses and possibly financial data about prospective benefactors.

The threat of theft is greatest for records stored in users' work areas where systematic handling procedures are seldom implemented and security provisions may be weak or absent. Centralized repositories, by contrast, tend to be more secure. Theft is a concern for records in all formats; but microforms and electronic media are compact and more easily concealed than paper documents, and their high storage densities increase the amount of information affected by a single incident of theft.

Tampering is a leading cause of corruption of recorded information, but not all record formats are equally vulnerable. With microforms, tampering is difficult and detectable. The contents of individual microimages cannot be altered, and insertion or removal of images requires splicing of film, which is readily apparent. By contrast, information in paper documents can be added to, obliterated, or changed, although such modifications can often be detected by skilled forensic examiners. The potential for unauthorized tampering with electronic records has been widely discussed in publications and at professional meetings. Records stored on rewritable media— such as magnetic disks, magnetic tapes, and certain optical disks—are subject to modification by unauthorized persons in a manner that can prove very difficult to detect. Such unauthorized modification may involve the deletion, editing, or replacement of information. Further, viruses and other malicious software can damage computer-stored records.

Qualitative Risk Assessment

Regardless of the specific threats involved, risk assessment may be based on intuitive, relatively informal qualitative approaches or on more structured, formalized quantitative methods. The methods are not mutually exclusive; they can be used in combination to evaluate the risks to which specific vital records are subject and to produce a prioritized list of vital records for which protective measures are recommended.

Qualitative risk assessment is the simpler of the two approaches. It relies principally on group discussions involving knowledgeable persons. **Qualitative risk assessment** is particularly useful for identifying and categorizing physical security problems and other vulnerabilities. A risk assessment team or committee, preferably led by a records manager, identifies and evaluates the dangers to specific vital records series from catastrophic events, theft, misfiling, or other threats.

Qualitative Risk Assessment Considerations

- Geophysical and political factors such as the likelihood of destructive weather or the possibility of warfare or civil unrest
- Reported problems with destruction or loss of records
- Number and types of employees who have access to records
- Records handling procedures that may result in damage to or loss of records
- Physical security, building construction, and access controls in records storage areas
- Proximity of records storage areas to laboratories, factories, or other facilities that contain flammable materials or hazardous substances
- Availability of fire control apparatus and fire department services
- Ability to reconstruct recorded information through backup procedures or other methods

A qualitative risk assessment is usually based on a physical survey of locations where vital records are stored, combined with a review of security procedures already in place. The risk assessment team may consider any of the items listed in the sidebar.

Although the nature and frequency of destructive weather, misfiles, theft of records, or other adverse events are examined and evaluated, qualitative risk assessments do not estimate their statistical probabilities or the financial impact of resulting losses. Instead, consequences and probabilities are evaluated in general terms. Consequences associated with the loss of specific records series, for example, may be categorized as devastating, serious, limited, or negligible. Similarly, the likelihood of significant information loss associated with specific threats may be described as very low, low, medium, high, or very high.

In the project team's assessment, these evaluative designations should be accompanied by definitions or a clarifying narrative. The greatest concern is for vital records with high exposure to threats that have a high probability of occurrence with sudden, unpredictable onset—for example, researchers' notebooks stored in laboratory areas where flammable chemicals are routinely used in scientific experiments, or confidential product specifications and pricing information stored in file cabinets or left on desktops in unsecured office areas.

Quantitative Risk Assessment

Quantitative risk assessment is based on concepts and methods originally developed for product safety analysis and subsequently adapted for computer security applications. Like its qualitative counterpart, quantitative risk assessment relies on site visits, discussions, and other systems analysis methodologies to identify risks, but it uses numeric calculations to estimate the likelihood and impact of losses associated with specific vital records series. The losses are expressed as dollar amounts, which can be related to the cost of proposed protection methods. Compared with qualitative methods, quantitative risk assessment provides a more structured framework for comparing exposures for different vital records series and prioritizing vital records protection recommendations.

Although various quantitative assessment techniques have been proposed by risk analysts and others, all are based on the general risk assessment formula.

The risk assessment formula measures risk, sometimes called the **annualized loss expectancy (ALE)**, as the probable annual dollar loss associated with a specific vital records series. The total expected annual loss to an

Risk Assessment Formula

$$R = P \times C$$

where:

R = the risk associated with the loss of a specific vital records series due to a catastrophic event or other threat

P = the probability that such a threat will occur in any given year

C = the cost of the loss if the threat occurs

organization is the sum of the expected annualized losses calculated for each vital records series.

Quantitative risk assessment begins with the determination of probabilities associated with specific events and the calculation of annualized loss multipliers based on those probabilities. Quantitative risk assessment has a subjective component in so far as the qualitative risk assessment approach is typically used to determine the probabilities. Program unit personnel or others familiar with a given records series are asked to estimate the likelihood of occurrence for specific threats. Whenever possible, their estimates should be based on the historical incidence of adverse events, which can be accurately determined in some cases but only approximated in others. Reliable frequency information is easiest and most conveniently obtained for incidents such as burglaries, fires, power outages, equipment malfunctions, software failures, network security breaches, and virus attacks for which security reports, maintenance statistics, or other documentation exists. The frequency of potentially destructive geophysical or political events, such as hurricanes or terrorist attacks, may likewise be documented in books, newspapers, or other published sources.

In the absence of written evidence or experience, probability estimates must be based on informed speculation by persons familiar with the circumstances in which a given vital records series is maintained and used. Often, a records manager must ask a series of probing questions, followed by lengthy discussion, to obtain usable probability estimates. As an example, the records manager may ask employees of a human resources department whether the inability to locate essential personnel files is likely to occur once a year. If the answer is yes, the records manager should ask whether such an event is likely to occur once every half year, once a quarter, once a month, and so on. This procedure can be repeated until a satisfactorily specific response is obtained.

Once probabilities are estimated, annual loss multipliers can be calculated in any of several ways. Using one method, a calamitous threat to vital records with a given probability of occurrence is assigned a probability value of 1. Other threats are assigned higher or lower values, based on their relative probability of occurrence. As an example, a threat estimated to occur once a year is assigned a probability value of 1, which serves as a baseline for other probability estimates. An event estimated to occur once every three months (four times a year) is assigned a probability value of 4, while an event with an estimated frequency of once every four years is assigned the probability value of 0.25.

Applying the formula given previously, the probability value is multiplied by the estimated cost of the loss if the event occurs. Factors that might be considered when determining costs associated with the loss of vital records include, but are by no means limited to, the following:

- The cost of file reconstruction, assuming that reconstruction is possible
- The value of canceled customer orders, unbillable accounts, or other business losses resulting from the inability to perform specific business operations because needed records are unavailable
- The cost of defending against or otherwise settling legal actions associated with the loss of vital records

Quantitative risk assessment is an aid to judgment not a substitute for it. The risk assessment formula is an analytical tool that can help records managers clarify their thinking and define protection priorities for vital records.

As an example, assume that a hospital, based on previous experience, estimates that one incident occurs per year in which a patient's folder—essential to mission-critical medical care—is lost through misfiling, a clinician's failure to return the folder to the medical records area following treatment, or for some other reason. A probability (P) of 1 is assigned to the risk that a patient folder will be lost in this manner. If the estimated cost (C) is $3,000 to reconstruct medical records contained in the lost folder by obtaining copies of records from physicians' offices, reexamining the patient, repeating medical tests, or other means, the risk (annualized loss expectancy) is 1 times $3,000.

Again based on its experience, the hospital estimates one chance in ten years that as many as 50 patient folders will be destroyed by flood, fire, or destructive weather. A probability (P) of 0.1 is assigned to that risk, indicating that this type of loss is one-tenth as likely to occur as the loss of one patient folder per year for reasons described previously; but the risk affects many more folders. If the cost (C) to reconstruct lost patient records is $3,000 per folder, the damage will total $150,000. The risk (annualized loss expectancy) is 0.1 times $150,000, or $15,000.

These calculations indicate that destruction of patient records by a catastrophic event, while having a much lower probability of occurrence, poses a more significant risk than loss of patient records by misfiling or other reasons. Consequently, the catastrophic event should be made a higher priority for vital records protection. Greater attention should be given to protecting records against fire, flood, or destructive weather than to implementing procedures that will prevent misfiling of patient folders.

Risk Control

Risk control is an important component of any vital records program. The purpose of risk control is to safeguard vital records. Where vital records protection is part of a broader business continuity and disaster recovery plan, risk control measures may also safeguard facilities, computer hardware and software, laboratory equipment, and other resources. Regardless of scope, risk control encompasses preventive and protective measures.

As in the example given in the previous section, some recorded information may be reconstructable in the event of a disaster, but the high cost of such reconstruction makes it a last-resort component of risk control. Prevention is the first line of defense against risk. Preventive measures are designed to minimize the likelihood of damage to vital records from one or more of the threats enumerated in the preceding discussion. Preventive measures apply to both working copies and security copies of vital records. By contrast, protective measures typically apply only to security copies, sometimes described as **backup copies**, of vital records. Protective measures permit the reconstruction of essential information and the restoration of business operations if one or more vital records series is destroyed, damaged, or lost.

Whether prevention or protection is involved, risk control begins with heightened security awareness formalized in organizational policy and procedures, which must be communicated to every employee who works with vital records. Information security should be the responsibility of every employee. A directive from senior management to line managers or other key personnel in individual program units should acknowledge the mission-critical importance of vital records and emphasize the need to safeguard them. Risk control guidelines should be conspicuously posted in areas where vital records are stored or used. One person in each program unit should be assigned specific responsibility for the implementation of risk control guidelines. Ideally, that person will also serve as the program unit's records management liaison. Program unit managers should be instructed to review risk control policies and procedures at staff meetings. The records manager should be available as a resource person to address such meetings and clarify risk control policies and procedures. To publicize the vital records initiative, the records manager can prepare articles on vital records and the importance of risk control for employee newsletters, intranet Web pages, or other in-house publications.

Preventive Measures

Preventive risk control measures address the physical environment where vital records are stored and used. To the greatest extent possible, storage facilities for vital records should be located in areas where floods and destructive weather are unlikely. Locations near chemical factories, utility plants, airport landing patterns, and other potential hazards should also be avoided. Vital records repositories should be situated away from high-traffic locations, preferably in buildings or portions of buildings without windows. Often, records managers have little control over the geographic locations where working copies of vital records are maintained, but they can specify storage locations for backup copies. Storage areas for vital records must be properly constructed and include appropriate smoke detection and fire-extinguishing equipment, as discussed in Chapter 4.

Protective Measures

Protective measures permit the reconstruction of vital records to support the restoration of mission-critical operations in the event of a disaster. Such measures have historically relied on specially designed storage enclosures

Preventive Risk Control Measures

The following preventive risk control measures promote the physical security of vital records against malicious destruction or unauthorized access.

- One storage location is easier to secure than many. In this respect, centralized records repositories are preferable to decentralized ones. Where vital records are maintained in user areas, security is difficult to enforce and easily compromised.
- Access to vital records storage areas should be limited to a single supervised entrance. Other doors should be configured as emergency exits with strike bars and audible alarms.
- Access should be restricted to authorized individuals who have a specific business reason for entering such areas. Badges should identify authorized individuals.
- Employees should be instructed to challenge and report suspect persons who enter vital records repositories.
- All containers should be examined on entry into or removal from the vital records repository.
- Janitorial services in the vital records repository must be performed in the presence of authorized employees.
- Areas where vital records are stored or used should never be included in building tours.
- Vital records should be filed in locked drawers, cabinets, or other metal containers until needed and returned to their filing locations immediately after use.
- A "clean desk" policy is recommended. Vital records must never be left unattended on work surfaces, and all vital records must be put away at the end of the workday.
- Confidential personal data, trade secrets, or other sensitive information should not be

continued on page 140

- stored in mobile computing devices, which are easily stolen. If using mobile devices is unavoidable, they must never be left unattended.
- Vital electronic records stored on networked computers can be accessed, and possibly damaged, by remote users. Physical security measures must consequently be supplemented by safeguards against electronic intrusion.
- Access to vital electronic records and their associated software should be controlled by passwords or personal identification numbers.
- Access to computer workstations must be restricted to authorized employees. Computer workstations should be turned off—and locked, if possible—when not in use. They should never be left unattended while operational. System software should automatically terminate a computer session after a predetermined period of inactivity.
- Mission-critical applications and vital electronic records should be isolated from publicly accessible computer resources in organizations connected to the Internet.

and purposeful duplication of records for off-site storage. These measures are most effective when combined.

Specially designed filing cabinets, vaults, and other storage enclosures provide on-site protection of vital records against certain threats. Vital records can be protected against theft, for example, by storing them in locked file cabinets, safes, or other containers, although simple keylocks offer little resistance to a skilled intruder. Containers with high-security keylocks or combination locks are preferable.

Underwriters' Laboratories rates file cabinets, safes, and other containers for their resistance to break-in by prying, drilling, chiseling, hammering, sawing, or other means. A container with a TL-30 rating, for example, will resist attack against the door and front face by high-speed drills, saws, pry bars, grinders, or other mechanical or electrical penetrating tools for 30 minutes. A container with a TRTL-30 or TRTL-60 rating will resist attack against the door and front face by cutting or welding torches and mechanical or electrical tools for 30 or 60 minutes, respectively. A container with a TXTL-60 rating will resist attack against the door and front face by torch, mechanical or electrical tools, and explosives for 60 minutes. Other Underwriters' Laboratories ratings measure resistance to an attack against all surfaces. As discussed in Chapter 4, Underwriters' Laboratories also rates insulated storage containers, which offer some protection against fire by limiting the records' exposure to potentially destructive heat for a defined time period.

Although tamperproof and fire-resistant storage containers can prove useful in certain situations, the most effective approach to vital records protection involves the purposeful preparation of backup copies for storage at a secure off-site location. Microfilming is usually the best practice for production of backup copies of vital paper records. Compared to full-size photocopies, microfilm copies are usually faster and cheaper to produce, and they require less storage space at the off-site location, which is an important consideration where backup copies will be housed in a commercial records center that charges by the amount of space consumed. A cubic-foot container can store over ninety 215-foot rolls of 16mm microfilm, which can contain almost half a million letter-size pages reduced 24×. By contrast, a cubic-foot container can store about 1,200 letter-size photocopies. When records are microfilmed for retention purposes, additional backup copies can be produced at a small incremental cost.

The production of backup copies of essential electronic records at predetermined intervals is routine operating procedure in most mainframe and minicomputer installations and for information stored on network servers. However, backup operations may be performed sporadically, if at all, in desktop computer installations where procedures are typically less routinized and users may be unaware of the need for backup copies. For effective vital records protection, backup responsibilities must be clearly delineated. Backup schedules must be established and rigidly enforced.

Off-site storage repositories for vital records may be established and operated by a business, government agency, or other organization on its own behalf. Alternatively, a commercial records center or data vault may be utilized for off-site storage. In either case, the off-site facility must be secure. Some vital records repositories are located underground in salt, limestone, or iron mines. The best facilities combine natural restrictions on accessibility with armed guards and electronic surveillance apparatus for stringent perimeter security.

Backup copies of vital records must be stored at a sufficient distance from the working copies so that they are unaffected by the same natural disasters or destructive events. The storage facility must be close enough, however, for convenient delivery of vital records as well as timely retrieval of backup copies to support disaster recovery. For pick-up and delivery of records, some in-house and commercial storage facilities offer courier services equipped with environmentally controlled trucks or vans. Some facilities also support electronic vaulting in which backup copies of vital electronic records are transmitted to off-site storage over high-speed telecommunications facilities.

The typical vital records repository has suitable storage facilities for paper documents, microforms, and electronic media, although some data vaults exclude paper records to minimize the danger of fire. Environmental specifications appropriate to the type of media being stored and the retention period for recorded information must be observed. Backup electrical generators should be available to maintain environmental controls in the event of power outages.

Auditing for Compliance

Once vital records are identified and appropriate loss control methods specified, the implementation of preventive and protective measures for designated records series will usually be the responsibility of personnel in the program unit that maintains the records. Periodic audits should be performed to confirm compliance. Such audits may be conducted by records management staff or delegated to another organizational unit, such as an internal audit department, that has other compliance-oriented responsibilities. In such cases, auditing for vital records compliance can be coordinated with financial or other auditing activities, thereby simplifying the scheduling of audits as well as saving both time and labor. Internal auditors can report the results of vital records compliance audits to the records manager for follow-up and corrective action where indicated. To gain the attention of top management, the internal audit reports should also be distributed to those persons who receive reports of important financial audits.

Chapter 7

Managing Active Records I: Document Filing Systems

As discussed in preceding chapters, the systematic management of inactive records emphasizes timely destruction of obsolete records and cost-effective storage of recorded information that must be retained for specific periods of time. The systematic management of vital records emphasizes protection and recoverability of mission-critical information assets. By contrast, the systematic management of active records is principally concerned with the organization of recorded information for retrieval when needed. By definition, active records are likely to be retrieved until the matters to which they pertain are resolved.

Active records may be organized for retrieval in two ways: They can be filed, or they can be indexed. An **index** is a list of names, identifiers, subject terms, or other descriptors together with references (pointers) to the documents with which the descriptors are associated. **Filing**, the subject of this chapter, organizes information by identifying related records and placing them in close physical proximity to one another—in the same folder, in the same drawer, in the same cabinet, and so on. Broadly defined, a **file** is a collection of related records that are stored and used together. *Indexing*, by contrast, creates lists of descriptive words or phrases that apply to specific records without regard to their physical arrangement. Filing relies principally on manual methods that physically group and arrange related records so that they can be located when needed. Automated document storage and retrieval technologies, which are discussed in Chapter 8, usually employ indexing as an alternative to filing; but the two approaches are not mutually exclusive. Manual filing systems can have an indexing component, and some computer-based document management systems use filing concepts to organize electronic records.

As the name implies, a **filing system** provides a coherent, methodical approach to the organization of records in a specific application or situation. To be truly systematic, a filing system must encompass all components related to the organization of records. Those components include, but are not necessarily limited to, written policies and procedures, clerical and supervisory personnel, filing equipment, filing supplies, and office space or other facilities where filing activities will be performed or where filed documents will be stored. Among their responsibilities, many records managers plan, implement, and, in some cases, operate filing systems for specific collections of records. Such initiatives involve, but are not necessarily limited to, preparing policies and procedures that define a filing system's purpose, scope, and operating characteristics; developing filing arrangements that can effectively address users' retrieval requirements; selecting or advising about the selection of appropriate filing equipment and supplies; and supervising file room operations. This chapter examines records management principles and practices that guide these activities. The chapter begins with a discussion of centralized filing, followed by surveys of file arrangements, equipment, and supplies. The chapter is written from an analytical and managerial perspective. It emphasizes essential concepts; it does not explain how to file. The section on alphabetic filing, for example, examines important characteristics and considerations that affect the implementation and performance of alphabetic arrangements. It does not provide a detailed explanation of alphabetic filing rules, which are well covered in other publications.

Although principles and practices discussed in this chapter were originally developed for paper documents, they also apply to photographic records, such as film negatives and microforms, and to electronic documents such as word processing files, e-mail messages, spreadsheets, presentation aids, and computer-aided design files. Modern computer operating systems use filing models and terminology to organize recorded information; media directories and subdirectories are conceptualized as folders, for example, while local hard drives and network file servers are the electronic counterparts of in-office filing cabinets and centralized file installations, respectively. The filing system principles and practices presented here do not apply to all electronic records, however. Database records, which are organized and retrieved by the software that creates and maintains them, are a notable exception. Although filing concepts can be applied to electronic document images, most imaging implementations employ the indexing principles and practices discussed in Chapter 8.

Central Files

In many companies, government agencies, and other organizations, records associated with selected business processes, operations, or activities are consolidated for filing in a single location where authorized persons can access them. Widely encountered examples include student transcripts in an academic institution, patient records in a hospital or medical clinic, deeds and mortgages in a county clerk's office, client files in a social services agency, incident reports in a police department, claims processing records in an insurance company, litigation files in a law firm, customer account records in a financial services company, laboratory notebooks in a pharmaceutical company, and engineering drawings in a manufacturing company. Such consolidated collections of records are often described as **central files**, but that phrase encompasses a variety of filing configurations. Recordkeeping can be centralized at any level in an organization. A central file may serve an entire enterprise, one or more divisions or departments, a workgroup or project team, or any subset or combination thereof. Central filing concepts are applicable to paper, photographic, and electronic records. In computer installations, databases, word processing documents, spreadsheets, or other information may be centralized on network file servers at the workgroup, departmental, or enterprise levels.

Information sharing is a major motive for centralized filing. As their defining characteristic, central files are shared files. Where recorded information must be available to more than one worker, consolidated document repositories are usually preferable to decentralized filing arrangements in which records relating to a particular business process, operation, or activity are scattered in multiple locations. Often such decentralized files are kept in the work areas of individual employees. Thus, members of a project team may each keep their own records relating to those aspects of a project for which they are responsible. Each team member possesses a subset of project information. Individual files may be organized differently, even idiosyncratically. If a team member is absent from work, reassigned, or otherwise unavailable, locating documents needed by others can be difficult or impossible. A well-organized central file of project documents can address this problem by providing a single, authoritative, presumably complete repository of recorded information about all aspects of a project. Such a repository increases the likelihood that team members will have full access to information about the project's purpose, scope, and activities, including accomplishments and problems outside of their areas of direct responsibility. The repository might be centralized in the project team's work area or combined with other project files at the department, division, or enterprise level.

Other advantages of centralized filing are based on a straightforward principal: Recorded information is easier to manage in one location than in many locations. In particular:

- Centralized file rooms can be configured for economical high-density storage. When compared with decentralized filing of an equivalent quantity of records in cabinets scattered throughout office areas, consolidated files typically require less floor space, equipment, and supplies.

- Centralized filing permits more efficient and effective use of administrative personnel when compared to decentralized arrangements in which administrative employees perform filing in addition to word processing, answering the telephone, making photocopies, arranging meetings, and other tasks, which have high visibility and often must be performed immediately. In such situations, filing may be treated as a low-priority activity that can be deferred until other work is completed. In a centralized installation, by contrast, filing is the top priority. Central file room employees have narrowly focused duties, which simplifies training, facilitates work scheduling, encourages accuracy and reliability as experience is gained with a particular collection of records, and promotes accountability.

- Because records are kept in a single location and serviced exclusively by designated employees, centralized filing facilitates the implementation of uniform file arrangements and consistent recordkeeping procedures, including timely purging of obsolete records with elapsed retention periods.

- By making a single complete repository of recorded information available to authorized persons, a central file can minimize duplicate recordkeeping.

- Compared with decentralized filing arrangements, central files provide better security for confidential records. Central file rooms are typically supervised during normal business hours. To restrict access at other times, they can be equipped with locks, alarms, and other anti-intrusion mechanisms. Central file room employees can log all retrieval requests, ensure that access to specific records is limited to authorized persons, and keep track of records that have been removed from the file room.

To realize these advantages, a central file must have a written policy that defines the file's purpose and scope. The policy must identify the business applications that the central file will serve, the types of records to be included in the central file and, where applicable, the types of records that are excluded. The policy must be supported by clear written procedures that specify who is responsible for submitting records to the central file, and when and how they are to be submitted. Generally, employees who create or receive documents or other records that come within the scope of a central file should be instructed to submit one copy of such records as soon as possible after the records are created or received. To ensure file completeness, all relevant records must be submitted. Where doubt exists about the appropriateness of submitting a specific record to the central file, it should be sent. The central file staff will reject inappropriate records and return them to the submitter.

The advantages of centralized filing generally outweigh the most widely cited disadvantage: A central file area may not be located in convenient proximity to all authorized users. As a result, employees often withhold records they consult frequently, thereby compromising the completeness of a central file. To address this problem, employees may be allowed to keep convenience copies of records submitted to a central file. The quantity of such convenience copies should be limited, and they should be discarded when no longer needed. The problem of proximity does not apply to centralized filing of electronic records on network servers. As discussed in Chapter 8, automated document storage and retrieval systems employ central filing concepts but nullify proximity concerns by providing electronic access to records when needed.

File Arrangements

A **file arrangement** places logically related records into a predetermined sequence for retrieval when needed. Records may be arranged by the name of a person or organization to which they pertain; by a numeric identifier for a case, project, or transaction; by date; by a code that represents the way a name is pronounced; by a geographic unit; or by subject categories. The following sections describe these file arrangements, emphasizing their most important characteristics and the type of records management applications and retrieval requirements for which they are best suited.

Alphabetic Filing

An often cited records management aphorism advises filing system planners to select an arrangement that corresponds to the way in which records are requested. Although that advice is necessarily oversimplified, it frequently applies to alphabetic arrangements, which are well suited to records requested by the name of a person or organization. Examples include personnel files, student records, patient records, and customer files. Alphabetic arrangements are also widely, but less successfully, used for topical subject files. As discussed later in this chapter, hierarchical subject arrangements are often preferable for that purpose.

Basic *alphabetic filing* concepts are straightforward and familiar. Letters are ranked in alphabetic sequence from A to Z. File arrangement is determined by the spelling of filing units, which consist of personal names, corporate names,* subject headings, or other words or phrases that represent the contents of folders, documents, index cards, microfiche, or other objects. In most cases, the filing unit is contained within or inscribed upon the object to be filed. Tabs of file folders, for example, are labeled with names or other words that identify the documents they contain. Alphabetization is performed word by word and, within words, letter by letter. If the first words on two folder tabs are identical, alphabetization is based on the second words; if the second words are identical, alphabetization is based on the third words; and so on. If the first letters of two words are identical, alphabetization is based on the second letter; if the second letters are identical, alphabetization is based on the third letter; and so on.

Some alphabetic filing practices are so widely observed that they require little comment—personal names, for example, are customarily reversed so that the initial filing unit is the surname—but rules are necessary to ensure consistent filing practices and facilitate retrieval in special situations. Common examples include, but are not limited to, the following:

- Hyphenated surnames, such as *Smith-Kline*
- Surnames that begin with a prefix, such as *Van* or *Von*, followed by a space
- Personal names with suffixes, such as *Jr.* or *MD*
- Acronyms and abbreviations, such as *ARMA* and *Corp.*
- Company names that begin with *The*
- Government names that begin with common expressions, such as *Department of* or *City of*
- Corporate and government names with embedded prepositions, such as *Commonwealth of Kentucky*
- Company names, such as *3M Company* or *Amazon.com*, that include numbers, punctuation marks, or other nonalphabetic characters.

---

*   *Anglo-American Cataloging Rules,* Second Edition, published by the American Library Association, defines a corporate body as an organization or group of persons that is identified by a particular name and that acts or may act as an entity. This broad definition encompasses businesses, government agencies, professional associations, educational and cultural institutions, labor unions, community groups, and clubs, among other organizations.

Although library publications, such as the *ALA Filing Rules*, published by the American Library Association, and the *Library of Congress Filing Rules*, provide comprehensive alphabetization guidelines, they are principally intended for catalog entries and other bibliographic records that describe books or other publications.[**] The ANSI/ARMA 1-1995 standard, *Alphabetic Filing Rules*, is a more useful authority for business records. It provides specific recommendations with clear examples for alphabetization of personal and corporate names and for preparation of cross-references for abbreviations and acronyms. Records managers responsible for planning and supervising alphabetic filing operations can accept the ANSI/ARMA guidelines in their entirety or adapt them for their own purposes. In either case, written alphabetization procedures and staff training sessions, repeated periodically, are essential for successful implementation of an alphabetic file arrangement.

Alphabetic file arrangements are compatible with both drawer- and shelf-type filing equipment discussed later in this chapter. Guides or other dividers, marked with single- or double-letter alphabetic designations, can separate groups of individual folders and draw the user's eye to the desired alphabetic section of a drawer or shelf. Alphabetic file arrangements can also employ color coding for misfile detection.

Numeric Filing

Numeric arrangements are widely used for case files, customer order files, financial records, insurance policy and claim files, and other records that are numbered and that, when needed, are requested by an identifying number. Numeric arrangements are also used for name files or other alphabetic files that are converted to numeric codes for filing purposes. Advocates of this approach contend that numeric coding increases privacy and decreases training requirements and filing labor. Compared with alphabetic arrangements, numeric filing requires fewer rules to cover special situations, although a name-to-file-number index must be created in most cases.

Sequential numeric filing is the simplest and most widely encountered type of numeric arrangement. As its name indicates, a sequential numeric filing system features a consecutive arrangement of numbered folders with higher numbered folders placed after lower numbered ones. Thus, the folder for case number 403581 comes after the folder for case number 403580 and before the folder for case number 403582. Like alphabetic arrangements, sequential numeric systems are compatible with drawer- and shelf-type filing cabinets. Preprinted or customized guides can be used to subdivide drawers or shelves into readily identifiable segments. Numeric identifiers can be color-coded to simplify misfile detection.

Sequential numeric filing systems are easily learned and implemented, but several significant disadvantages can limit their usefulness:

- In many filing installations, numeric identifiers are sequentially assigned to newly created folders as cases are opened, orders are received, financial transactions are

---

[**] Some library filing practices may be confusing or unacceptable for business applications. For example, *ALA Filing Rules* equate names that begin with "Mc" and "Mac," so that "McDougal" and "MacDougal" are treated as identical spellings. Both are filed after names that begin with "Mab."

processed, insurance policies are written, or claims are submitted. According to the previously discussed concept of an information life cycle, records are consulted most frequently when they are newest and the matters to which they pertain are unresolved. Where file numbers are sequentially assigned, the highest numbered and presumably most active folders will be clustered together in drawers or on shelves. In busy filing installations, those areas can become congested. Administrative workers may have to stand in line to retrieve folders from those drawers or shelves and to replace them when they are returned to the filing area. By contrast, access to filing cabinets containing lower numbered folders, which are older and less active, is usually much easier.

- As a related limitation, this unbalanced distribution of retrieval and refiling activity prohibits the assignment of particular cabinets, drawers, or shelves to designated administrative employees, a technique that promotes accountability for accurate filing procedures.

- Sequential numeric filing systems usually require the time-consuming movement or "backshifting" of folders to make room for newly created records as older records are purged from drawers or shelves.

The *terminal-digit filing* method was developed to address these limitations. It is intended for large records repositories, such as a medical records room in a hospital, a central policy file in an insurance company, or a cumulative student records file in a university registrar's office. A terminal-digit filing installation is divided into 100 primary sections, each of which is subdivided into 100 secondary sections. Primary sections may be file cabinets, drawers, or sections of shelving units. They are identified by the digits 00 through 99. Within each primary section, the secondary sections are identified by file guides, which are labeled with the digits from 00 through 99. The terminal-digital method is based on a nonsequential numeric arrangement. Case numbers, account numbers, claim numbers, or other numeric folder identifiers are transposed for filing in specific primary and secondary sections. The transposition is based on the following procedure:

- The folder identifier is divided into three sets of digits. Terminal-digit filing works best with six-digit numeric identifiers that can be divided into three pairs of two digits. Thus, the case number 403581 would be divided for filing and retrieval purposes into 40-35-81. The third pair (81)—the terminal-digits—is considered the primary filing unit, the middle pair (35) is considered the secondary filing unit, and the first pair (40) is considered the tertiary filing unit. As noted previously, the terminal-digit method is intended for large filing installations. Six-digit numeric identifiers can accommodate up to one million folders. Terminal-digital filing with shorter or longer numeric identifiers is possible but not optimal. Shorter numeric identifiers must be padded with zeros, in front or back, to reach the six-digit length. Longer identifiers, such as social security numbers, can be truncated to six digits, but that approach may yield duplicate folder numbers. Alternatively, the secondary or tertiary filing units can have more than two digits.

- The numeric identifier is read backwards in primary, secondary, and tertiary unit sequence. Thus, the folder for case number 40-35-81 will be filed as if it read 81-35-40. Note that the case number, claim number, or other numeric identifier on the folder tab is not actually changed. The number is transposed for filing and retrieval purposes only.

- The folder is placed into the appropriate primary section behind the appropriate secondary file guides. For case number 403581, the folder will be filed in primary section 81 behind secondary guide 35 where it will be the fortieth folder, surrounded by folders for case numbers 393581 and 413581.

As their defining characteristic, terminal-digital transpositions radically alter the sequence of folders within cabinet drawers or on shelves. In a sequential numeric arrangement, the folder for case number 403581 would be filed in primary section 40 behind secondary guide 35 where it would be the eighty-first folder, surrounded by folders for case numbers 403580 and 403582. (See Figure 7-1.) Where numeric identifiers are sequentially assigned to newly created folders, the terminal-digit method evenly distributes the newest and presumably most active records throughout a filing installation, thereby eliminating contention and congestion resulting from clustering of active records within a few drawers or shelves. Distribution of the most active records or folders is the principal advantage of terminal-digit filing. In a large, active file room, administrative workers may be assigned to specific groups of cabinets with reasonable assurance that filing, retrieval, and refiling workloads will be equitably distributed. Because records are evenly distributed within primary sections and behind secondary file guides, backshifting of folders following purging of older records is not necessary. Identifying older records eligible for destruction or transfer to off-site storage can be difficult, however, because these files will be scattered throughout the terminal-digit arrangement.

Although terminal-digit filing procedures may seem initially confusing, they are soon mastered with practice. The terminal-digit system's proponents argue that it is easier to use, faster, and more accurate than sequential numeric filing. As with sequential numeric filing, terminal-digit systems are compatible with drawer- and shelf-type file cabinets. Numeric identifiers can be color-coded to simplify misfile detection.

Middle-digit filing is a variant form of nonsequential numeric arrangement. Like the terminal-digit method, it divides a six-digit folder identifier into three pairs of digits, but the middle pair is considered the primary filing unit, followed by the first pair then the terminal pair. Thus, the folder for case number 403581 would be read as 35-40-81 for filing or retrieval. The folder would be filed in primary section 35 behind file guide 40 where it would be the eighty-first folder. Middle-digit filing offers the same advantages as terminal-digital filing. Compared with sequential numeric filing, newly created folders and administrative workloads are more evenly distributed throughout a filing installation, and no need exists to backshift folders when older records are purged. Because they are scattered throughout a middle-digit filing installation, however, identifying older records that are eligible for destruction or transfer to off-site storage can be difficult.

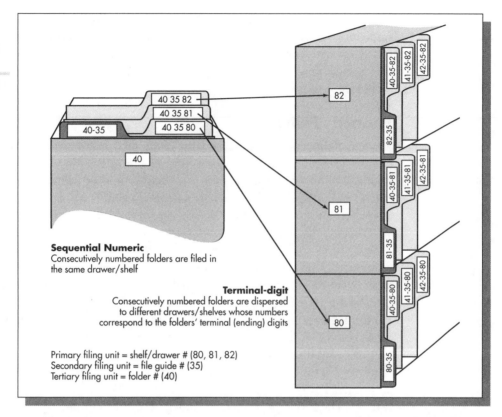

Sequential Numeric
Consecutively numbered folders are filed in the same drawer/shelf

Terminal-digit
Consecutively numbered folders are dispersed to different drawers/shelves whose numbers correspond to the folders' terminal (ending) digits

Primary filing unit = shelf/drawer # (80, 81, 82)
Secondary filing unit = file guide # (35)
Tertiary filing unit = folder # (40)

Alphanumeric filing systems, in which folder identifiers combine alphabetic characters and numeric digits, are sometimes categorized as numeric filing methods, but they have more in common with alphabetic arrangements. Depending on the filing rules in use, numeric digits may be sorted before or after alphabetic characters.

Chronologic Filing

In *chronologic filing*, a variant form of numeric filing, records are arranged by date. Early filing systems consisted of simple chronologic log books that listed all records created or received by an organization. Typically, the records themselves were also filed in chronologic order. Although some organizations continue to log all or selected documents chronologically, that approach typically supplements other filing methodologies. As their principal limitation, chronologic logs are not compatible with demanding retrieval requirements. To identify a given document, large portions of a log must be examined.

Today, chronologic filing is most often used for copies of outgoing correspondence, which are also stored in a subject file. Sometimes described as *reader files*, chronologic correspondence files were originally developed to keep selected employees advised about important developments, as reflected in outgoing correspondence. They also provide a convenient method of identifying correspondence that cannot be located in a subject file. Before photocopiers were invented, reader files consisted of carbon copies on lightweight paper described as "onionskin."

Chronologic filing can be used for transaction files, including so-called *tickler* or *suspense* systems in which records are filed by the date on which they must be consulted or acted upon. Whether used for correspondence or transaction records, chronologic files are organized by year with subdivisions, if necessary, for each day within the year.

Phonetic Filing

Phonetic filing was developed for large name files where surnames may sound alike but are subject to spelling variations or frequent misspellings. In a primitive form of phonetic filing, one of the possible spellings of a given surname is selected for use and all variant spellings of that surname are filed under that form. Cross-references are placed into the file to direct the user from variations to the accepted spelling.

The *Soundex method* offers a more sophisticated and effective approach to phonetic filing. Sometimes described as the *Russell Soundex method*, it was initially developed by Robert Russell, who received a patent for an alphanumeric coding scheme for phonetic filing of personal names in 1918. In 1936, Remington Rand proposed a refined version of the Russell Soundex method for a name index to microfilmed records of the 1900 U.S. Census. Soundex was subsequently used to index records of the 1880 and 1920 Censuses, in indexing projects involving twentieth-century immigration records, and to index other records created and maintained by federal and state government agencies. Over the years, computer scientists and others have developed Soundex variants with improved capabilities or special features. The *Daitch-Mokotoff Soundex* system, for example, is particularly useful for European surnames. Soundex systems have been applied to medical records, birth and death records, prison inmate records, bank customer records, insurance policy holder files, and other records that might otherwise be arranged alphabetically by name. They are also used by database management systems, Internet search engines, and other software that prepares name indexes.

Remington Rand's version of Soundex filing is the most widely encountered form of this file arrangement. Described as the *American Soundex* method, surnames are converted to a four-character alphanumeric code that generally results in the identical filing of similar sounding names of different spellings. In Soundex coding, the first letter of the surname becomes the first alphanumeric code character. All vowels and the consonants *h*, *w*, and *y* are ignored, and the first three remaining characters are converted to numeric digits using the following table:

Letters	Code Number
B,F,P,V	1
C,G,J,K,W,S,X,Z	2
D,T	3
L	4
M,N	5
R	6

Thus, the surname *Johnson* would be coded as J525, as would *Jonson*, and *Jahnsen*. If a name lacks a sufficient number of consonants, the code is completed with zeros. *Smith* is coded as S530, as is *Smythe*. Double letters are treated as a single character, as are adjacent characters with an equivalent numeric value in the Soundex table. American Soundex coding can yield confusing results. *Mailer, Miller, Mueller,* and *Mahler* are each coded as M460 despite noticeable differences in pronunciation. *Peterson* and *Petersen* are each coded as P362, but so are *Peters* and *Petrosian*. On the other hand, phonetically identical names may be coded differently. Examples include *Kohn* (K500), *Cohn* (C500), *Moskowitz* (M232), and *Moskovitz* (M213).

Soundex codes are filed according to rules for alphanumeric arrangements. In large filing installations, many folders will have the same Soundex code. The file folder tab is consequently inscribed with both the Soundex code and the person's name.

Geographic Filing

Geographic filing arrangements are recommended where records are requested by location. In a geographic arrangement, documents are filed by street addresses, counties, municipalities, states or provinces, countries, postal codes, tax map subdivisions, or combinations of these geographic designations. Although less commonly used than alphabetic and numeric arrangements, geographic filing is well suited to a variety of records. Political, topological, weather, and road maps produced by cartographers, geologists, meteorologists, petroleum exploration and mining companies, urban planners, and property surveyors are obvious candidates for geographic arrangement, but some business documents are filed geographically as well. Municipal building departments, for example, typically maintain property folders that are arranged by section-block-lot designations or by street address. Individual folders may contain ownership information, property descriptions, building permit applications, code enforcement complaints, and other records for a given property. A social services agency that serves a large geographic area may group case files by the counties or municipalities in which clients live. An operator of fast food restaurants may file records relating to its store locations by country, then by state or province, then by the name of the franchisee. In an insurance agency or office equipment dealer, customer files may be grouped by predetermined sales territories, which may be based on ZIP Codes, municipal boundaries, or other geographic parameters.

Although place names are typically sequenced alphabetically, geographic arrangements sometimes combine alphabetic and numeric filing rules. Street names, for example, are arranged alphabetically, and individual addresses for a given street are sequenced numerically. Geographic arrangements are easily expanded, but large geographic files can have multilevel subdivisions that require complicated combinations of file guides.

Hierarchical Subject Files

Many corporations, government agencies, and other organizations have a need to file documents that relate to specific organizations, events, activities, initiatives, products, or other topics. The contents of such subject files are as varied as the organizations that maintain them and the business operations they support. Subject files may include, but are by no means limited to the following types of records:

- Correspondence and reports
- Budgets and financial information
- Policies and procedures
- Agendas, minutes, handouts, or other materials distributed at meetings
- Planning documents
- Information about contractors and suppliers
- Competitive intelligence
- Information about government agencies', community groups', or other organizations' product specifications and brochures
- Press releases
- Copies of articles or other publications

The purpose and value of subject files likewise vary. They may provide indispensable support for highly focused business operations, or they may contain general reference or background information that is seldom consulted.

As mentioned briefly previously, alphabetic arrangements are compatible with subject filing. In such filing installations, folders labeled with topical headings are arranged, dictionary fashion, in alphabetic order. As an example of this approach, consider a hypothetical subject file of technical and competitive intelligence information in a company that sells magnetic and optical storage media for computer, video, and audio applications. This subject file includes specification sheets, product literature and reviews, copies of publications, and other documents pertaining to specific storage technologies and products. A typical alphabetic section of such a file might include folders with the following topical headings:

AIT	Maxell audio tapes
CD-RW	Mini-DV tapes
DAT	Optical disks
DLT	QIC formats
DVD-R	Recordable CDs
DVD-RAM	Removable hard disks
DVD-RW	Super DLT
DVD+R	Travan tapes
DVD+RW	Verbatim tapes
Floppy disks	VHS cassettes
Imation media	Zip cartridges
LS-120 SuperDisks	8mm data tapes
LTO Ultrium tapes	8mm video tapes
Magneto-optical disks	

This approach to subject filing has several significant shortcomings. The folder list comingles general headings, such as "floppy disks," and more specific headings, such as "Zip cartridges," in a single alphabetic sequence. Information about related subjects, such as the various types of magnetic tapes, is scattered throughout alphabetic sections of the file. None of the general headings are subdivided to reflect specialized facets of a given topic, and, other than expansion within a given alphabetic section, no framework exists for creating new headings. In practice, some folder will likely contain many documents while others will have only a few pages.

Hierarchical subject filing systems, sometimes called *classification systems,* are designed to address these problems. Rather than arranging topical headings in alphabetic sequence, hierarchical systems create a tree-like structure of logically related categories that represent general and specific facets of a given subject or activity. Hierarchical filing systems are conceptually similar to library classifications systems, such as the Dewey Decimal System and the Library of Congress classification system, that organize published information about a wide range of subjects. Like their library counterparts, hierarchical filing systems for records management group related documents and provide a flexible framework for the incorporation of new subjects at various levels in the filing hierarchy. Some hierarchical filing systems—such as the Modern Army Recordkeeping System and its predecessors, the Army Functional Filing System and the War Department Decimal System—are ambitious enterprise-wide solutions to the problem of organizing paper documents. Most hierarchical filing systems, however, have a narrower scope. They are designed to organize documents associated with a specific business activity.

Hierarchical filing systems for records management are typically custom-developed for specific collections of documents. In most cases, a hierarchical filing system replaces an ineffective alphabetic subject arrangement. As a first step, the existing topical headings are studied and divided into top-level categories. For the hypothetical file of magnetic and optical storage media cited above, a hierarchical subject file might include three top-level categories. For example:

Top-Level Subject Categories
Computer media
Video media
Audio media

Each of these top-level categories would be subdivided into second-level categories. For example:

Second-Level Subject Categories
Computer media
    Magnetic disks
    Magnetic tapes
    Optical disks
Video media
    Videocassettes
    Optical disks
Audio media
    Audio cassettes
    Optical disks

These second-level categories may be further subdivided into third-level categories. For example:

Third-Level Subject Categories

Computer media
    Magnetic disks
        Floppy disks
        Removable hard disk cartridges
    Magnetic tapes
        Digital linear tape (DLT)
        Digital audio tape (DAT)
        LTO Ultrium
    8mm data tapes
        QIC tapes
    Optical disks
        Compact disks
        DVD media
        Magneto-optical disks

Third-level categories may require additional subdivisions. For example:

Fourth-Level Subject Categories

Computer media
    Magnetic disks
        Floppy disks
            Standard formats
            Proprietary formats
        Removable hard disk cartridges
    Magnetic tapes
        Digital linear tape (DLT)
            Conventional DLT
            Super DLT
        Digital audio tape (DAT)
        LTO Ultrium
        8mm data tapes
            Conventional 8mm cartridges
            Advanced intelligent tape (AIT)
            Mammoth cartridges
        QIC tapes
            Older QIC formats
            Travan formats
    Optical disks
        Compact disks
            CD-R
            CD-RW
        DVD media
            DVD-R
            DVD-RAM
            DVD-RW
            DVD+R
            DVD+RW
        Magneto-optical disks

If warranted by the quantity and characteristics of documents to be filed, some fourth-level categories may be subdivided. For example:

Fourth-Level Subject Categories, Subdivided

Magnetic disks
    Floppy disks
        Standard formats
        Proprietary formats
            LS-120 SuperDisk cartridges
            Zip cartridges
    Removable hard disk cartridges
Magnetic tapes
    Digital linear tape (DLT)
        Conventional DLT
        Super DLT
    Digital audio tape (DAT)
    LTO Ultrium
    8mm data tapes
        Conventional 8mm cartridges
        Advanced intelligent tape (AIT)
            AIT-1
            AIT-2
            AIT-3
        Mammoth cartridges
    QIC tapes
        Older QIC formats
        Travan formats
            TR-1
            TR-2
             TR-3
             TR-4

Following library models, some hierarchical filing systems assign numeric or alphanumeric designations to categories. Decimal subdivisions are sometimes used to represent the hierarchical interrelationship of categories. For example:

Numeric Subject Category Designations with Decimal Subdivisions

1 Computer media
    1.1 Magnetic disks
        1.1.1 Floppy disks
            1.1.1.1 Standard formats
            1.1.1.2 Proprietary formats
                1.1.1.2.1 LS-120 SuperDisk cartridges
                1.1.1.2.2 Zip cartridges
        1.1.2 Removable hard disk cartridges
    1.2 Magnetic tapes
        1.2.1 Digital linear tape (DLT)
            1.2.1.1 Conventional DLT
            1.2.2.2 Super DLT
        1.2.2 Digital audio tape (DAT)
        1.2.3 LTO Ultrium
        1.2.4 8mm data tapes
            1.2.4.1 Conventional 8mm cartridges
            1.2.4.2 Advanced intelligent tape (AIT)

continued on page 158

```
            1.2.4.2.1 AIT-1
            1.2.4.2.2 AIT-2
            1.2.4.2.3 AIT-3
          1.2.4.3 Mammoth cartridges
        1.2.5 QIC tapes
          1.2.5.1 Older QIC formats
          1.2.5.2 Travan formats
            1.2.5.2.1 TR-1
            1.2.5.2.2 TR-2
            1.2.5.2.3 TR-3
            1.2.5.2.4 TR-4
      1.3 Optical disks
        1.3.1 Compact disks
          1.3.1.1 CD-R
          1.3.1.2 CD-RW
        1.3.2 DVD media
          1.3.2.1 DVD-R
          1.3.2.2 DVD-RAM
          1.3.2.3 DVD-RW
          1.3.2.4 DVD+R
          1.3.2.5 DVD+RW
        1.3.3 Magneto-optical disks
```

As its principal feature and most attractive characteristic, the hierarchical approach to subject filing is truly systematic. Encompassing all facets of a given application, the logical organization and subordination of subject categories mirrors the application's scope and provides a place for every document—the more general the document, the higher its place in the hierarchy; the more specific the document, the lower its place in the hierarchy. In the previous example, technical specification sheets, brochures, copies of publications, or other documents about DVD-R media will be filed in the 1.3.2.1 category. Documents that deal with several different DVD formats—the catalog of a vendor that sells both DVD-R and DVD-RW formats, for example—will be filed one level up in the 1.3.2 category. Documents that deal with DVD and compact disk media will be filed in the 1.3 category, which encompasses all optical disks. File categories are selected from a master list that must be updated periodically as categories are added, revised, or deleted.

Hierarchical filing systems provide useful retrieval functionality. In particular, hierarchical filing systems facilitate browsing of related documents, which are physically grouped within categories. In alphabetic subject arrangements, by contrast, related documents may be scattered in multiple folders, each labeled with a different topical heading. Hierarchical subject arrangements also permit the retrieval of documents at varying levels of specificity. In the above example, all information about magnetic tapes can be obtained by examining the entire 1.2 category with its various subdivisions, while documents relating to specific magnetic tape formats can be retrieved by consulting the appropriate third- or fourth-level categories.

Hierarchical subject filing systems are readily expandable. New categories can be introduced at any level in the hierarchy without affecting other categories, and existing categories can be subdivided as necessary. In the previous example, fourth-level categories may be added if new DVD formats are introduced, and existing DVD categories may be subdivided, if desired, to differentiate specific products or vendors. Such subdivisions may be needed to manage large quantities of documents in a given category.

As their principal disadvantage, hierarchical subject filing systems are time-consuming and difficult to construct. They typically require a comprehensive understanding of the subject area with which the documents to be filed are associated. Thus, to develop a hierarchical subject filing system for a company that sells magnetic and optical storage media, a records manager must be familiar with the storage media industry and with information storage requirements for computer, video, and audio applications. As a further limitation, hierarchical systems provide only one place for filing a given document. It is consequently best suited to correspondence, reports, or other documents that deal with a single subject. If a document deals with multiple subjects, it is typically filed in the category for the principal subject. This limitation can be addressed by copying documents for filing in multiple categories, a common approach that greatly increases the size of a file, or by making cross-references among related categories, a procedure that must be followed faithfully to be effective. A simple method of cross-referencing involves copying the first page of a long document for filing in multiple categories. An annotation on the first page indicates the location of the complete document.

Filing Equipment and Supplies

To be readily retrievable when needed, records must be properly arranged, but an effective filing installation also requires appropriate equipment and supplies. Properly selected, filing equipment and supplies can clarify file arrangements, enhance productivity in filing and refiling operations, simplify the identification and retrieval of records when needed, protect records from damage, and prevent unauthorized access to recorded information. The following sections describe the most common types of filing cabinets, file folders, and accessories. The discussion emphasizes features and functions that affect the utility of these filing system components in specific records management applications.

Vertical Files

Vertical-style drawer-type filing cabinets, simply known as *vertical files*, were introduced in the late nineteenth century as alternatives to cabinets that stored folded documents in small compartments. Wooden cabinets, the original configuration, were ultimately supplanted by metal construction. Often preferred in installations where functionality is more important than aesthetics or where wall space is limited, vertical files are the most widely encountered storage containers for office records. They are available in models that measure 15 inches wide for letter-size pages and 18 inches wide for legal-size documents. Letter-size cabinets are preferable to legal-size models, which cost more, require more expensive filing supplies, and occupy more floor space. Special vertical filing cabinets are available for small records, such as index cards and microforms, or for large records such as computer printouts.

A typical letter- or legal-size vertical file cabinet measures 27 or 28 inches deep and provides about 25 linear inches of filing space per drawer. Within each drawer, documents are filed from front to back. A follower block mechanism keeps folders upright when a drawer is partially full. Cabinet capacity depends on several factors, including the number of drawers, document characteristics, and the ratio of pages to file folders. A reasonably full vertical file drawer can hold 2,000 to 2,500 pages allowing space for folders and file guides. Very full drawers may contain more than 3,000 pages. The number of drawers per cabinet ranges from two to five. The four-drawer vertical file is the most common configuration. (See Figure 7-2.) Five-drawer cabinets offer greater storage capacity without an increase in floor space consumption, but the

Vertical File Cabinet with Folder Tabs Aligned on the Right

Figure 7-2

(Courtesy: Smead)

top drawer can be hard to reach and, when fully extended, may tip the cabinet forward. Two- and three-drawer vertical files are typically employed in desk-side or under-desk installations.

ANSI/BIFMA X5.3, *American National Standard for Office Furnishing—Vertical Files*, presents technical specifications developed by the Business and Institutional Furniture Manufacturer's Association. Desirable features include 22-guage steel construction (wood cabinets remain available to meet special décor requirements), drawers that open and close easily, counterweights or other mechanisms that prevent tipping when multiple drawers are open at the same time, and full-height drawers that keep documents in place and permit the use of hanging file folders without special frames. Although most vertical file cabinets are lockable, some models are equipped with combination locks or pick-resistant key locks for extra protection. Federal Specification FF-L-2740 presents requirements for combination locks for secure file cabinets. Some vertical file cabinets have Class 5 and Class 6 GSA security ratings that satisfy the requirements of Federal Specification AA-F-358H for file cabinets that store classified documents. Class 5 cabinets are rated for resistance to forced entry. Class 6 cabinets are not.

Insulated vertical files provide fire protection, but they are up to ten times more expensive than conventional models. Like the fire-resistant safes discussed in Chapter 4, insulated file cabinets for paper records are rated by Underwriters Laboratories for the period of time, in hours or fractions thereof, that interior drawer temperatures will remain below 350 degrees Fahrenheit (175 degrees Celsius) when exposed to fire temperatures up to 1,700 degrees Fahrenheit (920 degrees Celsius). Cabinets that pass the test are described as Class 350 products. Thus, a Class 350-1 hour cabinet will maintain interior drawer temperatures below 350 degrees Fahrenheit for one hour. Underwriters Laboratories imposes more stringent fire-resistance requirements for file cabinets that store electronic media. Described as Class 125 products, such cabinets must maintain an interior temperature below 125 degrees Fahrenheit (53 degrees Celsius) with a relative humidity below 85 percent for a specified period of time. File cabinets that combine fire- and impact-resistance are recommended for installations above ground level. Cabinets that pass Underwriters Laboratories' impact test will remain intact when exposed to high temperatures for 30 minutes then dropped onto concrete rubble from a height of 30 feet.

Lateral Files

With vertical filing cabinets, depth exceeds width. With lateral drawer-type cabinets, simply known as *lateral files*, width exceeds depth. Most lateral files measure 18 inches deep. The most popular cabinet widths are 30 and 36 inches. Some manufacturers also offer lateral cabinets that measure 42 inches wide. Although vertical files are available in letter- and legal-size models, lateral file drawers can accommodate both letter- and legal-size pages. (See Figure 7-3.) Documents are usually filed from side to side within each drawer. Alternatively, a drawer can be divided into sections for front-to-back filing.

Lateral file capacity depends on several factors, including the number and width of drawers, document characteristics, and the ratio of pages to file folders. A 36-inch lateral cabinet drawer provides about 33 linear inches of side-to-side filing space. A

Lateral Filing Cabinet

Figure 7-3

(Courtesy: Herman Miller)

reasonably full drawer can hold 2,600 to 3,300 pages, allowing space for folders and guides. A very full drawer may contain more than 4,000 pages. A 30-inch lateral cabinet drawer provides about 27 inches of side-to-side filing space. A reasonably full drawer can hold 2,500 to 3,000 pages, allowing space for folders and guides. A very full drawer may contain more than 3,600 pages. As with vertical files, the number of drawers per cabinet ranges from two to five. Two- and three-drawer models may be installed under desks or, when fitted with a countertop, used as credenzas. Four- and five-drawer models are the popular configurations. With five-drawer models, the top drawer is usually a roll-out shelf.

Lateral files are often preferred over vertical files for aesthetics, particularly in open plan offices where filing cabinets will be used as room dividers. Some vendors claim that lateral files make more efficient use of floor space than vertical cabinets, but that claim is not correct for letter-size documents. A four-drawer 36-inch lateral file occupies 4.5 feet of floor space and provides 132 linear inches of filing space, or about 30 filing inches per square foot. A four-drawer 30-inch lateral file occupies 3.75 feet of floor space and provides 108 linear inches of filing space or 28.8 filing inches per square foot. By comparison, a four-drawer letter-size vertical file occupies 3 square feet of floor space and provides 100 linear inches of filing space or about 33 filing inches per square foot. Lateral files are slightly more efficient for storing legal-size documents. The floor space requirements and cabinet capacities cited above apply equally to letter- or legal-size pages. By contrast, legal-size vertical filing cabinets require more floor space than letter-size models. A four-drawer legal-size vertical file occupies 3.5 square feet of floor space and provides 100 linear inches of filing space or about 28.5 filing inches per square foot.

Technical specifications for lateral files are presented in ANSI/BIFMA X5.3, *American National Standard for Office Furnishings—Lateral Files.* Like vertical files, lateral files are available in secure and fire-resistant configurations, although the selection of available products is not as great as it is for vertical cabinets. Lateral files are usually more expensive than vertical files of comparable capacity and construction.

Shelf Files

Whether vertical or lateral in design, drawer-type files are poorly suited to large active filing installations. Vertical and lateral cabinets require wide aisles to accommodate extended drawers. The total floor space requirement is usually 2.5 to 3 times the cabinet's base dimensions. Thus, a letter-size vertical file occupies 3 square feet of space on its base, but the total floor space commitment is about 7.5 to 9 square feet when space is reserved for extended drawers and room for users to stand while accessing open drawers. Further, filing and retrieval productivity are degraded by the time and effort required to pull out and replace drawers. As an added complication, only one person can conveniently access a given cabinet at a time. To prevent tipping, some vertical and lateral cabinets have safety mechanisms that prohibit simultaneous opening of multiple drawers.

Shelf files, sometimes described as *open-shelf filing cabinets,* address these problems. Typically, the filing equipment of choice in large, active centralized file rooms, shelf files are bookcase-like units in which folders are filed from side to side on steel shelves. Multiple units may be joined together, back-to-back and/or side-to-side. Movable dividers help keep folders upright on shelves, which may measure 30, 36, or 42 inches wide. Side-tab folders, which face outward, are preferred for visibility. The shelves themselves may be fixed or adjustable; the latter type is useful where shelf files will store paper records along with microforms, magnetic tapes, or other nonpaper media. With some products, the shelves slide forward for easier access. Some units feature receding front panels that can close over shelves for improved confidentiality and/or appearance. Such configurations resemble lateral drawer-type files, with which they are sometimes confused. (Some lateral cabinets, as previously noted, are fitted with one roll-out shelf in place of the top drawer.) The front panels may be equipped with key locks. Front panels can also protect records from dust.

Compared to vertical and lateral drawer files, shelf files offer greater storage density through more effective use of available floor space. Shelf files are taller than drawer-type cabinets—six-shelf, seven-shelf, or even eight-shelf configurations, which exceed seven feet in height, are available. (See Figure 7-4.) By contrast, the height of drawer-type cabinets rarely exceeds five feet. Shelf files for office records are available in 15- and 18-inch depths for letter- and legal-size folders, respectively. A letter-size

Shelf Filing Installation

Figure 7-4

(Courtesy: Iron Mountain)

unit with six 36-inch shelves occupies 3.75 square feet of floor space and provides 210 filing inches, or about 56 filing inches per square foot—twice as much as lateral or vertical files that occupy the same amount of floor space. A legal-size unit with eight 30-inch shelves occupies 4.5 square feet of floor space and provides 280 filing inches or about 62 filing inches per square foot—again, twice as much as lateral or vertical files that occupy the same amount of floor space. More significantly, shelf cabinets do not require wide aisles to accommodate extended drawers. Compared to vertical or lateral files, more cabinets can be installed and many more records stored in a given area. Because paper records are heavy—about 2.5 pounds per filing inch for letter-size pages—a structural engineering inspection is typically necessary to confirm that the weight of shelving units and records is within floor loading limits.

Floor loading is an important consideration in mobile or compacted shelving installations where shelf files are mounted on tracks. *Mobile shelving systems* increase storage density by drastically reducing aisle space. In a typical installation, a single aisle is allocated to a bank of double-sided shelving units. The end units in the bank are typically anchored in place. The other units slide on tracks. To access a given shelving unit, the adjacent units are moved aside manually or through motorized controls to create an opening. Safety mechanisms restrict the movement of shelving units when someone enters the opening. In a variant form of mobile shelving, single-sided shelving units are installed two or three rows deep on tracks. Shelving units in the front rows slide from side to side to provide access to the units behind them. (See Figure 7-5.) As their principal advantage, mobile shelving systems can increase

Shelf Filing Cabinets with Side-Tab Folders and Roll-Out Shelves for Suspended Folders

Figure 7-5

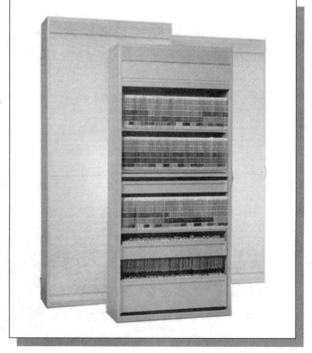

(Courtesy: Russ Bassett)

the records storage capacity of a given area by as much as 50 percent when compared to stationary shelf files and by more than 100 percent when compared to vertical or lateral drawer-type files. Although stationary shelf files are usually less expensive than vertical or lateral drawer-type cabinets on a cost-per-filing-inch basis, mobile shelving is considerably more expensive to acquire and install than stationary filing equipment of any type. Mobile shelving should consequently be reserved for filing installations where large quantities of paper records must be stored in a relatively small amount of space. (See Figure 7-6.) A structural engineering evaluation is mandatory, and floor reinforcement or other costly building modifications may be necessary before mobile shelving can be installed.

Shelf files, whether stationary or mobile, are compatible with alphabetic and numeric file arrangements, and they are the only type of cabinets suitable for terminal-digit filing and for color-coding for misfile detection. Stationary and mobile shelf filing installations are expandable within the confines of available space. Compared to drawer-type filing equipment, however, shelf files are more difficult to move. Often, they must be fully or partially disassembled for transport then reassembled at the new destination. Because mobile shelving would require disassembly and reassembly, it is not practical where file room relocations are likely. Further, shelf files may not be acceptable for confidential records. Shelving units may be fitted with lockable doors, but such locking mechanisms cannot satisfy stringent security requirements. Unlike vertical or lateral drawer-type cabinets, shelf files are not available in fire-resistant models.

**Mobile Shelf
Cabinets**

Figure 7-6

(Courtesy: Spacefile)

Motorized Files

With vertical, lateral, and shelf files, users must go to a specific cabinet and open a drawer or consult a shelf to retrieve desired records. As their name implies motorized files utilize mechanical and/or electronic components to deliver records to users. Motorized files were particularly popular during the 1960s and 1970s when computerized document storage and retrieval systems were largely experimental and very expensive. They remain available, and when properly selected and implemented, they offer fast retrieval, effective security for confidential information, and good storage density for paper records.

The vertical motorized file, the most widely encountered example, dates from the early 1960s. It consists of shelves mounted on a revolving transport mechanism inside a large cabinet. Cabinet heights and shelf widths vary. The shelves may store letter-size folders or documents, legal-size folders or documents, or computer printouts. Special models are available for index cards, microforms, checks, fingerprint cards, and other small records. To retrieve or replace a folder or document, the operator consults an index to determine its shelf location. The index may be manually prepared or computerized. In either case, the operator enters the shelf number at a calculator-style keypad. The transport mechanism revolves to position the indicated shelf at an opening, allowing the operator to remove or replace the desired folder or document.

The vertical motorized file exhibits the advantages and limitations of mechanized filing equipment. Given a suitable index, folders or documents can be located quickly. The newest models can operate under computer control. Following an index search, a computer program initiates shelf movement, eliminating the need to key-enter shelf numbers. To protect confidential information, the opening where records are retrieved or replaced may be covered by a locked door when the vertical motorized file is not in use. A vertical motorized file can store a given quantity of records in about one-third the floor space occupied by vertical or lateral drawer-type cabinets, but vertical motorized files cost substantially more to purchase and maintain than manual files of comparable capacity. Further, as previously noted, high-density storage of large quantities of paper records has structural implications. Floor reinforcement or other expensive site preparation may be required prior to installation of vertical motorized files. Like mobile shelving, vertical motorized files are difficult to move, which makes them a poor choice for departments that change locations frequently. Although vertical motorized files are reliable, downtime is always possible and, over a period of years, inevitable. An equipment malfunction can render records completely inaccessible. As a final, often overlooked limitation, a vertical motorized file works best with a trained equipment operator who will handle all document retrieval requests.

Special Filing Equipment

Most drawer- and shelf-type cabinets are intended for office records, especially letter- or legal-size pages. A variety of special filing equipment is available for smaller and larger records. Vertical files are available for index cards, checks, microforms, tabulating cards, and other small documents. A vertical drawer-type filing cabinet that measures 15 inches wide by 52 inches high by 27 inches deep can store up to 15,000 microfiche or 4-by-6-inch index cards. Some shelf files are specifically designed for X-ray films, which are larger and heavier than office documents.

Flat files are drawer-type cabinets for flat storage of unfolded engineering drawings, architectural plans, maps, prints, circuit diagrams, and other large documents measuring up to 36 by 48 inches (E-size). Flat file cabinets are typically configured with 5 to 10 drawers, each measuring 1.5 to 3 inches deep. A flat file drawer that measures 2 inches deep can hold about 100 drawings when reasonably full. Flat file cabinets with shallow drawers, which store fewer drawings, are more expensive but easier to access. Drawer dividers allow flat files to be used for smaller documents. Hanging files are useful for drawings and large documents that are consulted frequently. The drawings are suspended from rails or clamps. As their name indicates, roll files store rolled drawings or other large documents. Although flat files are preferable for preservation of drawings, roll files are often the only practical storage equipment for drawings that are larger than 36 by 48 inches.

Shelf files have been used for decades in centralized magnetic tape libraries associated with mainframe and mid-range computer installations. Depending on cabinet design, magnetic tape reels may rest on shelves separated by wire racks that maintain the reels in an upright position; alternatively, tape reels may be suspended from clips inserted in a specially designed hanger bar. A 50-inch shelf can hold about 50 reels of magnetic tape wrapped in tape-seal belts and suspended from clips. Shelf capacities are reduced when wire racks are used. A typical cabinet contains five or six shelves, the latter configuration approaching a height of 7 feet. Similar high-capacity shelf files are available for half-inch data cartridges, which have replaced magnetic tape reels in mainframe and mid-range computer installations.

For maximum versatility, several manufacturers offer mixed-media storage units that use interchangeable shelves and racks to accommodate different sizes and types of electronic media within the same cabinet. (See Figure 7-7.) Such a cabinet might, for example, contain one or more hanging bars for magnetic tape reels, several racks for half-inch data cartridges, and additional shelves for hard disk cartridges or optical disks. If desired, shelves and hanging frames can be included for binders, computer printouts, file folders, microfilm, and microfiche trays, thereby permitting storage of electronic media and related human-readable documentation in the same cabinet. Three styles of media cabinets that will accommodate various forms of electronic media and microforms are shown in Figure 7-8.

Drawer-type vertical and lateral filing cabinets are poorly suited to magnetic tape reels, but they are available for smaller media, including data cartridges, videocassettes, audiocassettes, hard disk cartridges, diskettes, and optical disks. A typical 10-drawer unit measures approximately 26 inches wide by 30 inches deep by 60 inches high. Using dividers to partition drawers into multiple rows for media filing, such a cabinet can store approximately 1,250 half-inch data cartridges, 1,300 quarter-inch data cartridges, 2,300 quarter-inch minicartridges, 650 videocassettes, 2,700 audiocassettes, or 12,000 diskettes.

Computer
Printout Cabinet

Figure 7-7

(Courtesy: Steelcase)

Tub files house frequently referenced records in an open cabinet that is accessed from the top. Often mounted on casters, tub files can store paper documents, microforms, or electronic media. A *tub desk*, as its name suggests, combines a tub file with a work surface. *Carousel files* consist of storage racks or bins mounted onto turntables that can be manually rotated. They are available for microforms, magnetic tape cartridges, audiocassettes, videocassettes, diskettes, optical disks, and other media.

File Folders

File folders keep logically related documents together. Manila folders are the most common filing supplies. Manufactured from paperboard and characteristically light tan in color, they are available in letter, legal, metric, and special sizes that, when folded along a designated score line, are slightly larger than the documents they will contain. A letter-size manila folder, for example, measures approximately 11.75 inches wide by 9 inches high, excluding the tab, which typically bears a label or other identifying markings and adds about one-half inch to the folder's height or width. Folders with top tabs are intended for drawer-type vertical or lateral files. Folders with side tabs, also known as *end tabs*, are intended for shelf files. Legal-size manila folders measure 9 by 14.75 inches, excluding the top or side tab. Folder characteristics are described in several national and international standards, including ISO 623, *Paper and Board—Folders and Files—Sizes*; CAN/CGSB 53.30, *File Folders*, published by the Canadian General Standards Board; BS 1467, *Specifications for Folders and Files*, published by the British

Electronic Media and Microform Cabinets

Figure 7-8

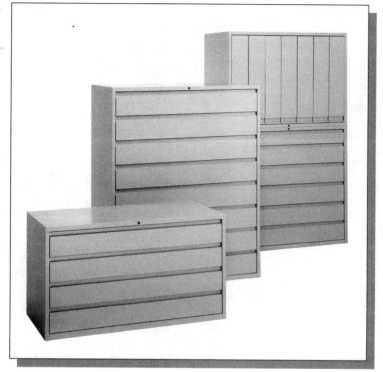

(Courtesy: Russ Bassett Company)

Standards Institution; and DIN 821 P1, *Files and Folders—Dimensions*, and DIN 821 P3, *Files and Folders—Concepts*, both published by the Deutsches Institut fuer Normung.

File folders must be able to withstand repeated handling without tearing or other damage. Durability is determined, in large part, by folder thickness, which is measured in points, where one point equals 0.001 inch. An 11-point manila folder is suitable for many office records, but thicker 14-point or 18-point folders offer greater durability for files that will be consulted frequently over long periods of time. Where greater thickness is required, 20- or 25-point folders are manufactured from pressboard, which is heavier and more durable than paperboard. Most pressboard folders feature expanding box-like bottoms that can accommodate many pages. Some products, described as classification folders, have interior dividers or pockets to separate documents into predefined groups (See Figure 7-9). As might be expected, thick folders are more expensive than thin ones. Some vendors offer economical lightweight manila folders that are less than 11 points thick, but such products are rarely suitable for records management applications.

As with other types of papers, the life expectancy of file folders is determined by their acidic content. Acid-free file folders are available for valuable documents with long retention periods. Their characteristics are described in ASTM D2201, *Standard Specification for File Folders for Storage of Permanent Records*. Specifications for file folders have also been published by the U.S. National Archives and Records Administration, the U.S. Library of Congress, and other archival and library agencies.

**Examples of File
Folders for
Special Purposes**

Figure 7-9

(Courtesy: Smead)

Suspended folders hang from rails built into or installed into file drawers (See Figure 7-10). The top edges of suspended folders are equipped with metal rods that have hook-shaped ends for that purpose. Suspended folders slide along the rails, facilitating the insertion or removal of records. Suspended folders may be constructed of paperboard, recycled paper products, or plastic. The top edges have slots for the insertion of plastic tabs. Suspended folders are available in a variety of sizes and configurations, including folders with box-shaped bottoms, internal dividers, and internal pockets. Documents can be inserted directly into suspended folders or enclosed in manila folders, which are inserted into suspended folders. As a potentially significant limitation, suspended folders take up more space than conventional folders. They can decrease drawer capacity by 10 to 25 percent, depending on application characteristics.

Color-Coding

Identifying information can be written or typed directly onto a folder tab. More often, the information is written, typed, or computer-printed onto a pressure-sensitive, adhesive label, which is then affixed to the tab. **Color-coding** is often used to identify file folders or records with specific attributes. Some labels feature color strips that can be used to signify specific folder attributes, such as destruction dates or access restrictions, that are not reflected in the file arrangement. In a terminal-digit filing installation, where records with different retention periods are characteristically scattered rather than clustered together, different colors can identify the years when specific folders are to be purged. Similarly, colors can identify folders that contain confidential records or

**Vertical Filing
Cabinet
Containing
Suspended
Folders**

Figure 7-10

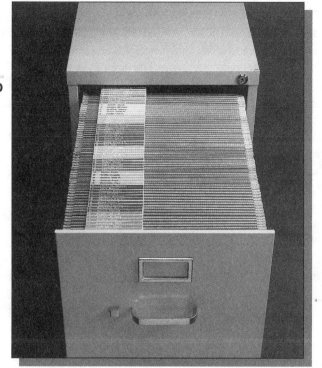

(Courtesy: Smead)

folders that cannot be removed from a designated area. Colored folders can be purchased for such purposes, or colored stickers can be affixed to manila, pressboard, or suspended folders.

A more complex form of color-coding is used to minimize misfiling and simplify misfile detection in large alphabetic and numeric filing installations. This form of color-coding is intended for shelf files with side-tab folders. Colors are assigned to specific numeric digits or letters of the alphabet. Folder tabs display color bands that represent alphabetic or numeric identifiers. In numeric filing installations, color-coding is typically limited to the first three numbers in a folder identifier. Thus, for a folder tab labeled with the identifying number 362415 only the digits 3, 6, and 2 will be color-coded. In alphabetic name files, color-coding is usually applied to the first two or three letters of the surname and, if needed, the person's first initial. When folders are properly filed, their tabs present uninterrupted bands of color. Misfiled folders, which interrupt the continuous color bands, are readily detectable, provided that the misfiling involves the color-coded digits or letters. Undetectable misfiles are limited to the remaining digits or letters, which narrows the area of the file that must be searched.

To implement color-coding, several vendors offer preprinted adhesive color strips that can be affixed to side-tab folders. Alternatively, software is available for custom-printing of color-coded labels from computer-generated lists of numeric or alphabetic file identifiers. In either case, numeric filing installations require a maximum of ten different colors. In alphabetic filing installations, which require more colors, the same color may be assigned to two different letters.

Filing Accessories

File guides enhance the appearance and usability of filing installations. They divide drawers or shelves into readily identifiable sections, making locating the section where documents will be filed or retrieved easier. File guides are available in letter- and legal-size for drawer- and shelf-type cabinets. They are usually constructed of 25-point pressboard with three or five tab positions along the top edge. Some products feature metal reinforced tabs. File guides can be purchased with preprinted alphabetic characters, numeric digits, or days of the week for alphabetic arrangements, numeric arrangements, and tickler files, respectively. In hierarchical subject filing systems, file guides can identify and demarcate topical categories and subcategories. Guides with tabs in the first or left position can identify primary categories. Guides with tabs with positions to the right identify secondary categories, and so on.

Out guides, also known as *charge-out cards*, are pressboard cards in the shape of a file folder with the word OUT printed on the tab, usually in red letters or in white letters on a red background. When a folder is removed from a drawer or shelf, the out guide is inserted into its place. The body of the out guide is a printed form with spaces for recording the date a folder was removed, the name of the person who removed it, and other information. A variant version, usually made of red vinyl, features a pocket for temporary filing of records to be added to the removed folder when it is returned.

Out guides are most effective in supervised centralized filing installations where staff members will ensure that they are completed each time a folder is removed. Even then, out guides are merely placeholders. A manual charge-out system provides little information about how many records have been removed from a filing installation and which folders have not been returned as expected. Where greater control over records is required, computer software can charge out folders or individual documents, keep a record of charge-out transactions, and check items in when they are returned. Such software is modeled after library circulation control systems, which have been widely computerized for over three decades. When a charge-out transaction occurs, the folder's bar code number, a borrower's identifier, and the date are entered into a computer database. To simplify data entry, bar code labels can be affixed to folders and, if item removal is permitted, individual documents. Among its useful capabilities, charge-out software can: (1) define access privileges and restrictions for specific types of records and employees; (2) limit the number of records that an employee can remove at one time; (3) impose time limits on charge-out periods for specific types of records; (4) generate lists of items not returned by a specified time; (5) print overdue notices; (6) block charge-out transactions for employees who have not returned records; and (7) produce statistical summaries of charge-out activity for specific time periods, folders, or borrowers.

Some Filing Guidelines

Filing cabinets and supplies are a filing system's building blocks, but, to be effective, they must be used appropriately. The following list presents widely cited advice for that purpose. Although they are typically associated with paper filing systems, most of the guidelines are also applicable to electronic records.

Guidelines for Filing Paper and Electronic Records

1. Prepare a detailed written description for each filing installation.
   - Define the purpose and scope of the installation.
   - Indicate the layout of the filing area and the arrangement of records within cabinets.
   - Specify how filing and retrieval will be performed for particular types of records.
2. Label all drawers, shelves, file guides, and folders clearly to indicate their contents.
   - Drawer and shelf labels should indicate the span of folders contained therein.
   - At a minimum, folder labels should include a name, identifying number, subject heading, or other descriptor, along with a date where meaningful.
3. Make filing a high-priority activity.
   - Records should be filed as soon as possible after they are created or received. Filing backlogs impede access to important information resources.
   - Records should be filed so that they can be located quickly and reliably when needed.
4. Sort records into the same sequence as the file arrangement before interfiling them, especially when large quantities of records will be added to existing folders.
   - Where customer records are arranged alphabetically by the customer's name, for example, newly received documents should be sorted into alphabetic order before filing. Sorting racks are available for that purpose.
5. Avoid overcrowding of filing cabinets.
   - Allow several inches of working space within drawers or shelves.
   - Remove inactive records from filing cabinets as specified in retention schedules. Active records will be easier to identify when needed.
6. Do not file multiple copies of documents unless a demonstrable need exists for them.
7. Use middle cabinet drawers or shelves for the most active records where practical. Those drawers and shelves are easy to reach.
   - Reserve top and bottom drawers or shelves for storing older records, which are less likely to be retrieved.
8. Use file guides to demarcate a file drawer or shelf into readily identifiable subdivisions. Do not create subdivisions or prepare file guides until they are needed.
   - File subdivision requirements depend on the quantity of records. Subdivisions may need to be added over time as the quantity of records increases.
   - The number of file guides per drawer or shelf depends on the file arrangement and the level of retrieval activity; the more active the records, the more file guides needed.
9. Replace damaged folders as soon as possible.
10. Place the most recently received documents in the front of a folder.
    - Select folders with prongs where documents must be kept in order or to prevent removal of individual pages.
11. Conventional manila folders can hold about three-quarters of an inch of paper. Subdivide folders by date or topic when they approach capacity. Include the folder sequence number on the folder labels.
    - Place several related manila folders into one suspended folder to keep them together.
    - Use box-bottom folders if subdivision of records within conventional folders is impractical or undesirable. Box-bottom folders are also useful for multipage documents, such as bound reports, that cannot be subdivided.
12. Color-coding can simplify detection of misplaced folders within alphabetic and numeric file arrangements, but color-coding cannot prevent filing of documents into the wrong folders.
    - When documents cannot be located in a given folder, check the folders surrounding it and the bottom of the file drawer or shelf.
13. Consider using binders rather than folders for small quantities of related records that are consulted frequently and that must be conveniently and quickly available when needed.
    - For accessibility, binders should be stored on shelves rather than in drawer-type cabinets.
    - Binders must be clearly labeled to indicate their contents.
14. Advise employees about safety precautions when using filing equipment.
    - Repair cabinets with sharp or rough edges.
    - Make sure cabinets and shelves are level to avoid accidental opening of drawers and to keep records from sliding off shelves.
    - Close filing cabinet drawers completely after use. Never leave an open drawer unattended.
    - Avoid overloading the top drawers of a cabinet to prevent tipping, particularly if the bottom drawers are partially full or empty.
    - Avoid filling drawers to capacity to reduce the effort required to open them.
    - Open only one drawer of a given filing cabinet at a time. (Some cabinets have antitipping mechanisms to prevent simultaneous opening of multiple drawers.)
    - Use a step-stool, if necessary, to access high shelves or the top drawers of a cabinet.
    - Never climb onto shelves or onto open cabinet drawers.
    - Empty filing cabinets before moving them.
    - Do not stack filing cabinets on top of one another.

Chapter 8

Managing Active Records II: Automated Document Storage and Retrieval

As discussed in the preceding chapter, paper filing systems present significant challenges. Large filing installations can occupy large amounts of office space. File arrangements can be difficult to develop and implement, particularly where records are retrieved by subject. Written procedures must clearly delineate filing responsibilities and methods. Centralized filing is recommended for efficiency and effectiveness, but some users may be poorly served by centralized installations. Filing equipment and supplies must be compatible with file arrangements, retrieval activity, and installation constraints. Keeping track of records that have been removed from filing installations can be difficult. Filing errors are inevitable and their detection is difficult, even when color-coded folders are used.

Some office tasks, such as typing, have been successfully addressed with computerization; however, filing is the least likely to be automated, even in organizations that make extensive use of information processing technology for other purposes. Although documents are routinely created by word processing software and distributed as e-mail messages and attachments, they continue to be filed and retrieved manually. Typewriters, where present, have long been relegated to preparation of forms and addressing business envelopes, but filing equipment and supplies remain well-established fixtures in even the most modern offices.

Nonetheless, effective computer-based alternatives to manual filing systems have been available for many years. Collectively characterized as *automated document storage and retrieval systems*, they employ indexing rather than filing concepts. As briefly defined in Chapter 7, an *index* is a list of names, identifiers, subject terms, or other descriptors together with references (pointers) to the documents with which the descriptors are associated. The physical arrangement of records, the most important consideration in filing installations, is immaterial if an index is available. Indexes group logically related documents conceptually rather than physically.

In automated document storage and retrieval implementations, the index is a computer database. The documents themselves may be stored electronically, in microform, or, less commonly, in paper form. As its principal advantage, a computer-based index permits complex retrieval operations that cannot be conveniently performed, and may not even be possible, with conventional paper filing methodologies. Compared with filing, computer-based indexes can be searched more quickly and are better suited to documents that may be requested by multiple parameters or combinations thereof—author, subject, and/or date, for example—or documents of varied subject content that cannot be adequately represented by a single topical heading.

This chapter surveys three automated document storage and retrieval technologies that rely on computer-based indexing as an alternative to paper filing systems. The technologies are electronic document imaging, computer-assisted microfilm retrieval, and text retrieval. The most important characteristics of each technology are described, and the advantages and limitations of each technology for records management applications are emphasized. The chapter begins, however, with an overview of basic document indexing concepts, including the identification of indexing parameters and selection of index values.

Document Indexing Concepts

The successful implementation and distinctive capabilities of automated document storage and retrieval technologies depend on the characteristics and effectiveness of indexing concepts and procedures employed in particular applications. If documents are not indexed accurately, they cannot be retrieved reliably. Research studies spanning three decades confirm that indexing errors, particularly the omission or inappropriate use of subject terms, are a leading cause of retrieval failures in computer-based information systems. The following discussion summarizes document indexing concepts and procedures, emphasizing analytical and application development principles that are most significant for records management applications.

Indexing Parameters

An **indexing parameter** is a category of information by which documents will be indexed for retrieval. The identification of appropriate indexing parameters or categories is an essential first step in planning and implementing an automated document storage and retrieval system. If a document is not indexed by a given parameter, it cannot be retrieved by that parameter. The identification of indexing parameters often precedes the selection of hardware and software components. It may occur at an early stage of planning and analysis when application requirements are initially delineated. Thus, when preparing a proposal to replace paper filing methodologies with an automated document storage and retrieval system, a records manager will usually include a suggested list of indexing parameters or an equivalent description of the proposed system's indexing characteristics, although such preliminary indexing decisions may be modified or refined in later stages of system implementation.

An automated document storage and retrieval system creates and maintains a computer database that serves as an index to documents, which may be stored electronically, in microform, or even in paper form. The index database contains one record for each document included in a given application. Database records are divided into fields that correspond to indexing parameters selected for that application. One of the fields contains a pointer to the document to which the index record refers. Depending on the locations and formats in which documents will be stored, the pointer could be a document control number, a microform and frame number, the name of a file that contains an electronic document image, the name of a text file, or some other document identifier.

Within index records, fields are customarily divided into two groups: key fields and nonkey fields. *Key fields*, the most important type, correspond to the indexing parameters identified for a particular application. They may contain names, numeric identifiers, subject terms, dates, or other information by which documents will be retrieved. *Nonkey fields*, by contrast, contain descriptive information that is important but will not be used for retrieval. The information contained in nonkey fields is displayed when database records are retrieved through searches involving key fields. Nonkey fields are especially useful where document indexing capabilities are incorporated into broader database management applications. In such situations, the information contained in the nonkey fields within database records may satisfy many retrieval requirements. In an application involving human resources documents, for example, database records may include nonkey fields for employees' job titles, addresses, and telephone numbers, thereby eliminating the need to consult the documents to obtain such information. As an additional advantage, information contained in nonkey fields can facilitate relevance judgments where many documents are retrieved by a given index search. Database records that index technical reports, for example, may include abstracts, tables of contents, annotations, or other document summaries in nonkey fields. That information can help searchers determine which documents should be consulted.

When developing indexing procedures for a given collection of documents, a records manager studies the target application and prepares a database plan for consideration by prospective users. The plan includes a list of suggested key and nonkey fields that will be reviewed, revised as necessary, and ultimately approved by interested parties. Key fields are typically identified by interviewing users to determine their retrieval requirements and by observing existing filing practices and retrieval methodologies. For nonkey fields, the records manager must consult with users to determine additional descriptive information to be displayed when database records are retrieved.

To illustrate these concepts, the following list presents possible key and nonkey fields for indexing correspondence, reports, and other commonly encountered office documents that might be included in a hierarchical subject filing system of the type described in the preceding chapter:

☐ Date	key field
☐ Date entered	nonkey field
☐ Document type	key field
☐ Author	key field
☐ Author affiliation	key field
☐ Recipient	key field
☐ Recipient affiliation	key field
☐ Subject(s)	key field
☐ Notes	nonkey field

In this example, all the suggested fields are key fields except "notes" and "date entered." The "notes" field may contain a document summary, evaluative comments, instructions for further action, or other descriptive information. The "date entered" field indicates the date that a document was indexed. The "date" field, which is a key field, stores the date on which a given document was written, assuming that the document is dated, or the date it was received, for documents that are date-stamped upon receipt. Date information is frequently used to narrow retrieval operations to specific time frames. The "document type" field identifies particular types of office records, such as correspondence, memoranda, budgets, or reports. Retrieval can consequently be limited to a particular type of document.

The "author" and "recipient" fields, which contain personal names, may not be applicable to all documents. The "recipient" field is typically associated with correspondence, memoranda, and other documents received from external sources. Although personal names are important, authors and recipients may be more meaningfully identified by the internal departments or external organizations with which they are affiliated. The manager of an engineering project, for example, may need to retrieve all correspondence to or from a given contractor or supplier, regardless of the specific author or recipient of the correspondence. The "subject(s)" field contains words or phrases that represent the subject content of a document, one of the most important retrieval parameters for office records. This field is typically a multivalue field because many documents cover multiple topics. In this respect, indexing methodologies address one of the principal limitations of hierarchical subject filing systems. As discussed in Chapter 7, such systems are best suited to documents that deal with a single subject. When a document addresses multiple topics, cross-references must be made or copies must be filed under all applicable subject headings. In theory, documents can be indexed with dozens of subject terms at varying levels of specificity, but such exhaustive indexing is seldom required.

Index Values

An index database is sometimes characterized as *metadata* because it contains information about information (the documents being indexed). Indexing is based on the premise that the content or other characteristics of documents can be adequately represented by descriptive labels that serve as document surrogates. Indexing involves an analysis of document characteristics and the determination of appropriate labels for designated indexing parameters. For purposes of this discussion, the descriptive labels associated with specific indexing parameters are termed *index values.* Indexing parameters, as previously discussed, are defined for an application as a whole; index values describe specific documents in a manner determined by those parameters. Index characteristics and indexing methods are presented in various standards and related publications, including ISO 999, *Information and Documentation, Guidelines for the Content, Organization, and Presentation of Indexes;* ISO 5963, *Documentation— Methods for Examining Documents, Determining their Subjects, and Selecting Indexing Terms;* NISO TR-02, *Guidelines for Indexes and Related Information Retrieval Devices,* and BS 6529, *Recommendations for Examining Documents, Determining their Subjects and Selecting Index Terms.*

Often, the values appropriate to specific indexing parameters can be identified by a cursory examination of documents. This type of examination is appropriate, for example, with dates, authors' names, and recipients' names used to index office correspondence and memoranda. Such documents are usually formatted in a manner that highlights the indicated information. Interdepartmental memoranda, for example, are often created on special stationery that includes labeled heading areas for dates and names. That information is also prominently featured in e-mail messages. Similarly, purchase orders and other standardized business forms contain labeled sections for dates, purchase order numbers, vendor names, and other information. The date, author(s), title, and originating department usually appear on the cover of a technical report. The title block of an engineering drawing typically contains the drawing number, date, project number, producer, and revision number in labeled boxes. The drawing's size, material, and number of pages can usually be determined by physical examination.

In such straightforward situations, appropriate index values can be quickly and easily extracted from documents by administrative or data entry personnel who have limited knowledge about the document collection and the records management application with which it is associated. Subject indexing, however, is more difficult. Documents must be read to determine what they are about, and that determination must be expressed in words or phrases that are variously called *subject terms, subject headings, subject descriptors, subject identifiers,* or *subject keywords.* Because subject indexing is an intellectually demanding and potentially time-consuming task, simpler indexing parameters—such as names, dates, and numeric identifiers—are preferable, but subject indexing is often unavoidable. Subject indexing is unavoidable, for example, with correspondence, reports, policy statements, standard operating procedures, proposals, and technical specifications.

In some applications, subject terms are selected from a predefined list of authorized words or phrases. Such an indexing aid is variously called a *thesaurus* (plural form: thesauri) or a *subject authority list.* The characteristics of thesauri are covered by national and international standards, including ANSI/NISO Z39.19, *Guidelines for the Construction, Format, and Management of Monolingual Thesauri,* ISO 2788, *Documentation—Guidelines for the Establishment and Development of Monolingual*

Thesauri, and ISO 5964, *Documentation—Guidelines for the Establishment and Development of Multilingual Thesauri*. Thesauri have been developed for published reference books and online databases that index articles in specialized subject areas, such as aeronautics, medicine, petroleum engineering, education, or pharmaceuticals. The time and cost associated with thesaurus creation and maintenance, however, are major impediments to their use in nonscholarly applications.

A *name authority list* is a variant form of thesaurus. It establishes approved forms for personal and corporate names to be used as index values. It also provides cross-references from unauthorized forms, such as abbreviations and acronyms, to approved forms. Compared to thesauri, name authority lists are easier to construct and maintain.

Index Data Entry

Once names, subject terms, or other index values are selected, they must be converted to computer-processable form for inclusion in the index database. As in other computer applications, key-entry of field values is the most prevalent data entry methodology. The data entry workstation typically displays a formatted screen with field names and adjacent blank spaces for entry of index values. The data entry operator fills in the blanks, using the tab key or another designated key to advance from field to field. Key-entry rates are affected by operator skill, data entry procedures, source document characteristics, and other factors. Entered data must be checked for incorrectly keyed characters and any errors corrected. Errors can be detected by proofreading displayed or printed data or by double-keying, in which index data is typed twice and the operator is alerted to discrepancies in the first and second typing. Double-keying is more accurate but takes longer than proofreading. Double-keying is often reserved for selected information, such as numeric values, that is difficult to proofread or for indexes to critical documents where data entry errors are intolerable.

Electronic Document Imaging

The foregoing concepts can be used to index paper files arranged by control number, but that arrangement is rarely advisable. Even when effectively indexed for retrieval, paper documents are difficult to control and, in large quantities, occupy a large amount of floor space. Computer-based indexing methods work best where documents are converted to nonpaper formats such as electronic images, microimages, or character-coded text. **Electronic document imaging** technology records documents as digitized images onto computer storage media for retrieval, distribution, or other purposes.

In publications and vendor presentations, the phrase electronic document imaging is often shortened to *document imaging* or simply *imaging*, but such abbreviated designations are imprecise. Broadly defined, *document imaging* encompasses any technology that produces pictorial copies (images) of office records, reports, business forms, publications, engineering drawings, and other source documents for storage, retrieval, distribution, or other purposes. Document imaging technologies include photocopying, which makes full-size or near-size reproductions of documents, and micrographics, which records source documents as miniaturized images on microfilm, microfiche, or other microforms as described in Chapter 5. The term *imaging* is even broader; it can be applied to such diverse technologies as computer drawing and painting software, computerized cartography, computer-aided design products, multimedia presentations, medical imaging systems, remote sensing, and machine vision systems.

Terminology aside, electronic document images are usually produced by scanning paper documents or paper-like records such as the vellum or polyester sheets used for engineering drawings, architectural plans, overhead transparencies, and certain artwork. In some cases, input to an electronic document imaging system consists of microimages or electronic images produced from paper records by a previously implemented document imaging system. As discussed in Chapter 5, document images recorded on microfilm, microfiche, or aperture cards may be scanned for conversion to electronic formats. Alternatively, images created by a previously implemented electronic document imaging system may be converted to a format required by its replacement.

Regardless of input source, electronic document imaging systems create and maintain a computer database that serves as an index to stored images. The index is searched to identify document images that meet specified retrieval parameters. Depending on application requirements and system components, retrieved images may be displayed, printed, or distributed to support particular business operations.

Advantages for Records Management

Electronic document imaging systems are designed as completely computerized replacements for paper filing systems or micrographics systems. As such, electronic document imaging technology offers significant benefits for records management applications. These benefits include, but are not necessarily limited to, the following:

- **Improved Productivity:** Manual searching through paper files can be time-consuming and labor-intensive. As its principal benefit for most records management applications, an electronic document imaging system provides rapid online access to recorded information needed for specific purposes, thereby saving employees' time and improving productivity. Tedious, time-consuming file browsing is eliminated. Compared to conventional filing methods, electronic document imaging systems provide more varied and effective indexing capabilities. Required documents can be quickly identified and retrieved at desktop workstations for display or printing. Document images can also be routed electronically for reference, action, or other purposes.

- **Improved File Integrity:** Office records, engineering drawings, and other documents contain information required for day-to-day business operations as well as for decision-making, long-term planning, and other analytical activities. To be useful for those purposes, document collections must be complete and reliable. Missing documents are unacceptable. As discussed in Chapter 7, keeping track of records that have been removed from a paper filing installation can be difficult. An imaging implementation can create a complete, well-organized, and authoritative repository of documents pertaining to specific business operations, projects, or other matters. Because images are not removed from files for reference purposes, document tracking requirements are eliminated. File integrity is assured. Assuming that they are properly indexed, electronic document images cannot be lost or misfiled.

- **Convenient Remote Access:** Assuming that appropriate computing and networking arrangements are utilized, document images can be accessed by authorized persons at any time from any location, including international locations. Document images can be available during the evening, on weekends, or at other times when offices are closed. Images can be retrieved by employees who are working at home or traveling.

- **Improved Security:** Access to electronic document images can be restricted to specific employees or other authorized persons. Access can be strictly controlled by personal identifiers, password privileges, and other computer-based security measures. Because employees will rely on images for reference or other purposes, the number of paper documents maintained in office areas will be greatly reduced, thereby minimizing the exposure of sensitive or proprietary information to unauthorized employees or visitors. If desired, printing of specific document images can be prohibited or limited to designated persons.

- **Reduced Photocopying:** Because document images are accessible online, photocopying requirements should be significantly reduced. Organizations need not produce multiple copies of documents for distribution to employees. Instead, document images can be routed as e-mail attachments. When preparing for business travel, employees can download images of needed records to mobile computing devices rather than producing photocopies.

- **Version Control:** An electronic document imaging system can provide effective version control for engineering drawings, technical reports, and other documents that are subject to revision. Version identifiers can be included in index information. Index records can clearly indicate version numbers when documents are retrieved. If desired, retrieval can be limited to the most recent version of a document.

As a high-performance retrieval technology, electronic document imaging is most suitable for records that will be consulted frequently and that must be immediately available when needed. Imaging systems can identify and retrieve documents quickly for online display or printing. That advantage pertains to active records exclusively. Because inactive records are rarely consulted, retrieval speed is inconsequential. Compared to paper records, an electronic document imaging implementation can drastically reduce office space requirements and minimize the future purchase of filing cabinets for a given quantity of records, but conversion of paper documents to electronic images solely to manage storage requirements is inadvisable. In particular, the costly conversion of inactive records to electronic document images must be avoided. As an added complication, the limited stability of computer storage media and the adverse impact of hardware and software obsolescence on the future retrievability of electronic document images pose significant problems for long-term or permanent retention of records in image formats. As discussed in preceding chapters, off-site storage or microfilming are usually more economical choices for managing inactive records. Off-site storage is invariably more economical than electronic document imaging for inactive records that will be retained for less than 10 years, and depending on the circumstances, 15 years or longer. Microfilming is usually a better choice than electronic document imaging for inactive records that require long-term or permanent retention.

Creating Images from Documents

As previously noted, electronic document images are produced by scanning paper documents or, less commonly, by scanning microform images. Borrowing terminology utilized in microfilming and data entry, the paper documents to be scanned are described as *source documents*. They may be typed, printed, handwritten, or hand drawn. Source documents may contain textual or graphic information in black and white, gray tones, or color. These variations aside, image production begins with source document preparation followed by scanner operation and inspection of scanned images, with rescanning as necessary. Scanners convert paper source documents to electronic images suitable for computer processing and storage. Typical work steps in a document imaging installation are illustrated in Figure 8-1.

Document preparation for scanning is comparable to preparation of source documents for microfilming. Work steps and productivity estimates discussed in Chapter 5 are applicable to imaging implementations. At a minimum, correspondence, memoranda, reports, case files, and other records must be removed from file cabinets, folders, or other containers; unfolded if necessary; and stacked neatly in the correct sequence for scanning. Torn pages must be mended or photocopied prior to scanning. Staples and paper clips must be removed from source documents for some document scanners. Even when not required, removing fasteners improves the productivity of scanner operators and enhances the appearance of electronic document images.

Document scanners are available in sheetfed and flatbed configurations. **Sheetfed scanners** are sometimes described as *pass-through* or *pull-through scanners*. Pages to

Document Imaging Work Steps

Figure 8-1

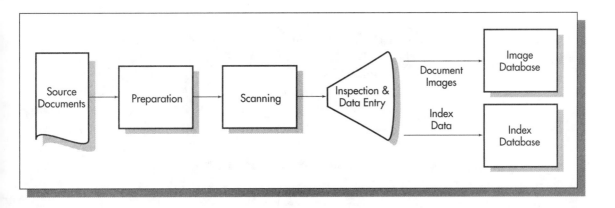

be scanned are inserted into a narrow opening from which they are transported individually across a scanning mechanism that includes optical and photosensitive components. Depending on equipment design, the scanned pages are ejected at the back or bottom of the machine. A **flatbed scanner**, by contrast, features a flat exposure surface on which pages are individually positioned for scanning. Most models feature a glass exposure surface on which pages are placed face down, the scanning components being located beneath the glass surface. Much less commonly, flatbed scanners employ an overhead design in which individual pages are positioned face up for scanning by optical and photosensitive components positioned at the top of a vertical column, in the manner of planetary cameras described in Chapter 5.

Sheetfed scanners, which have dominated electronic document imaging implementations since the industry's inception, are recommended for most records management applications. Models are available for office records up to 11 by 17 inches in size and for large-format documents such as engineering drawings. Compared to flatbed scanning, sheetfed operation is faster and yields higher labor productivity; pages can be inserted into a sheetfed scanner's transport mechanism at a much faster rate than they can be positioned onto a flatbed scanner's glass exposure surface. To minimize operator involvement, most sheetfed scanners can be equipped with an automatic page feeder as a standard feature or optional accessory. (See Figure 8-2.) Flatbed scanners are necessary, however, for bound volumes or fragile documents. Several manufacturers offer special book scanners for such applications. For maximum flexibility, some document scanners support both sheetfed and flatbed input methods. An operator can remove or lift the scanner's sheetfeed mechanism to reveal a flat glass surface on which bound volumes or fragile documents can be positioned.

Following scanning, electronic document images are typically routed to a temporary file, pending inspection and, if necessary, rescanning. The purpose of inspection is to ensure that electronic document images are sufficiently legible and usable for

Document Scanner

Figure 8-2

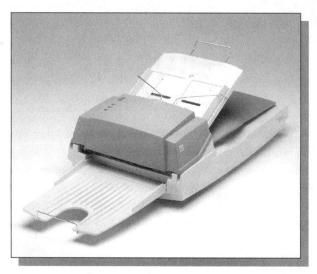

(Courtesy: Eastman Kodak)

their intended purposes, which may include display, printing, facsimile transmission, or optical character recognition. Obvious mechanical and legibility problems that necessitate rescanning include excessive page skewing, double feeding of pages, pages scanned upside down or backwards, pages with folded corners, obliteration of information within pages, insufficient clarity or contrast, blotches or other blemishes, and curved or jagged lines within images. Depending on the application, inspection may encompass all electronic document images or be limited to a predetermined sample. Careful inspection of all images is critical if paper documents will be discarded following scanning.

Any of the image production steps previously discussed can be performed in-house or outsourced to a service bureau. A *document imaging service bureau* is a business that performs one or more imaging operations to customer specifications using the customer's own source documents. A service bureau may offer any combination of image production and support services, including consulting for application selection and systems design, document preparation, source document scanning, image inspection, index planning and data entry, and media duplication. Depending on the service bureau and customer requirements, imaging operations may be performed at the service bureau's facilities or at the customer's location, although on-site implementations are more costly and may limit the types of services to be offered.

As noted in other chapters, outsourcing arrangements are increasingly popular in records management operations. Many organizations contract with service bureaus for at least one phase of image production. Service bureaus can, for example, scan documents that were prepared in-house. They can likewise inspect and index images produced by an in-house scanning department. Even organizations with extensive in-house imaging operations use service bureaus to supplement or enhance their own capabilities in unusual situations. Imaging service bureaus are particularly useful for high-volume work that must be completed in a short time or for tasks, such as image reformatting or microform scanning, that require special equipment, software, or technical expertise unavailable in house.

Image Storage

Although electronic document images offer a compact alternative to paper files, they can require large amounts of computer storage—far more, for example, than word processing files or e-mail messages of comparable content. Even though they are routinely compressed following scanning, images produced from letter-size pages can each require 50,000 to 60,000 bytes of storage; at that rate, the contents of a four-drawer file cabinet containing about 10,000 pages will require 500 to 600 megabytes of computer storage. A million-page document collection, which is far from unusual in records management applications, will require 50 to 60 gigabytes.

Fortunately, developments in computer storage technology have kept pace with these demands. As a type of computer-processible information, document images can be recorded on any storage medium with sufficient capacity. For most records management applications, however, the only practical choices are hard drives or optical disks. Hard drives are increasingly the preferred media for document image storage. They offer a favorable combination of capacity, familiarity, and cost. Over the last decade, hard drive capacities have improved dramatically and their prices have plunged. Hard drives for entry-level desktop computers can store several hundred thousand digitized images, and network servers can accommodate multimillion-page imaging applications. Document images recorded onto hard drives are typically backed up on magnetic tape for offline storage.

Electronic document imaging and optical disk technologies have been closely associated since the early 1980s. Given the then limited storage capacities of hard drives, the development of high-capacity optical disks was a precondition for successful commercialization of electronic document imaging technology. The earliest optical disks provided gigabyte-level storage at a time when most hard drives stored less than 100 megabytes. In recent years, hard drives have caught up, but optical disks still offer impressive storage capacities. For many electronic document imaging implementations, recordable compact disks, DVDs, and other optical disk formats offer an attractive combination of voluminous storage capacity, good retrieval performance, low media cost, and removability for distribution or off-site storage, although hard drives have faster access times for reading and writing information. Even where optical disks are used for document images, hard drives are the principal storage devices for index data, which must be retrieved as quickly as possible.

Image Retrieval

Image retrieval operations begin with a search for database (index) records—and, by implication, document images—that will satisfy specified information requirements. The index records contain pointers to document images that may be stored on hard drives or on optical disks. The nature and complexity of database searches depend on the retrieval functionality supported by database management programs. Searchable fields, previously defined as key fields, are determined by the indexing plan developed for a particular imaging implementation. A typical search specification includes a field name, a field value, and a relational expression, such as "equal to," "greater than," or "less than." Field values may be words, phrases, numbers, dates, or other index information to be matched. They may be key-entered into a search form or selected from a scrollable list of previously entered or permissible field values.

As an initial response to a search specification, most electronic document imaging systems display a count of the number of index records and, by implication, the number of document images that satisfy the specification. Depending on this response, the searcher may reconsider the retrieval strategy and modify the search specification, broadening it if too few index records are identified or narrowing it if the number of retrieved records is excessive. Following examination of index records, the searcher may request one or more document images, which will be retrieved and displayed. Image retrieval workstations equipped with large-screen monitors can display two letter-size page images side by side in their entirety. More often, however, a portion of a document image is displayed in a scrollable window on a conventional computer monitor. Although electronic document imaging is widely marketed as a paperless office technology, most installations include one or more printers for production of paper copies for reference, distribution, or other purposes.

Legal Status of Electronic Document Images

Corporations, government agencies, and other organizations are understandably concerned about the legal status of information generated and stored by electronic document imaging technology. Their concerns are greatest where paper documents will be destroyed following scanning, leaving electronic document images stored on computer media as the only available versions of documents to satisfy evidentiary or legally mandated retention requirements. Space savings through elimination of paper files and cost reduction through discontinuation of microfilming operations are often-cited justifications for electronic document imaging implementations. Such justifications are based on the assumption that the electronic document images are substituted for original paper records or microfilm copies. If such substitution is not legally acceptable, paper copies must be retained and/or microfilm operations continued.

All current thinking about the legal status of electronic document images is based on the following premise: Electronic document images are true copies of the documents from which they were made, a **true copy** being one that accurately reproduces an original document. As such, electronic document images are subject to existing legal statutes and provisions of case law that pertain to copies of documents. The most frequently cited legal statutes were discussed in Chapter 5:

- *The Uniform Photographic Copies of Business and Public Records as Evidence Act* permits the substitution of photographic copies for original documents for judicial or administrative purposes, provided that the copies are produced in the regular course of business and that no laws or regulations require retention of the original documents. Where these conditions are satisfied, the Uniform Photographic Copies of Business and Public Records as Evidence Act permits, but does not mandate, the destruction of original documents.

- *Rule 1003 of the Uniform Rules of Evidence and Federal Rules of Evidence* provides for admission of duplicate records in evidence unless serious questions are raised about the authenticity of original records from which the copies were made or, in specific circumstances, admitting a copy in lieu of an original is judged unfair. Rule 1003 does not require that duplicate records be produced in the regular course of business. It does not authorize or prohibit destruction of original records.

The applicability of these laws to electronic document images is based on interpretation rather than explicit provisions because both laws predate electronic document imaging technology. The Uniform Photographic Copies of Business and Public Records as Evidence Act was written in 1949. The Uniform Rules of Evidence were written in 1953 and revised in 1974. (The Federal Rules of Evidence were passed by Congress in 1975.) Although the Uniform Photographic Copies of Business and Public Records as Evidence Act specifically mentions photocopying and microfilming, it does not provide an exhaustive list of acceptable reprographic technologies, nor does it exclude technologies that are not mentioned. The Act applies to any copying process that "accurately reproduces or forms a durable medium for so reproducing" original documents. In its definition of duplicate records, the Uniform Rules of Evidence and Federal Rules of Evidence mention photographic and electronic recording among "the equivalent techniques which accurately reproduces the original." Electronic document images satisfy the requirements of these broad definitions.

To clarify matters further, a growing number of government agencies have modified their existing laws concerning duplicate records to more specifically encompass electronic document images. Since the early 1990s, several regulatory agencies, including the Securities and Exchange Commission and the Nuclear Regulatory Commission, have revised their retention requirements to specifically incorporate guidelines or opinions concerning the acceptability of electronic document images for certain types of records. Similarly, Federal Acquisition Regulations let government contractors substitute electronic document images for paper records in most cases, provided that the images are accurate reproductions of the original records and that they are conveniently indexed. Contractors must retain the original records for one year following scanning for periodic validation. Many state archives have promulgated guidelines for electronic document imaging implementations by state and local government records subject to their authority. In some cases, electronic document imaging is permitted for state and local government operations involving records that will be retained for relatively brief periods of time—typically, ten years or less. Some states impose no restrictions on electronic document imaging implementations that involve the destruction of paper records following scanning, provided that a satisfactory retention plan is developed.

COLD Technology

As a standard or optional feature, some electronic document imaging systems can store and retrieve page-formatted computer output. As such, they incorporate capabilities offered by so-called **computer-output laser disk (COLD)** systems, which record computer-generated reports onto computer storage media for online access rather than printing them onto paper. When they were first introduced, COLD installations recorded computer-generated reports onto optical disks, hence the laser disk designation. Newer COLD implementations, however, utilize hard drives or optical disks.

Although often associated with electronic document imaging, COLD is not an imaging technology. COLD information is recorded in the character-coded form associated with data and text files. Unlike a conventional computer database, however, COLD information is formatted as report pages, much as it would be transmitted to a paper printer or COM recorder. When retrieved, the information is displayed in a printout-page format.

Records managers have long recognized the storage and retrieval problems associated with computer-generated reports, which are among the bulkiest business records. With large pages packaged in thick binders, computer-generated reports are characteristically difficult to handle. Many reports are printed in multiple copies at frequently intervals, daily or weekly in some cases. Computing departments must allocate resources to these print jobs and distribute the reports to user departments when completed. Computer-output microfilm, as discussed in Chapter 5, addresses some of these problems. Like COM, COLD technology provides compact storage of voluminous reports, but it provides other advantages as well. COLD implementations eliminate the time and labor required to produce and distribute paper printouts or COM-generated microforms. By making reports available online, COLD technology promotes information sharing in network installations. Users can also browse through report pages. Reference copies of specified pages can be printed on demand. As a potentially useful feature, report pages can be exported to other application programs as text files; as an example, a table from a computer-generated report can be incorporated into a word processing document or transferred into a spreadsheet.

Computer-Assisted Retrieval (CAR)

Computer-assisted retrieval (CAR) technology is conceptually similar to electronic document imaging but differs from it in one crucial aspect. Like electronic document imaging, CAR uses a computer database to index document images, but the images are recorded onto microforms. The index includes pointers to the microform and frame locations of document images associated with specific index terms.

The possibility of automated microimage retrieval was discussed in the mid-1940s. The earliest implementations recorded index codes onto microfilm adjacent to the document images to which they pertained. Despite significant limitations, they played an important role in information retrieval at a time when computers were more expensive and less versatile than they are today. True CAR systems, which integrate computer and micrographics components, date from the 1960s. As their defining characteristic, they combine the compaction of microforms with the ability of computers to rapidly manipulate index information.

Although CAR systems permit fast, reliable retrieval of documents, CAR is rarely the technology of choice for automated document storage and retrieval. Completely computerized approaches, which were not available when CAR technology was introduced, offer higher performance, greater convenience, better product selection, and, in some cases, lower costs. Increasingly, records managers look to electronic document imaging rather than CAR to replace paper files, and a number of CAR systems installed in the 1970s and 1980s have been replaced by electronic document imaging. Nonetheless, a sufficient number of CAR installations remain in operation to warrant its inclusion in this chapter. Further, as discussed next, CAR and electronic document imaging technology can be effectively combined in certain records management applications.

CAR Components

A computer-assisted retrieval system includes micrographics and computer subsystems. Each subsystem creates and maintains a database. The micrographics database is a collection of microimages. Although any type of microform can be used, most CAR implementations record documents onto 16mm microfilm, which is loaded into self-threading cartridges to simplify handling and speed retrieval. Documents are microfilmed by cameras that place small rectangular marks, called *blips* or *image count marks*, beneath all or selected microimages. Specially designed reader/printers and reader/scanners count the blips and in so doing count the frames. A computer database links index terms to microimages that are identified by their cartridge and frame addresses. At retrieval time, the computer database is searched to determine the existence and microform addresses (cartridge and frame numbers) of documents associated with specific index terms. When a microform address is determined, an operator mounts the designated microfilm cartridge into a blip-counting retrieval unit and enters the frame number into a keypad intended for that purpose. The desired microimage is displayed for viewing, printing, or scanning, depending on the retrieval unit's capabilities.

The CAR retrieval process is convenient but not fully automated. Some reader/printers and reader/scanners can be optionally equipped with a CAR interface for direct connection to the computer where the index database resides. Following an index search, pertinent frame numbers are transmitted directly to the blip-counting retrieval device, thereby eliminating key-entry. The operator must still manually select and mount the appropriate microfilm cartridge, however. Jukebox-type units for automatic selection and mounting of microfilm cartridges were introduced in the 1970s, but they are no longer available.

Integration with Electronic Document Imaging

CAR and electronic document imaging systems employ conceptually similar approaches to document storage and retrieval. With both technologies, a computer database serves as an index to document images. With both technologies, an information systems planner must determine indexing categories and define indexing procedures by analyzing application characteristics and determining user requirements. (Indexing concepts and methods are technology-independent; CAR and electronic document imaging systems may employ identical database management software.) Both technologies employ multistep retrieval procedures that involve database searching followed by display or printing of specific document images. The two technologies offer similar benefits, including rapid retrieval and compact document storage.

Given these similarities, CAR and electronic document imaging systems offer excellent opportunities for integrated implementations in which the respective strengths of the two technologies complement each other. CAR and electronic imaging technologies can be combined in a given installation. A single computer database can index document images stored in either microform or electronic formats. A database search can identify microimages or electronic images that satisfy specific retrieval requirements. Retrieval workstations can include computer and micrographics display and printing components: a computer monitor for electronic images and a reader/printer for microimages.

Among its advantages, an integrated approach can avoid costly backfile conversions in electronic document imaging installations where documents were previously microfilmed or where the electronic document imaging system will replace a CAR system. Older documents can remain in microform, while new documents are scanned for computer storage. Initially, the integrated implementation will rely heavily on microimages. As time passes, however, electronic images will account for an increasingly large and important percentage of the total document collection. If desired, the microform component can be phased out by using reader/scanners to digitize microimages for computer storage as they are retrieved. Microimages that have not been converted to electronic form within a predetermined period of time (three to five years, for example) presumably have limited reference value and can be retired from the system.

Text Retrieval

A **text retrieval system**—variously described as a *full-text retrieval system*, a *text information management system*, a *textbase management system*, or a *text data management system*—is a special category of database management software. Like conventional database management programs, text retrieval software can store and process collections of structured records where information is organized into fields. As their defining characteristic, however, databases created by text retrieval programs can store and index long, unstructured text segments, including complete documents as well as abstracts, annotations, and other document surrogates. The text segments are stored in character-coded form. Each letter of the alphabet, numeric digit, punctuation mark, and other symbol is represented by a predetermined sequence of bits. Most text retrieval programs support the American Standard Code for Information Interchange (ASCII) or its ANSI variant, which includes accented characters, special punctuation marks, and such commonly encountered business characters as the trademark and copyright symbols.

Character-coded documents may be generated by word processing programs, electronic messaging systems, or other computer applications. Alternatively, the content of paper records may be converted to character-coded text by optical character recognition (OCR), or, as a last resort, key entry. In any case, text retrieval programs support full-text retrieval by creating indexes to every significant word in database records. The indexes can rapidly identify and retrieve text segments that contain specified character strings. Typical work steps utilized in text retrieval are illustrated in Figure 8-3.

Text retrieval software has been commercially available since the 1970s. The earliest products were designed for mainframe and minicomputer installations, which dominated information retrieval applications at that time. Text retrieval software for personal computers was introduced in the 1980s. Suitable for standalone computers or network installations, highly functional products are widely available from multiple suppliers.

Like electronic document imaging, text retrieval technology provides a completely computerized approach to document storage and retrieval, but the two technologies encode and store documents in different ways. Electronic document imaging systems store digitized facsimiles that preserve the appearance as well as the content of source documents. Text retrieval products, by contrast, store the content of documents in character-coded form; they do not preserve their original appearance, although some text retrieval programs will preserve formatting in documents generated by popular

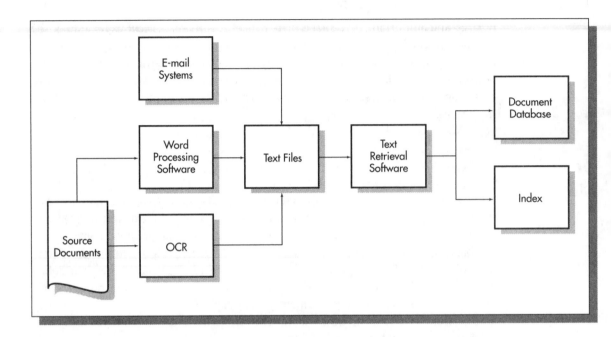

word processing software. By definition, text retrieval products are limited to textual records. They are obviously unsuitable for graphic documents, such as engineering drawings, maps, and photographs, which contain little if any text. Text retrieval technology can be selectively applied to compound documents that combine text with embedded illustrations, signatures, and other significant graphic elements. Where the appearance of a paper document has significant informational or evidentiary value, however, electronic document imaging is the preferred technology for computerized storage and retrieval.

Potential for Records Management

Historically, text retrieval applications have been more closely associated with librarianship than with records management. Since the 1970s, libraries, archives, and related organizations have used text retrieval software to manage a variety of documents, including proprietary research reports, as well as conference presentations, preprints, reprints, and other publications in specific subject areas. Most installations have been in industrial, technical, medical, and law libraries where complex retrieval operations required powerful search capabilities. Records management awareness and applications have been slow to develop, despite potentially significant advantages offered by text retrieval technology. Those advantages include the following:

1. **Automatic Indexing:** Electronic document imaging and computer-assisted retrieval technology rely on manual methods to identify and key-enter index terms for specific documents. In straightforward business applications, index values, such as dates and authors' names, may be easily identified and extracted from source documents. Often, however, indexing involves significant intellectual effort. In some applications, specialized subject knowledge is required to

accurately index documents. Given its labor-intensive nature, manual indexing can involve prohibitively high costs. Manual indexing is particularly costly when backfile conversions involve large quantities of un-indexed documents. Even where cost is not an issue, manual methods are ineffective in applications, such as litigation support, where large quantities of documents must be indexed within a short period of time. Addressing these limitations, text retrieval programs extract index terms from documents automatically. Each word in a document is compared to a list of insignificant words. Words not on the list are considered valid index terms. They are recorded in an index database, together with pointers to the documents that contain them. This process eliminates indexing and data entry labor, thereby speeding implementation and reducing costs. Where appropriate, indexing may be augmented by appending additional words or phrases to documents or by combining the full text of documents with predefined index fields.

2. **Enhanced Retrieval:** Like electronic document imaging, text retrieval technology provides convenient on-line access to complete documents. As their most widely discussed advantage, text retrieval systems permit full-text retrieval—that is, the retrieval of documents that contain specific words or phrases. Text retrieval software can perform straightforward searches or complex retrieval operations. Documents identified by an index search can be displayed, printed, or distributed as attachments to e-mail messages.

3. **Compatibility:** Compared to electronic document imaging, text retrieval technology has limited hardware and software dependencies. Text retrieval technology is compatible with widely encountered computer configurations. Special peripheral devices are not required. Character-coded documents can be stored on any computer media with adequate capacity and performance characteristics; in most cases, documents and index data are stored on hard drives for fast retrieval. Character-coded documents can be displayed on any computer monitor. Hard copies can be produced by any printer. Character-coded documents are reasonably portable. Stored as straightforward text files, they can be transferred from one text retrieval program to another, although they must be re-indexed.

4. **Compact Storage:** Text retrieval technology provides the most compact form of document storage. A single-spaced letter-size page stored as character-coded text will occupy 3,500 to 4,000 bytes as compared with 50,000 to 60,000 bytes for the same page stored as an electronic document image. Additional storage space is required for full-text indexes, which typically increase storage requirements by a factor of 1.75 to 2.5. Thus, a single-spaced letter-size page with indexes will occupy 5,250 to 10,000 bytes. Even when allowing for index information, the amount of space required by character-coded pages is a fraction of the space required by their image counterparts. One million pages stored as character-coded text, including full-text indexes, will require just 5.25 to 10 gigabytes of computer storage, as compared with 50 to 60 gigabytes of computer storage for the same quantity of records stored as electronic images, 100 four-drawer file cabinets for the same quantity of records in paper form, or 200 reels of 16mm microfilm.

5. **Bandwidth Requirements:** Because they are smaller than electronic document images, character-coded pages require much less transmission time in networked computer installations. Transmission time is an important consideration where the volume of document retrieval activity is high, very long documents must be distributed electronically, and/or available bandwidth is limited.

Indexing and Retrieval Functionality

Text retrieval software imports documents from the computer applications that create them. All programs discussed in this chapter can import text-only files from word processing programs, e-mail systems, or other applications. Many text retrieval programs can import files in native formats associated with popular word processing programs and other software packages, including database management and spreadsheets programs. Increasingly, text retrieval programs can import Web pages saved as HTML files.

Text retrieval programs index database records, including lengthy text segments as well as field values, where present. The indexes permit full-text retrieval, the programs' distinguishing characteristic and most users' principal motive for implementing them. Indexing is performed automatically and quickly as documents are imported or field values are entered. When databases are updated, reindexing or other reorganization may be necessary, although some text retrieval programs update indexes dynamically.

Text retrieval programs are notable for their powerful and flexible retrieval functionality, which is a particularly important consideration in records management applications with complex retrieval requirements. By definition, text retrieval programs can retrieve documents or field values that contain specified words or phrases, but this capability may be implemented in several ways. To serve users of varied knowledge and experience, most programs support novice and advanced retrieval modes. The *novice mode*, which relies heavily on dialog boxes, usually supports a subset of a given program's retrieval functionality. It is suitable for inexperienced users and straightforward searches. The *advanced mode*, as its name suggests, supports complex retrieval requirements. With some text retrieval programs, the advanced mode is command-oriented and requires some study to use effectively.

Text retrieval functionality has improved steadily and significantly since the technology's inception. Capabilities considered unusual a decade ago are now commonplace. All text retrieval programs, for example, support Boolean operators, relational expressions, and, subject to some variation, proximity commands to search for phrases or specified words in the same sentence or paragraph. Most programs also support search term truncation, fuzzy retrieval for spelling variants and other near matches, and automatic searching of predefined synonyms, abbreviations, acronyms, and related concepts. Less common retrieval capabilities include negative proximity commands, hypertext searching of words in previously retrieved records, phonetic matching, term weighting for relevance ranking, and quorum operators, which will match some but not all words from a specified list.

All text retrieval programs respond to search commands with a list of documents that satisfy specific retrieval parameters. Any listed document can be selected for a complete display with search terms highlighted. Alternatively, some programs will display "answer passages"—short document segments that contain search terms surrounded by several lines of context. Some text retrieval programs can display documents in the computer applications that originally created them. When a word processing document is retrieved, the program that created it is automatically launched and the document is displayed with appropriate formatting, as if it had just been typed.

Limitations

Despite its attractive features, several limitations have impeded the widespread implementation of text retrieval technology in records management applications. First and foremost, text retrieval programs require character-coded documents. Although a large and growing percentage of recorded information is generated in character-coded form by word processing software, e-mail systems, or other computer programs, many documents exist only in human-readable paper form. Human-readable paper is the case with documents received from external sources and with older documents that predate the proliferation of word processing software or where the word processing versions have been discarded or are no longer usable because of damaged media, format incompatibilities, or discontinued software. Such documents must be converted to character-coded form by retyping them or, where possible, by optical character recognition (OCR).

Retyping, although invariably effective, is so labor-intensive and time-consuming that it should be reserved for small quantities of very important documents; even then, the cost of retyping may be prohibitively high. With optical character recognition, documents are first scanned to produce electronic images. OCR software then analyzes the images to recognize the characters they contain and convert them to character-coded form as if they had been typed. OCR operations require less labor than typing, but scanning operations are not labor-free. Documents must be properly prepared, pages must be inserted into and removed from scanners, and images must be inspected. Additional labor is required to proofread recognized text and correct any errors detected.

Labor aside, OCR's effectiveness ultimately depends on its ability to accurately recognize characters. Although OCR technology has improved dramatically over the last ten years, accurate recognition depends on document characteristics. The best results are obtained with high-contrast documents that contain sharply defined, dark characters on a light, preferably white, background. Unfortunately, records managers seldom have control over the quality or typographic characteristics of recorded information. Office files may include photocopies, faxes, and other documents that are faded, speckled, or otherwise marginally legible. OCR is not a reliable conversion method in such cases.

Document conversion methods aside, text retrieval technology has some functional limitations. Befitting its name, it is better suited to retrieval rather than retention of recorded information. As described previously, text retrieval technology captures the contents of documents but not their appearance, which can be meaningful in some situations. Many documents contain signatures, handwritten annotations, or other information that cannot be converted to character-coded form but that may need to be preserved. Thus, character-coded versions cannot substitute for paper documents in every case. Paper documents or image versions (electronic or microfilm) must be retained.

Text Retrieval and Electronic Document Management

In the broadest sense, the phrase *electronic document management* encompasses any technology involved with storage, retrieval, or control of recorded information contained in documents. By that definition, text retrieval is an electronic document management technology, as is electronic document imaging. The phrase is used more narrowly, however, to denote a group of software products that automate certain document management functions. Such products define documents broadly to include word processing files, electronic messages, spreadsheets, graphics, Web pages, and other computer files.

Electronic document management system software support full-text indexing, storage, and retrieval capabilities. Compared with text retrieval programs, however, electronic document management products support a broader range of features and functions for preparation, organization, tracking, and distribution of recorded information.

Electronic document management products also incorporate electronic document imaging capabilities, including document scanning, field-based indexing, database searching, and image display and printing.

Electronic Document Management Software Features

- The ability to import files created by popular office productivity software and other application programs
- Creation and maintenance of large document repositories on magnetic or optical storage media
- Comingling of character-coded text, document images, Web pages, spreadsheets, presentations, video recordings, audio recordings, and other types of recorded information within a given repository
- Collaborative preparation, editing, and annotation of documents by authorized members of predefined workgroups
- Library services for cataloging, indexing, and saving documents in a variety of formats
- Document check-out capabilities that limit access to documents being edited by other authorized users
- A browser interface for Internet and intranet implementations
- Document viewers that support a variety of file formats
- Display of retrieved documents within their native applications where appropriate
- Archiving services that move documents to specific storage media based on age, reference activity, subject matter, or other characteristics
- Version control that traces the development of reports, policy statements, standard operating procedures, or other documents subject to revision
- Audit trails that record information about input, editing, retrieval, or other document-related actions

Glossary

The following list contains brief definitions of selected terms used in this book. Except for a few grammatical changes, the definitions are identical to those presented in the chapters where the terms are introduced. The relevant portions of individual chapters should be consulted for a fuller explanation and discussion of specific terms. This glossary is provided for the reader's convenience. It is not a comprehensive list of records management terms nor is it intended as a substitute for other glossaries, such as ANSI/ARMA 10, *Glossary of Records and Information Management Terms*, ANSI/AIIM TR-02, *Glossary of Document Technologies*, ISO 6196, *Micrographics—Vocabulary*, or ISO 12651, *Electronic Imaging—Vocabulary*.

A

active record—a record that is consulted frequently and must be conveniently available for that purpose. A record needed to perform current operations; subject to frequent use and usually located near the user. It can be accessed manually or online via a computer system.

administrative retention criteria—retention criteria based on an organization's operational requirements. Such criteria are concerned with the availability of records for long-term administrative consistency and continuity, as well as for day-to-day operations of individual program units.

annualized loss expectancy (ALE)—the probable annual dollar loss associated with the loss of a specific vital records series. The total expected annual loss to an organization is the sum of the expected annualized losses calculated for each vital records series.

aperture card—a tabulating-size card with an opening that contains one frame of 35mm microfilm.

arrangement—the physical sequence of records or groups of records within a series.

automated information system—hardware and/or software components designed to perform one or more information processing operations.

B

backup copy—a copy of a record created specifically for vital records protection or disaster recovery.

breaking files—the practice of subdividing a records series chronologically to simplify the identification of records eligible for retention actions.

C

camera films—microfilm intended for original microphotography in source document cameras and COM recorders.

central files—a collection of records consolidated for storage in a single location where authorized persons can access them. The files of several organizational units physically and/or functionally controlled and managed under a centralized service.

certificate of destruction—a record that documents the disposal of specific records in conformity with an organization's formally established retention policies and schedules.

computer-assisted retrieval (CAR)—a technology that uses a computer database to index document images recorded onto microforms. Systems that combine the document storage capabilities of micrographics with the indexing and retrieval capabilities of a computer database.

computer-output laser disk (COLD)—a technology that records computer-generated reports onto optical disks or other computer storage media for online access rather than printing them onto paper.

computer-output microfilm (COM)—microforms produced from computer-processible information. The process that converts and records data from a computer onto microfilm in human-readable format.

COM recorder—a device that produces computer-output microfilm and converts the results of computer processing to human-readable form.

color-coding—the use of color to identify file folders or records with specific attributes.

cubic foot (of records)—a measure of the quantity of records or the contents of a records container with interior dimensions of 10 inches high by 12 inches wide by 15 inches deep.

D

data archiving—offline storage of inactive information, usually on magnetic tape and other removable media.

data migration—the process of periodically converting electronic records to new file formats and/or new storage media to satisfy long retention requirements.

departmental retention schedule—a retention schedule prepared for a specific department or other program unit and that is limited to records series actually held by that program unit.

duplicating films—microfilm designed to produce copies of other microforms; they are not suitable for use in microfilm cameras or COM recorders. Also known as *copy films* or *print films*.

E

electronic document imaging—the technology or process that records documents as digitized images on computer storage media for retrieval, distribution, or other purposes.

electronic document management system—a type of software product that automates the preparation, organization, tracking, and distribution of electronic documents.

electronic records—records that contain machine-readable information that is electronically encoded; examples include computer records, audio recordings, and video recordings. Records stored on electronic storage media that can be readily accessed or changed.

F

file—a collection of related records that are stored and used together.

file arrangement—the physical sequence of records or groups of records within a records series. The way in which logically related records are placed in a predetermined sequence for retrieval when needed. Records may be arranged alphabetically by the name of a person or organization; by a numeric identifier; by date; by a code that represents the way a name is pronounced; by a geographic unit; or by subject categories.

filing—the process of organizing information by placing related records into close physical proximity to one another.

filing system—the combination of policies, procedures, labor, equipment, supplies, facilities, and other resources that relate to the organization of records.

flatbed scanner—a flat exposure surface on which pages are individually positioned for scanning. Most models feature a glass exposure surface on which pages are placed face down, the scanning components being located beneath the glass surface.

functional retention schedule—a retention schedule that categorizes records series by the business functions to which they pertain.

G

general retention schedule—a retention schedule that specifies retention periods for designated records series, regardless of the particular program units where the records are maintained.

I

important records—records that support a program unit's business operations and help it fulfill its assigned responsibilities. The loss of such records may cause delays or confusion that impede a program unit's work, but it will not bring mission-critical business operations to a halt. Records that contain information pertinent to an organization that would need to be recreated or replaced if lost or destroyed.

inactive record—a record that is not consulted frequently but must be retained for legal, operational, or scholarly reasons. It does not have to be readily available.

index—a set of descriptive words or phrases that apply to specific records and that facilitates the retrieval of such records; a list of names, identifiers, subject terms, or other descriptors together with references (pointers) to the documents with which the descriptors are associated. A systematic guide that allows access to specific items contained within a larger body of information.

indexing parameter—a category of information by which records are indexed for retrieval.

information life cycle—the concept that information is subject to changing requirements for storage, retrieval, and distribution from its creation or receipt through destruction or permanent retention.

K

knowledge management—a multifaceted discipline concerned with the systematic management, utilization, and exploitation of an organization's knowledge resources. Knowledge management initiatives emphasize the value of an organization's intellectual capital—its inventions, patents, trade secrets, product formulations, customer intelligence, and well-established business processes.

L

legal retention criteria—retention criteria based on recordkeeping requirements specified in laws and regulations or on the need to keep records for possible use in legal proceedings.

life expectancy (LE) designation—a prediction of the minimum life expectancy, in years, for a given medium.

limitations of assessment periods—the fiscal counterparts of statutes of limitations. They prescribe the period of time that a government agency can determine taxes owed.

litigation hold—temporary suspension of destruction for records believed relevant for litigation or government investigations.

M

microfiche—a sheet of film that contains miniaturized document images in a two-dimensional grid of rows and columns. A microform in the shape of a rectangular sheet having one or more microimages arranged in a grid pattern that requires a reader for viewing and has an eye-readable heading area across the top

microfilm camera—a camera that produces highly miniaturized reproductions of paper documents.

microfilm duplicator—a device that produces copies of microforms.

microfilm jacket—a transparent carrier with sleeves or channels for insertion of single or multiple strips of 16mm or 35mm microfilm.

microfilm processor—a device that develops microfilm images following exposure.

microform—a photographic information carrier that contains highly miniaturized document images; types of microforms include roll microfilm, microfilm cartridges, microfiche, microfilm jackets, and aperture cards.

microform reader—a device that magnifies microimages for viewing.

microform reader/printer—a device that magnifies microimages for viewing or printing.

microform scanner—a device that produces electronic images from microimages.

micrographics—a document imaging technology that is concerned with the creation and use of microforms as storage media for recorded information; also known as *film-based* imaging. The technology by which information can be quickly reduced to a microform, stored conveniently, and then easily retrieved for reference and use.

micrographics service bureau—a business that performs one or more micrographics services to customer specifications using the customer's own documents, computer data, or other source material.

microimages—document images that are highly miniaturized and consequently require magnification for viewing or printing.

mission-critical operation—a business operation that an organization must perform.

N

nonrecords—information-bearing objects that are excluded from the scope and authority of an organization's records management program. Items that are not usually included within the scope of official records, e.g., convenience files, day files, reference materials, drafts, etc.

nonunitized microforms—microfilm reels or cartridges onto which unrelated documents are grouped on a single reel or cartridge. A user interested in one client's file must consult a microform that includes the records of other clients.

O

obsolete records—records that are no longer needed for any purpose.

office of record—the program unit that maintains the official copy for retention purposes.

official copy—the copy of a record that is designated to satisfy an organization's retention requirements for information that exists in multiple copies; also known as the *record copy.*

P

paper documents—records in paper form such as office files, business forms, engineering drawings, charts, maps, and computer printouts.

photographic records—records composed of photographic films, including photographic negatives and slides, motion picture films, filmstrips, and microforms.

pretrial discovery—the investigative phase of litigation when the opposing party can obtain access to recorded information believed relevant to its case.

program-specific retention schedule—a retention schedule limited to those records series that are actually held by a specific department, office, or other program unit.

program unit—a division, department, section, or other administrative unit that maintains recorded information.

Q

qualitative risk assessment—a method of assessment that is particularly useful for identifying and categorizing physical security problems and other vulnerabilities. It is usually based on a physical survey of locations where vital records are stored, combined with a review of security procedures already in place.

quantitative risk assessment—a method of assessment that uses numeric calculations to estimate the likelihood and impact of losses associated with specific vital records series. Losses are expressed as dollar amounts, which can be related to the cost of proposed protection methods.

R

record—an information-bearing object, regardless of physical medium or format, that comes within the scope and authority of an organization's records management program. Recorded information, regardless of medium or characteristics, made or received by an organization that is evidence of its operations and has value requiring its retention for a specific period of time.

record copy—the copy of a record that is designated to satisfy an organization's retention requirements for information that exists in multiple copies; also known as the *official copy.*

recorded information—any and all information created, received, maintained, or used by an organization.

recordkeeping requirements—records retention requirements specified in laws and government regulations.

records center—a specially designed, warehouse-type facility that provides safe, economical, high-density storage for records that are consulted infrequently but must be retained for legal or administrative reasons. A low-cost centralized area for housing and servicing inactive or semi-active records whose reference rate does not warrant their retention in a prime office space.

records inventory—a fact-finding survey that identifies and describes records maintained by all or part of an organization. A detailed listing that could include the types, locations, dates, volumes, equipment, classification systems, and usage data of an organization's records.

records management—a specialized business discipline concerned with the systematic analysis and control of recorded information, which includes any and all information created, received, maintained, or used by an organization in accordance with its mission, operations, and activities. The systematic control of all records from their creation, or receipt, through their processing, distribution, organization, storage, and retrieval to their ultimate disposition.

records retention scheduling—an aspect of records management work that determines how long records need to be kept.

records series—a group of logically related records that support a specific business or administrative operation and that are filed, indexed, evaluated as a unit for retention purposes, and/or used together.

reduction—a measure of the number of times a given linear dimension of a document is reduced through microphotography.

reference activity—the frequency with which a given records series is consulted for business or other purposes.

resolution—the measure of the ability of microfilm equipment and photographic materials to render fine detail visible within a microimage. It roughly equates to image sharpness.

retention schedule—a list of records series maintained by all or part of an organization together with the period of time that each records series is to be kept. May include retention in active office areas, inactive storage areas, and when and if such series may be destroyed or formally transferred to another entity such as an archives for historical preservation.

risk analysis—the process of evaluating the exposure of vital records to specific risks.

S

sheetfed scanner—a machine containing a narrow opening into which pages to be scanned are inserted. They are transported individually across a scanning mechanism that includes optical and photosensitive components. Depending on equipment design, the scanned pages are ejected at the back or bottom of the machine.

source document microfilming—the production of microforms from paper documents.

spoliation of evidence—destruction of evidence, including records that an organization knows or reasonably should know are relevant to impending or ongoing litigation or government investigations.

stability—the extent to which a given storage medium retains physical characteristics and chemical properties appropriate to its intended purpose. The period of time that a given medium will remain useful for its intended purpose. The ability of materials to resist decomposition.

statute of limitations—the period of time during which legal action can be taken pertaining to some matter.

storage copies—microforms used to produce one or more working copies that are placed into storage and seldom handled thereafter.

T

text retrieval system—a variant form of database management system that stores and indexes documents in character-coded form.

true copy—a copy that accurately reproduces an original document.

U

unitized media—microfiche, microfilm jackets, aperture cards, and other flat microforms are unitized because each client file is recorded on a separate microform. If space remains within a given fiche, it is left blank. A microfilm jacket is updateable.

V

vital record—a record that is indispensable to a mission-critical operation. A record identified as essential for the continuation or survival of the organization if a disaster strikes. Such records are necessary to recreate the organization's legal and financial status and to determine the rights and obligations of employees, customers, stockholders, and citizens.

vital records management program—a set of policies and procedures for the systematic, comprehensive, and economical control of adverse consequences attributable to the loss of mission-critical information.

W

working copies—microforms intended for display, printing, distribution, or other purposes and may be referenced frequently.

Finding More Information

A large and growing body of books, articles, conference papers, and other publications contain more detailed or otherwise different treatments of topics covered in this book. Although a comprehensive bibliography is beyond the purpose and scope of this book, this appendix provides some suggestions for further reading and research, with citations for illustrative English-language titles where applicable.

Library databases, which are widely searchable at library Web sites, are the best resources for citations to books and monographs about records management. Large national and academic libraries are likely to have the most complete holdings. The Library of Congress catalog (www.loc.gov), though not comprehensive, is a good starting point. "Records Management" is a Library of Congress subject heading. Other useful headings include "Records," "Business Records," "Public Records," "Records Retention," "Filing Systems" "Indexing," "Electronic Filing Systems," "Document Imaging Systems," "Micrographics," and "Archives." For an international perspective on records management, search the online catalogs of the National Library of Canada (www.nlc-bnc.ca), The British Library (www.bl.uk), and the National Library of Australia (www.nla.gov.au), all of which contain some unique titles.

Records management principles and practices are well covered in academic textbooks, most of which are intended for undergraduate courses in community colleges and four-year academic institutions. Examples include J. Read-Smith et al., *Records Management*, Seventh Edition (South-Western Publishing, 2002); J. Stewart and N. Melesco, *Professional Records and Information Management*, Second Edition (Glencoe McGraw-Hill, 2001); B. Ricks et al., *Information and Image Management: A Records Systems Approach*, Third Edition (South-Western Publishing, 1992, out of print); A. Henne, *Intensive Records Management* (South-Western Publishing, 1997), and M. Robek et al., *Information and Records Management*, Fourth Edition (Glencoe, 1995). Some of these books are accompanied by study guides and other supplementary publications that feature self-test questions, topics for discussion, exercises, and other useful content.

A number of business-oriented books treat records management from a practical rather than an academic perspective. Examples include E. Shepherd and G. Yeo, *Managing Records: A Handbook of Principles and Practices* (Facet, 2003); M. Langemo, *Winning Strategies for Successful Records Management Programs* (Information Requirements Clearinghouse, 2002); E. Parker, *Managing Your Organization's Records* (Library Association, 1999); J. Arn et al., *Records Management for an Information Age* (Delmar Publishers, 1998); J. Kennedy and C. Schauder, *Records Management: A Guide to Corporate Record Keeping*, Second Edition (Addison Wesley Longman Australia, 1998); C. Hare and J. McLeod, *Developing a Records Management Program* (ASLIB, the Association for Information Management, 1997); S. Diamond, *Records Management: A Practical Approach* (New York: AMACOM, 1995, out of print); I. Penn et al. *Records Management Handbook* (Ashgate, 1994); B. Wiggins, *Effective Document Management: Unlocking Corporate Knowledge* (Gower, 2000); J. Mims, *Records Management: A Practical Guide for Cities and Counties* (ICMA, 1996); and K. Sampson, *Value-Added Records Management: Protecting Corporate Assets and Reducing Business Risks,* Second Edition (Quorum Books, 2002).

Various business indexes and databases contain citations to articles about records management in professional journals, business magazines, newspapers, and other periodical publications. Examples of online databases likely to be available in many medium-size and larger academic and public libraries include *ABI-Inform, Business and Management Practices* (BaMP), *Business and Industry Database, Business Dateline, Globalbase, Information Science Abstracts, Library and Information Science Abstracts, Library Literature, Management Contents, Newsletter Database, PROMT, Trade and Industry Database,* and *Wilson Business Abstracts.* Articles indexed in these databases range from brief overviews of recordkeeping principles and concerns to detailed case studies that describe records management practices in specific companies, government agencies, or other organizations.

English-language periodicals that deal principally or exclusively with records management, or related topics such as archival administration, include *The Information Management Journal,* published by ARMA International; *Records Management Journal,* published in the United Kingdom by Emerald Group Publishing; *Records Management Bulletin,* published in the United Kingdom by the Records Management Society; *InfoRMAA Quarterly,* published by the Records Management Association of Australia; *American Archivist,* published by the Society of American Archivists; *Archivaria,* the journal of the Association of Canadian Archivists; *Archives,* published by the British Records Association; *Archival Science,* published by Kluwer; *Comma: International Journal on Archives,* published by K. G. Saur; *Crossroads,* a quarterly newsletter published by the National Association of Government Archivists and Records Administrators (NAGARA); *Prologue,* published by the National Archives and Records Administration; *ACARM Newsletter*, published in the United Kingdom by the Association of Commonwealth Archivists and Records Managers; *Archives and Manuscripts*, published by the Australian Society of Archivists; the *Journal of the Society of Archivists*, published in the United Kingdom by Carfax; and *New Zealand Archivist*, published by the New Zealand Society of Archivists.

The Internet is an indispensable source for information about records management practices, issues, and concerns. Thousands of Web pages feature records management policies and procedures, samples of records retention schedules, descriptions of recordkeeping products and technologies, position papers, and other useful items that would have previously required an impractical level of effort to identify and collect. The best single directory is the *Records and Information Management Resource List* (www.infomgmt.homestead.com). It categorizes and provides links to hundreds of sites about records management and related topics. The *UNESCO Archives Portal* (www.unesco.org/Webworld/portal_archives) likewise provides links to a variety of resources that deal with archives and records management. Internet search engines, such as Google or Alta Vista, are obvious starting points to locate pertinent Web sites, but the voluminous results they deliver can require time-consuming browsing. At the time of this writing, for example, a Google search for Web pages containing the phrase "records management" retrieved over 1.1 million items covering policies, procedures, practices, projects, and problems in varying levels of detail and with varying degrees of reliability and usefulness. When searches are narrowed to focus on specific topics, fewer items are retrieved, but the results are still unwieldy. For example, a Google search for "records management" and "vital records" retrieved over 10,600 items, while a search for "records management" and "retention schedules" retrieved over 10,800 items.

The Web sites of national, state, provincial, and municipal archival agencies contain much useful information about electronic records, including policies, procedures, retention schedules, and position papers, as well as online manuals and other publications. Examples include the Web sites of the U.S. National Archives and Records Administration (www.archives.gov), National Archives of Canada (www.archives.ca), National Archives of Australia (www.naa.gov.au), and British Public Records Office (www.pro.gov.uk). Many universities and some not-for-profit organizations likewise make their records management policies and retention schedules available at their Web sites.

As might be expected, the Web sites for professional records management and archival associations are valuable sources of information about many of the topics discussed in this book. Examples include the Web sites of ARMA International (www.arma.org), the Canadian Records Management Institute (www.rmicanada.com), the National Association of Government Archivists and Records Administrators (www.nagara.org), the Records Management Society of Great Britain (www.rms-gb.org.uk), the Records Management Association of Australia (www.rmaa.com.au), the Society of American Archivists (www.archivists.org), AIIM International (www.aiim.org), Aslib, the

Association for Information Management (www.aslib.co.uk), the Association of Canadian Archivists (www.archivists.ca), the Australian Society of Archivists (www.archives.org.au), the New Zealand Society of Archivists (www.archives.org.nz), the International Council on Archives (www.icr.org), and the Association of Commonwealth Archivists and Records Managers (www.acarm.org). The International Records Management Trust (www.irmt.org) emphasizes the problems of managing public records in developing countries, but much of the information available at its Web site is applicable to records management practice in other settings. The Nuclear Information and Records Management Association (www.nirma.org) deals with records management practice in the nuclear industry, which is subject to stringent recordkeeping regulations. The Association of Corporate Counsel Web site (www.acca.com) contains information of interest to corporate records managers.

Dozens of books and monographs deal with records retention laws and with advisable records management practices in specific industries or business situations. Examples include *Records Retention: Law and Practice* (Carswell, 1990); *Guide to Record Retention: The Lawyer's Role* (Business Laws Incorporated, 1986-), a subscription service that includes the *Corporate Counsel's Record Retention Report*, a monthly newsletter; *Records Retention for Financial Institutions* (American Bankers Association, 1995; a revised edition is in preparation at the time of this writing); J. Montaña et al., *The Sarbanes-Oxley Act: Implications for Records Management* (ARMA International, 2003); J. Barr et al., *Records Management in the Legal Environment: A Handbook of Practice and Procedure* (ARMA International, 2003); N. Morrissette, *Setting Up a Bank Records Management Program* (Greenwood Press, 1993); T. Stevenson, *Bank Records Retention Deskbook: Developing and Managing a Fail-Safe System for the Storage, Retrieval, and Protection of Vital Documents* (McGraw-Hill, 1991); R. Kirschner et al., *Record Retention Requirements for Taft-Hartley Welfare and Pension Funds as Required by ERISA, the Internal Revenue Service, and the Department of Labor* (International Foundation of Employee Benefit Plans, 1999); *AACRAO's Retention of Records: Guide for Retention and Disposal of Student Records* (American Association of Collegiate Registrars and Admissions Officers, 2000); M. Ruzicka and B. Weckmueller, *Student Records Management* (Greenwood, 1997); A. Pedersen, *NAFCU's Contingency Planning, Disaster Recovery, and Record Retention for Credit Unions* (Sheshunoff Information Services, 1998); J. Tomes, *Healthcare Records Management, Disclosure, and Retention: The Complete Legal Guide* (Healthcare Financial Management Association, 1994); C. Schwartz and P. Hernon, *Records Management and the Library: Issues and Practices* (Ablex Publishing, 1993); D. Stephens, *Information Management Issues in Mergers and Acquisitions* (ARMA International, 2000); and E. Brumm, *Managing Records for ISO 9000 Compliance* (ASQC Quality Press, 1995). These and other specialized topics are addressed in hundreds of articles that are indexed in the business databases cited previously.

A rapidly growing number of publications and Web sites deal with the special problems of managing electronic records. W. Saffady, *Managing Electronic Records*, Third

Edition (ARMA International, 2002), provides an overview of the field with suggestions for further reading. D. Stephens and R. Wallace, *Electronic Records Retention: New Strategies for Data Life Cycle Management* (ARMA International, 2002), deals specifically with retention of electronic records.

Books about vital records protection include V. Jones and K. Keyes, *Emergency Management for Records and Information Programs* (ARMA International, 2001), and J. Wellheiser and J. Scott, *An Ounce of Prevention: Integrated Disaster Planning for Archives, Libraries, and Record Centers*, Second Edition (Scarecrow Press, 2002).

Detailed treatments of micrographics and electronic document imaging technologies are provided in W. Saffady, *Micrographics: Technology for the 21st Century* (ARMA International, 2000) and W. Saffady, *Electronic Document Imaging: Technology, Applications, Implementation* (ARMA International, 2001).

William Saffady is a Professor at the Palmer School of Library and Information Science, Long Island University, where he teaches courses on information management topics. He previously held similar faculty positions at the State University of New York at Albany, Vanderbilt University, and Pratt Institute.

Dr. Saffady is the author of over three dozen books and many articles on records management, document imaging, information storage technologies, office automation, and library automation. Recent books published by ARMA International include *Electronic Document Imaging: Technology, Applications, Implementation, Managing Electronic Records,* Third Edition, *Micrographics: Technology for the 21st Century, Cost Analysis Concepts and Methods for Records Management Projects, Knowledge Management: A Manager's Briefing, The Value of Records Management: A Manager's Briefing, The Business Case for Systematic Control of Recorded Information,* and *Records and Information Management: A Benchmarking Study of Large U.S. Industrial Companies.*

In addition to teaching and writing, Dr. Saffady serves as an information management consultant, providing training and analytical services to corporations, government agencies, and other organizations.

ARMA International is the leading professional organization for persons in the expanding field of records and information management.

As of January 2004, ARMA has about 10,000 members in the United States, Canada, and 37 other countries around the world. Within the United States, Canada, New Zealand, Japan, Jamaica, and Singapore, ARMA has nearly 150 local chapters that provide networking and leadership opportunities through monthly meetings and special seminars.

ARMA's mission is to provide education, research, and networking opportunities to information professionals, to enable them to use their skills and experience to leverage the value of records, information, and knowledge as corporate assets and as contributors to organizational success.

The ARMA International headquarters office is located in Lenexa, Kansas, in the Kansas City metropolitan area. Office hours are 8:30 A.M. to 5:00 P.M., Central Time, Monday through Friday.

ARMA International
13725 W. 109th St., Ste. 101
Lenexa, Kansas 66215
800.422.2762 • 913.341.3808
Fax: 913.341.3742
hq@arma.org
www.arma.org